T0399891

Language for Behaviour and Emotions

This practical, interactive resource is designed to be used by professionals who work with children and young people who have Social, Emotional and Mental Health needs and Speech, Language and Communication needs. Gaps in language and emotional skills can have a negative impact on behaviour as well as mental health and self-esteem. *Language for Behaviour and Emotions* provides a systematic approach to developing these skills so that young people can understand and work through social interaction difficulties.

Key features include:
• A focus on specific skills that are linked to behaviour, such as understanding meaning, verbal reasoning and emotional literacy skills.
• A framework for assessment, as well as a range of downloadable activities, worksheets and resources for supporting students.
• Sixty illustrated scenarios that can be used flexibly with a wide range of ages and abilities to promote language skills, emotional skills and self-awareness.

This invaluable resource is suitable for use with young people with a range of abilities in one to one, small group or whole class settings. It is particularly applicable to children and young people who are aiming to develop wider language, social and emotional skills including those with Developmental Language Disorder and Autism Spectrum Disorder.

Anna Branagan is a speech and language therapist within a youth support team in Gloucestershire, working to enable vulnerable young people with speech, language and communication difficulties to access support more effectively. She also works within mainstream schools supporting inclusive practice in Worcestershire. Anna trained at Leeds Metropolitan University 25 years ago. She is co-author of bestselling Speechmark resources *Language for Thinking* (2nd edition, 2017), *Word Aware* (2nd edition, 2021) and *Word Aware 2* (2017).

Melanie Cross is a speech and language therapist who has worked with looked after children for many years. Her work has focussed on developing speech and language therapy services for children and young people with Social, Emotional and Mental Health needs (SEMH). This work has resulted in publications including *Children with Social, Emotional and Behavioural Difficulties and Communication Problems* (2nd edition, 2011), and she was the lead author of the Royal College of Speech and Language Therapists Clinical Guidelines on Social, Emotional and Mental Health. She is also a trainer, video interaction guider and supervisor.

Stephen Parsons is a speech and language therapist, trainer and author of practical language development resources for teachers and speech and language therapists. From 1996–2017, Stephen worked as a speech and language therapy service manager in Hackney and the City of London. With 30 years' experience in the field, he is co-author of bestselling Speechmark resources *Language for Thinking* (2nd edition, 2017), *Word Aware* (2nd edition, 2021) and *Word Aware 2* (2017). Stephen graduated in speech pathology from Flinders University before attaining an MSc in speech and language therapy from City University in 2000. He currently serves as Chair of NAPLIC, the UK association for professionals working with children and young people with Developmental Language Disorder.

Language for Behaviour and Emotions

A Practical Guide to Working with Children and Young People

Anna Branagan, Melanie Cross and Stephen Parsons

Routledge
Taylor & Francis Group

LONDON AND NEW YORK

First published 2021
by Routledge
2 Park Square, Milton Park, Abingdon, Oxon OX14 4RN

and by Routledge
52 Vanderbilt Avenue, New York, NY 10017

Routledge is an imprint of the Taylor & Francis Group, an informa business

British Library Cataloguing-in-Publication Data
A catalogue record for this book is available from the British Library

Library of Congress Cataloging-in-Publication Data
Names: Branagan, Anna, author. | Cross, Melanie, author. | Parsons, Stephen (Speech therapist), author. | Routledge (Firm)
Title: Language for behaviour and emotions : a practical guide to working with children and young people / Anna Branagan, Melanie Cross, and Stephen Parsons.
Other titles: Language for behavior and emotions Description: First Edition. | Abingdon, Oxon ; New York, NY : Routledge, 2020. | Includes bibliographical references.
Identifiers: LCCN 2020011279 (print) | LCCN 2020011280 (ebook) | ISBN 9780367491833 (Hardback) | ISBN 9780367331832 (Paperback) | ISBN 9780429318320 (eBook)
Subjects: LCSH: Language disorders in children. | Language disorders in adolescence. | Communicative disorders in children. | Communicative disorders in adolescence.
Classification: LCC RJ496.L35 B735 2020 (print) | LCC RJ496.L35 (ebook) | DDC 618.92/855—dc23
LC record available at https://lccn.loc.gov/2020011279
LC ebook record available at https://lccn.loc.gov/2020011280

ISBN: 978-0-367-49183-3 (hbk)
ISBN: 978-0-367-33183-2 (pbk)
ISBN: 978-0-429-31832-0 (ebk)

Typeset in SignaColumn-Light
by Apex CoVantage, LLC

Visit the companion website: www.routledge.com/cw/speechmark

To all young people with Developmental Language Disorder, especially those whose needs are not recognised and those who don't get opportunities to develop their language and emotional skills. We want to change that.

In particular, we would like to thank; the young people who put up with us trying things out on them and who gave us feedback on our early drafts. The wonderful Vicky Howells, Gill Grenyer and Emela Milne who tried things out for us and helped us think about what would be useful, Keri Knight who helped develop some of the assessments and last but by no means least a massive thank you to Maggie Burlington for all her proofreading.

To Kevin Foster, Steve Branagan and Steve Cross for being as patient and supportive as ever.

Contents

Introduction

Please note that for simplicity's sake we use the term 'young people' to refer to children and young people. We use the term 'children' when the research quoted specifically uses this term.

Aaron's story

Aaron is 13 years old. He struggled with reading and writing in primary (elementary) school, but since his transfer to his mainstream secondary (high) school the situation had deteriorated. His parents had consistently told him he was smart, as he could do lots of things well, but Aaron continued to tell himself he was 'thick' because he often did not 'get' things or took a long time to work out what to do. One day in class, Aaron realised he did not understand the work he had been set but was too self-conscious to ask for help. Aaron did not get much work done in this lesson and so was given a detention. Just one of several that week. When a supportive staff member spoke with him, Aaron was unable to explain what had happened, and so this staff member thought he was unmotivated and rude. This sort of thing kept happening, and adults began to talk about 'deterioration, consequences and repercussions', all words which Aaron did not understand. On many occasions, Aaron was asked to explain his actions, but by now his self-esteem was so low that he just looked down at the floor and gave minimal responses. He was getting more frustrated and angrier and began to lose his temper.

The authors have often encountered stories such as Aaron's (and far worse) in our practice, where a young person with identified Social, Emotional and Mental Health needs (SEMH) has their Speech, Language and Communication Needs (SLCN) unnoticed by all involved. Researchers have noted similar patterns on a wider scale (Hollo et al, 2014).

One study suggests that 81% of young people who present with SEMH and/ or behavioural problems also have SLCN, and this is mostly unrecognised (Hollo et al, 2014). Practitioners do not set out to disregard language and communication needs, but these difficulties can be hard to detect. SEMH can overshadow SLCN, and also practitioners may not know what SLCN looks like or even know that they should be looking for it. Many young people with

SEMH are talkative, but they may not have the skills required to understand complex language, talk about feelings, negotiate or explain the reasons behind their thinking. Their poor response to instructions can easily be labelled as being due to poor attention or a lack of cooperation (which it may be) rather than difficulty understanding the spoken words. Many young people with SEMH also lack the self-awareness and confidence to seek help and instead develop sophisticated 'camouflage' techniques.

Even when recognised, the interaction between SLCN and SEMH is complex and young people may present in very different ways (Conti-Ramsden et al, 2018). As a result, there is no 'rule book' about how young people will be affected but being aware of SLCN gives adults who work with young people with SEMH a starting point to offering more effective support.

The language and communication needs associated with SEMH can be complex and hard to spot, but the key areas to focus on are:

1   **Understanding language:** vocabulary, grammar and instructions. (Cohen et al, 2013; Bühler et al, 2018)

2   **Emotional literacy skills:** labelling of own feelings and those of others and managing own emotions with words. (Rieffe & Wiefferink, 2017; van den Bedem et al, 2018a)

3   **Inferencing and verbal reasoning:** 'reading between the lines' and working out what has not been explicitly stated (in conversation and reading) and verbalising one's own thinking. (Hollo et al, 2018)

4   **Narrative skills:** describing real events, including one's own life story, but also fictional stories. (Pearce et al, 2014; Colozzo et al, 2011)

5   **Social problem-solving:** using talk to think about how people interact with one another and how to sort out misunderstandings. (Wolters et al, 2014)

It is hard to predict exactly how these language and communication skills gaps will impact on any one young person but they can include negative effects on:

1	Academic success	Norbury et al, 2016
2	The ability to develop positive relationships. Children with SLCN can be at a greater risk of being bullied	Forrest et al, 2018; van den Bedem et al, 2018b
3	Literacy and behaviour	Westrupp et al, 2020; Petersen et al, 2013

4	Mental health	Im-Bolter et al, 2007; Salmon et al, 2016; Maggio et al, 2014
5	Self-belief	Botting et al, 2016
6	Accessing behaviour or mental health interventions	Im-Bolter et al, 2013

Successful social communication (saying the right thing to the right person in the right way) requires many of these skills, and young people with SEMH often find social communication very difficult. This adds to their difficulties because positive relationships are a buffer against mental health challenges (Perry, 2017).

There are young people with SEMH who have very good language skills, so having good language skills will not necessarily resolve SEMH. But for those with SLCN in addition to SEMH, identifying their needs and then targeting these areas in intervention will reduce some of the challenges they face. Behaviour management and support systems, such as talking therapies or restorative justice, are often verbally based, so developing language skills will better equip young people with SEMH to engage in these interventions. An increased awareness of potential SLCN will also help professionals differentiate interventions so that they are accessible and effective.

The *Language for Behaviour and Emotions* approach

This book provides a systematic approach to developing language skills so that young people are better at using words to solve social interaction difficulties.

As they mature, young people develop their language, thinking and emotional skills all together via interactions and conversations about real events. Conversations are critical for language development (Romeo et al, 2018) and, when we can talk to someone who really listens and does not judge us, we can relax, be creative and learn (Fredrickson, 2013). Stories underpin our understanding of the world as they promote learning about feelings, ourselves, other people, social problems and consequences. They also form the basis of nearly all of our communication with each other. With this in mind, this book provides a way to have structured conversations about social scenarios that will be accessible and engaging to learners. This approach specifically addresses many of the language skills that those with SEMH often have difficulty with. It also provides assessment tools, to focus the intervention and to monitor progress.

The key strands of the *Language for Behaviour and Emotions* (*LFBE*) approach are:

Note: The words adults use are very important, which is why when labelling all of the key language areas simple, young person friendly versions have been used, as well as technical terms. For example, 'saying when you don't understand' is a simpler way of saying 'comprehension monitoring'. We've also used these symbols throughout for clarity.

- What to do when things don't make sense (understanding language).
  - O Saying when you don't understand (comprehension monitoring).
  - O Understanding words (vocabulary).
  - O When people don't say what they mean (figurative language).
- Talking about feelings (emotional literacy).
  - O What's that feeling called? (naming emotions).
  - O Dealing with feelings (emotional regulation).
- Finding clues and explaining thinking (inference and verbal reasoning).
- The story (narrative).
- Bringing it all together and solving people problems.

How adults can help

Two traps to be aware of when using *LFBE* are, firstly viewing it as an intervention which is delivered in isolation and just focusing on skill development in the young person alone. Communication happens across the day and within a social context, so for it to be effective it is about everyone who works with the young person understanding the individual's language and communication profile better and implementing strategies to create a communicatively supportive environment. Secondly, language and communication needs cannot be 'fixed' by one person. Effective support requires positive engagement with the young person and collaboration with professionals and families to develop skills and strategies. Teamwork and sharing knowledge are therefore crucial.

What to do when things don't make sense (understanding) 🤯

Understanding language is a complex, multifaceted skill that we use every day and usually with very little thought. Most young people develop an understanding of language through daily interactions with family members, friends, teachers and sometimes other professionals. Some young people have specific difficulty learning language, no matter how positive their early interactions are. So, whilst most young people develop understanding well, a significant number do not, and this may be because they have Developmental Language Disorder (DLD). Around 7.5% of young people have DLD (Norbury et al 2016), and this percentage is much higher in those with SEMH.

General conversations with friends and family are not too demanding, but the classroom and other interactions with professionals place more demands on the young person, as the language used is grammatically more complex and uses more specialist vocabulary. In conversations, people tend to take relatively short turns, but in more formal situations, speakers may talk at length. Additionally, classroom language or behavioural interventions are more likely to be about abstract ideas or events and so lack the contextual clues that conversations with friends and family have.

Difficulties with understanding language can impact young people's learning, as they struggle to keep up with classroom dialogue. But these difficulties also impact on social relationships and self-esteem as the young people are aware of not being able to understand and feel left out. There are very few interventions that have proven to improve the understanding of spoken language, and the most successful have been delivered by highly trained specialists (Ebbels et al, 2019). As well as individual intervention, in-class support is crucial. If a professional is able to identify when a young person has not understood and modify his/her language accordingly then the impact of the young person's language needs can be mitigated. Unidentified and unsupported difficulties with understanding quite often have a poor long-term prognosis (Winstanley et al, 2017).

Within the *LFBE* approach three key areas relating to understanding have been identified:

- Saying when you don't understand (comprehension monitoring).

- Understanding words (vocabulary).
- When people don't say what they mean (figurative language).

Saying when you don't understand (comprehension monitoring)

If you have ever given an instruction and the young person has done the wrong thing despite nodding when you have asked 'do you understand?' then you have encountered someone who has not been monitoring their comprehension or at least has not been willing to admit that they do not understand.

Good comprehenders continually monitor their own understanding and build a mental picture, checking the incoming information they hear against what they already know (Oakhill et al, 2015). When a good comprehender hears something that does not match with their mental model, they query it. They have the confidence and language skills to do so. The converse is true of poor comprehenders. Their mental model may be more limited to start with, the information they hear may soon overwhelm them and so the gaps in their understanding increase. In a group situation or with an unsympathetic speaker, it is just too embarrassing or bothersome to ask. And so the gaps between the good and poor comprehenders grow.

Comprehension monitoring also prevents misunderstandings, because if a listener is unsure about what they just heard and then asks, the problem is averted. If a listener who has not checked their understanding proceeds, then this may impact negatively on the relationship.

In relation to SEMH, comprehension monitoring is particularly important, as lack of understanding which leads to poor compliance may get labelled as bad behaviour. Instead of doing the wrong thing, if the young person had instead said 'I don't understand' then they would probably be viewed more sympathetically.

This book provides strategies that can be implemented on a daily basis, as well as assessment and intervention tools which will enable practitioners to better support young people who have less developed comprehension monitoring skills. The support strategies and focussed intervention will promote the

development of young people's skills at identifying and saying when they don't understand.

Understanding words (vocabulary)

Like any specialism, SEMH comes laden with specialist vocabulary that people in the field use easily and without thought. Words such as 'responsibility', 'consequences' and 'perspective' are used commonly by practitioners, but to young people with SLCN these terms may be particularly problematic.

Vocabulary in general is challenging as there are just so many words, and the words any speaker knows are dependent on both their general word-learning ability and their experiences. It is hard to predict which words any young person will know, but due to their word-learning abilities those with Developmental Language Disorder (DLD) and other SLCN are likely to have difficulties with vocabulary. Those who have limited world experiences or who have missed periods of schooling may have surprising gaps in their word knowledge. Also, young people who have literacy difficulties (very common in those with SLCN because literacy builds on language skills) miss out on opportunities to learn new words from reading. It is important to note that just because a young person uses a few sophisticated words it cannot be assumed that their overall vocabulary is at an equivalent level. Practitioners are advised: if in doubt keep vocabulary simple, especially when the information being conveyed is important for the young person to understand.

In its entirety, vocabulary is vast and beyond the scope of this book. As a result, the assessment and intervention resources focus on the words typically used for behaviour management and words about thinking and emotions (for the latter see 'Talking about feelings' following for more details). For more comprehensive vocabulary resources refer to Parsons and Branagan (2016, 2021).

When people don't say what they mean (figurative language)

'Figurative language' refers to non-literal language, in which the speaker's intended meaning does not directly match the individual words' meanings. Similes, metaphors and idioms are all types of figurative language. Similes are when one thing is compared to another using 'like' or 'as' e.g.: 'You eat like a pig.'

Metaphors are similar to similes in that they compare two things but in a more direct manner and 'like' or 'as' are not used. For example, 'You are a pig when you eat.' Idioms are the sayings that can often be traced back centuries and quite often the meaning does not relate to the individual words at all. For instance: 'a pain in the neck' has nothing to do with necks and 'getting a grip' does not require any physical contact. Figurative language is used naturally by adults and, typically developing young children struggle with it, often to very humorous effect. However, young people with SLCN and SEMH might find it particularly challenging to understand, especially if they do not indicate when they do not understand, which then leads to misunderstandings, which then have further consequences.

Figurative language is common in literature, and so students with well-developed reading skills will have been exposed to this type of language more frequently than those with reading difficulties. Idioms are also highly culturally based, and great fun can be had deciphering the meanings of idioms from other languages, but young people who speak English as an additional language (English language learners) will not have the same exposure to English idioms, and so this creates a further barrier. Researchers have identified that young people with DLD may have particular difficulty with figurative language (Bühler et al, 2018; Seigneuric et al, 2016). Because they are harder to decipher and can lead so easily to communication breakdowns, idioms have been prioritised over similes and metaphors in this book.

The book also touches on exaggeration, sarcasm, 'white lies' and implied meaning. Both adults and young people use these, and when they are not understood, this can lead to confusion and social interaction difficulties. Adults can think that the young person is deliberating defying them, and misunderstandings with peers can lead to social awkwardness.

This book provides daily strategies, assessment and guidance for intervention for sarcasm, implied meaning and idioms.

Talking about feelings (emotional literacy)

Naming emotions and emotional regulation are addressed in this book under the headings:

- What's that feeling called?
- Dealing with feelings.

What's that feeling called? ⏸

Practitioners who work with young people with SEMH often notice that they use a limited range of emotion words. The young people might be limited to very simple terms, such as sad, happy, angry, when their typically developing peers have developed well beyond this. The reasons for this are complex, and it may be that some young people with SEMH and SLCN also have a condition called Alexithymia. Alexithymia is a condition in which a person is unable to identify or talk about emotions. Hobson et al (2019) explore in some detail the causality of Alexithymia, but one possible cause is that it has a linguistic basis. There is still much to learn about this condition, but the same authors report that linguistic input can improve emotion recognition in deaf children.

Labelling emotions may prove problematic for other groups, including young people with DLD (Rieffe & Wiefferink, 2017) and young offenders (Bowen et al, 2014), and as a result the latter authors call for specific interventions targeting emotion vocabulary in at-risk groups. Young people who are better at naming their own emotions and the emotions of other people tend to find it easier to make friends and have less anxiety and depression. Having good emotion knowledge has also been linked to academic success (Denham et al, 2012).

We also know that social and emotional skills matter for adult mental health and life satisfaction as well as for their work and health (Feinstein, 2015).

The scenarios which form a key part of this resource (see page 139) describe simple social situations. Each scenario is likely to involve a number of emotions, but all have one major emotion. When developing the scenarios, the authors used a list of emotions devised by Baron-Cohen et al (2010) which explores the typical development of emotion vocabulary. The early scenarios use emotions vocabulary that most typically developing four to six year olds are familiar with. The middle scenarios use vocabulary in the seven to 10 years old range, and the final scenarios target vocabulary up to 11–12 years of age with a few scenarios using 13–14 year old level emotions vocabulary.

In this book there are lots of resources to assess and develop emotion vocabulary, including visual supports, as well as the scenarios themselves. Vocabulary learning in a small group or individual session in isolation is unlikely to be effective, and so it is crucial that learning of emotion vocabulary is linked to school and home and as part of 'emotional coaching'.

The symbol ⏸ is a pause symbol: we need to pause to think about feelings.

Dealing with feelings (emotional regulation)

Put simply, emotional regulation is one's ability to modify or change one's own emotions. Although emotions have been discussed for millennia, the term 'emotional regulation' and associated thinking only emerged towards the end of the 20th century (Tamir, 2011). The ultimate goal of intervention is for those who were previously dysregulated to be able to independently self-regulate and thus manage their emotions in a more appropriate manner. Being able to identify and label emotions is a first step, but the emotional regulation process is highly dependent on language, as young people need to be able to verbally reflect, reason and discuss their thinking in order to develop skills and strategies. If a young person is able to put their own feelings into words, then this can calm them down (Torre & Lieberman, 2018). Similarly, if the young person is able to imagine how a problem might feel when they look back on it in the future, then this can lead to more positive feelings about it (Bruehlman-Senecal et al, 2016).

Van den Bedem et al (2018a) described how children with DLD are at risk of depression but, within this group, being able to identify one's own emotions and use positive self-regulation strategies such as asking people for help, leaving the situation, putting things in perspective and distracting yourself all help to reduce the risk of depression. Binns et al (2019) described the skilled role required to facilitate this process in children with SLCN.

In this resource, how young people deal with feelings can be assessed through the assessment scenarios, observation and discussion with the young person. As part of the intervention, a variety of emotion regulation strategies are offered that can be discussed in relation to the scenarios and social problem-solving in real life. It is also important to think about and remember positive emotions (Fredrickson, 2013), as we tend to be biased towards remembering difficult things, so we offer strategies for this too. There is some evidence that children who experience 'emotional coaching' as we describe it here are more cooperative (Brownell et al, 2013).

The symbol 🔴 is a dial. It represents the need to dial emotions up or down.

Finding clues and explaining your thinking (inference and verbal reasoning) 🔍

Inference refers to the listener's (or reader's) ability to 'read between the lines' and interpret the speaker's (or writer's) intended message which has not been explicitly stated. It requires the young person to understand the language they hear (or read) and match that to their own understanding of the situation even though the meaning may be hidden. Inference can be based upon non-verbal signals such as facial expressions, situational understanding (i.e.: what would I expect to happen if I was in the same setting?) and of course language. If we witnessed a young person returning home after an exam, slumping in a chair with a downturned mouth and only responding to questions tersely, we might pick up clues from the slumping, facial expression and short responses and add this to our existing knowledge of the stress of exams and infer that the young person is thinking that the exam did not go well. Or of course we could surmise that this is typical for this young person and not different from any other day! Inference is about integrating the available information but combining it with situational understanding, and so it requires empathy. It is a complex task and one which young people with SEMH have been identified as having difficulties with (Hollo et al, 2018).

Young people with SLCN often have less developed inference skills because they have weaker language and often also situational knowledge. Some will also have difficulties with understanding non-verbal communication. The resultant misreading of situations can lead to social isolation and miscommunication, which can feed into behavioural and mental health issues. If those who work with a young person know their inference strengths and needs, then the likelihood of negative interactions can be reduced.

In this context, verbal reasoning refers to the use of language as a tool to reflect upon thinking. Verbal reasoning includes skills such as: predicting, comparing, providing rationales, defining and explaining. Important verbal reasoning questions are 'why?' and 'how do you know?' To successfully answer the higher-level reasoning questions, a young person must have well-developed language skills and insight into their own and others' thinking. Thus there are many potential causes of breakdown. For instance, some may have difficulty understanding others' perspectives, whereas others may struggle to convey their intended meaning. Also, young people who can appreciate another person's perspective tend to be more popular (Slaughter et al 2015), but this skill is often difficult for young people with SEMH and SLCN (Nilsson & de López, 2016).

LFBE is based upon the seminal work of Blank, Rose and Berlin (1978) in which the classroom discourse was divided into four levels, starting with the most concrete 'Matching Perception', through the next two levels, 'Selective Analysis of Perception' and 'Reordering Perception', before ending with the most abstract, 'Reasoning About Perception'. The Blank et al framework was used as a basis for Parsons and Branagan's (2017) work, which applies the Blank method to simple social scenarios to develop verbal reasoning and inference skills. *Language for Thinking* (Parsons & Branagan, 2017) is one of the most widely used language interventions in the UK (Roulstone et al, 2012) and in developmental terms is a precursor to *LFBE*.

LFBE structures inference and verbal reasoning into four Language Levels. Those familiar with *Language for Thinking* (Parsons & Branagan, 2017) and Blank et al's (1978) levels may find the following table useful, but if you are not familiar with these approaches then it may be ignored. Blank et al's levels are not directly equivalent to the *Language for Thinking* (LFT) and *LFBE* Language Levels, but there are many similarities. The reason why Blank et al's Level 1 is not used within either LFT or *LFBE* is because paper-based resources such as this book are not appropriate for young people at this developmental stage, as they require hands-on real experiences. The addition of Level D onto the LFT levels is to reflect the needs of an older and more verbal client group, who are learning sophisticated reasoning and vocabulary.

Comparison of Blank, LFT and LFBE Levels

Blank Levels	LFT Language Levels	*LFBE* Language Levels
1	no equivalent	no equivalent
2	A	A
3	B	B
4	C	C
no equivalent	no equivalent	D

Outline of *Language for Behaviour and Emotions* Language Levels

Level A	At this level the young person selects information from what is provided, so it is very much based in the 'here and now'. The young person does not need to use any specific world knowledge, they just need to listen to what is said and look at what they can see and then identify the right information.
	More abstract questions may also be used but only if directly related to the child's own experiences: for example, 'How did you feel when . . .?'
	At this level the young person is selecting the right information, either from the story they are listening to, a picture they are looking at or remembering what has happened to them.
Level B	The young person selects information from what is presented and combines this with their world knowledge. They must organise their thoughts into a logical sequence. This stage requires simple inferences and predictions. Any inference about information not explicitly stated is simple and obvious.
Level C	This Language Level requires the young person to use 'language to predict, reflect on and integrate ideas and relationships' (Blank et al, 1978). This is true language for thinking. The key question at this level is 'why?', for example, 'Why will X happen?' and 'Why shouldn't . . .?' The young person is also expected to talk about a variety of possible outcomes that may not be immediately obvious (such as 'What would she do if . . .?') as well as reflect on his own understanding (e.g.: 'How can you tell?').
Level D	This is an extension of the Level C skills with more demanding reasoning and greater in-depth reflection. This Language Level requires precise analysis of the social situation as well as thorough, well-reasoned responses.
	The language load is increased by the use of complex vocabulary, such as 'evidence, conclusion, justify, suspect and consequences.'
	Multiple perspectives need to be analysed and/or require multiple steps. e.g.: 'what is the best solution for everyone?', 'If you consider it from XX's view, does that change your opinion? How?' and 'Tell me how they would resolve their differences. Talk through the steps.'

For many of the Language Level C and D questions there is no right or wrong response, it is about having a plausible view that is supported by the evidence. In group discussions with young people, it is beneficial to listen to various responses, discuss and compare. It is often illuminating, and it is important that we acknowledge the possibility of other perspectives about the same event

Inference is dependent on understanding the social situation as well as the language used, such as vocabulary and grammar. Inference is about making connections between the information that is seen and heard with wider understanding of the world. A deficit in either understanding of a particular setting, or the specific vocabulary and grammar, will impact on the ability to gather all of the information required to make connections and thus infer. For instance, if a scenario about paintballing was presented and one line said, 'The attendant called out, 'You have five minutes remaining.'' a young person may not be able to infer what this means either because they have never experienced paintballing or similar events, or it may be that they do not understand the word 'remaining' and so cannot infer what the attendant's motivation is. *LFBE* uses social situations that have been designed to be familiar to most young people, and the language is carefully selected to increase in challenge as progress is made through the scheme.

To provide young people with opportunities for developing verbal reasoning and inference skills, this book provides assessment tools and 60 illustrated scenarios as well as strategies which can be applied across the day.

The story (narrative)

Narrative is about connecting language together to tell a story. The story may be fiction, such as folk tales, or nonfiction, such as talking about witnessed events. Narrative is an important skill, as it is part of how we build our self-concept and make sense of the world. It is also linked to mental health as mentally healthy individuals can tell a coherent narrative about their own lives (Siegel, 2014). Securely attached children are able to tell longer and more coherent narratives than most insecurely attached children (Kelly, 2015), and many children with psychiatric difficulties have problems with using narrative, although these skills are important for access to therapies (Pearce et al 2014). Young people with SLCN often experience difficulties with forming narratives (Gillam & Gillam, 2016) and may struggle with the overall structure and miss key elements, as well as having difficulties with using vocabulary and grammatical structures. As Snow and Powell (2005) found, young offenders often find it difficult to tell a clear narrative, but being able to reliably tell a coherent narrative is important in criminal investigations. A young person who presents a poor narrative in court may be wrongly thought of as 'unreliable' when the cause of their difficulties is language-based.

Gillam and Gillam (2016), Joffe et al (2019) and others have found that narrative intervention can be effective. Narrative assessment and intervention can be a lengthy and intense process. Using the research literature as a basis, this book provides an assessment and intervention method which is easy to understand and can be quickly administered. This will meet the needs of many young people but some will need further assessment and specific intervention.

Bringing it all together and solving people problems ✓

This is the final strand of the *LFBE* approach that pulls together all of the other skill areas into one coherent functional skill.

Life requires all of us to establish and maintain many different, and different kinds, of interpersonal relationships. A key part of human development is learning how to manage these various relationships. Any parent or professional who has contact with young people will have plenty of first-hand knowledge about the amount of time spent talking about relationships. Once children move from the early years, their relationships with peers become more verbal, and so young people with SLCN often struggle with connecting with others. Researchers have shown that children with SLCN are at a greater risk of SEMH and for some this is due to problems in developing positive relationships with their peers and then fewer opportunities to learn about how to interact positively (Forrest et al, 2018). Having strong verbal capabilities becomes particularly important when there are interpersonal difficulties. If a young person is able to use words to persuade, negotiate and problem-solve, then they are able to prevent a situation from deteriorating further, whereas a young person who cannot use words may react physically or withdraw, both of which potentially contribute to greater problems. Some children who find it hard to solve problems with words can find themselves being rejected by other children (Wolters et al, 2014). And again, social problem-solving may be particularly difficult for adolescents with SEMH (Im-Bolter et al, 2013); it is easy to see why failure to socially problem-solve often exacerbates difficult situations. To successfully problem-solve social situations, a young person needs to understand what is said to them, be able to indicate when they do not understand, have a knowledge of their own and others' emotions, be able to regulate their own emotions, be able to infer intended meanings, explain their thinking and form well-constructed stories to explain events. If these skills sound familiar, it is because these are skills that have been addressed in the other strands of the *LFBE* approach. By building all of the preceding strands, young people should improve their ability to problem-solve real social situations. However, for many, this will not happen automatically. To support this process, a range of tools are available in the toolkit starting on page 263.

In summary

Many young people with SEMH also have SLCN even if those needs have not been identified. The relationship between language and behaviour is complex, but for young people with SEMH plus SLCN, this will compound issues and also make it more difficult to access support. Many young people who have SLCN are at risk of developing SEMH and so learning these particular language skills might help to reduce that risk.

There is no miracle cure for young people with SLCN, and for many, these difficulties will be lifelong. However, all who work with these young people can raise awareness, identify needs, develop skills and advocate to ensure this vulnerable group achieves the best possible outcomes.

**For details about training opportunities go to:
www.thinkingtalking.co.uk/LFBE/**

References, further reading and general resources

Specific resources are in each section of the toolkit

References

Baron-Cohen, S., Golan, O., Wheelwright, S., Granader, Y., & Hill, J. (2010). Emotion word comprehension from 4 to 16 years old: A developmental survey. *Frontiers in Evolutionary Neuroscience*, 2.

Binns, A. V., Hutchinson, L. R., & Cardy, J. O. (2019). The speech-language pathologist's role in supporting the development of self-regulation: A review and tutorial. *Journal of Communication Disorders*, 78, 1–17.

Blank, M., Rose, S. A., & Berlin, L. J. (1978). *The language of learning: The preschool years*. New York: Grune & Stratton.

Botting, N., Durkin, K., Toseeb, U., Pickles, A., & Conti-Ramsden, G. (2016). Emotional health, support, and self-efficacy in young adults with a history of language impairment. *British Journal of Developmental Psychology*, 34(4), 538–554.

Bowen, K. L., Morgan, J. E., Moore, S. C., & van Goozen, S. H. M. (2014). Young offenders' emotion recognition dysfunction across emotion intensities: Explaining variation using psychopathic traits, conduct disorder and offense severity. *Journal of Psychopathology and Behavioral Assessment*, 36(1), 60–73.

Brownell, C. A., Svetlova, M., Anderson, R., Nichols, S. R., & Drummond, J. (2013). Socialization of early prosocial behavior: Parents' talk about emotions is associated with sharing and helping in toddlers. *Infancy*, 18(1), 91–119.

Bruehlman-Senecal, E., Ayduk, Ö., & John, O. P. (2016). Taking the long view: Implications of individual differences in temporal distancing for affect, stress reactivity, and well-being. *Journal of Personality and Social Psychology*, 111(4), 610–635.

Bühler, D., Perovic, A., & Pouscoulous, N. (2018). Comprehension of novel metaphor in young children with developmental language disorder. *Autism & Developmental Language Impairments*, 3, doi:10.1177/2396941518817229.

Cohen, N. J. et al. (2013). Higher order language competence and adolescent mental health. *Journal of Child Psychology and Psychiatry*, 54(7), 733–744.

Colozzo, P., Gillam, R. B., Wood, M., Schnell, R. D., & Johnston, J. R. (2011). Content and form in the narratives of children with specific language impairment. *Journal of Speech, Language, and Hearing Research*, 54(6), 1609–1627.

Conti-Ramsden, G., Mok, P., Durkin, K., Pickles, A., Toseeb, U., & Botting, N. (2018). Do emotional difficulties and peer problems occur together from childhood to adolescence? The case of children with a history of developmental language disorder (DLD). *European Child & Adolescent Psychiatry*, 1–12.

Denham, S. A., Bassett, H. H., Way, E., Mincic, M., Zinsser, K., & Graling, K. (2012). Preschoolers' emotion knowledge: Self-regulatory foundations, and predictions of early school success. *Cognition & Emotion*, 26(4), 667–679.

Ebbels, S. H., McCartney, E., Slonims, V., Dockrell, J. E., & Norbury, C. F. (2019). Evidence-based pathways to intervention for children with language disorders. *International Journal of Language & Communication Disorders*, 54, 13–19.

Feinstein, L. (2015). *Social and emotional learning: Skills for life and work*. London: Early Intervention Foundation www.eif.org.uk/publications/social-andemotional-learning-skills-for-life-and-work/

Forrest, C. L., Gibson, J. L., Halligan, S. L., & St Clair, M. C. (2018). A longitudinal analysis of early language difficulty and peer problems on later emotional difficulties in adolescence: Evidence from the millennium cohort study. *Autism & Developmental Language Impairments*, 3, doi:10.1177/239694151879539.

Fredrickson, B. L. (2013). Positive emotions broaden and build. In P. Devine & A. Plant (Eds.), *Advances in experimental social psychology* (Vol. 47, pp. 1–54). San Diego, CA: Academic Press.

Gillam, S. L., & Gillam, R. B. (2016). Narrative discourse intervention for school-aged children with language impairment. *Topics in Language Disorders*, 36(1), 20–34.

Hobson, H., Brewer, R., Catmur, C., & Bird, G. (2019). The role of language in alexithymia: Moving towards a multiroute model of alexithymia. *Emotion Review*, 11(3), 247–261.

Hollo, A., Chow, J. C., & Wehby, J. H. (2018). Profiles of language and behavior in students with emotional disturbance. *Behavioral Disorders*, 44(4), 195–204.

Hollo, A., Wehby, J. H., & Oliver, R. M. (2014). Unidentified language deficits in children with emotional and behavioral disorders: A meta-analysis. *Exceptional Children*, 80(2), 169–186.

Im-Bolter, N., & Cohen, N. J. (2007). Language impairment and psychiatric comorbidities. *Pediatric Clinics of North America*, 54(3), 525–542.

Im-Bolter, N., Cohen, N. J., & Farnia, F. (2013). I thought we were good: Social cognition, figurative language, and adolescent psychopathology. *Journal of Child Psychology and Psychiatry*, 54(7), 724–732.

Joffe, V. L., Rixon, L., & Hulme, C. (2019). Improving storytelling and vocabulary in secondary school students with language disorder: A randomized controlled trial. *International Journal of Language & Communication Disorders*, 1460–6984, 12471.

Kelly, K. R. (2015). Insecure attachment representations and child personal narrative structure: Implications for delayed discourse in preschool-age children. *Attachment & Human Development*, 17(5), 448–471.

Maggio, V., Grañana, N. E., Richaudeau, A., Torres, S., Giannotti, A., & Suburo, A. M. (2014). Behavior problems in children with specific language impairment. *Journal of Child Neurology*, 29(2), 194–202.

Nilsson, K. K., & de López, K. J. (2016). Theory of mind in children with specific language impairment: A systematic review and meta-analysis. *Child Development*, 87(1), 143–153.

Norbury, C. F., Gooch, D., Wray, C., Baird, G., Charman, T., Simonoff, E., & Pickles, A. (2016). The impact of nonverbal ability on prevalence and clinical presentation of language disorder: Evidence from a population study. *Journal of Child Psychology and Psychiatry*, 57(11), 1247–1257.

Oakhill, J., Cain, K., & Elbro, C. (2015). *Understanding and teaching reading comprehension: A handbook*. Abingdon, Oxon: Routledge. Abingdon, Oxon: Routledge.

Parsons, S., & Branagan, A. (2021). *Word aware 1: Teaching vocabulary, across the day, across the curriculum* (2nd edition). Abingdon, Oxon: Routledge.

Parsons, S., & Branagan, A. (2016). *Word aware 2: Teaching vocabulary in the early years*. London: Speechmark Publishing.

Parsons, S., & Branagan, A. (2017). *Language for thinking: A structured approach for young children* (colour edition). Abingdon, Oxon: Routledge.

Pearce, P., Johnson, C., Manly, P., & Locke, J. (2014). Use of narratives to assess language disorders in an inpatient pediatric psychiatric population. *Clinical Child Psychology and Psychiatry*, 19(2), 244–259.

Perry, B., & Szalavitz, M. (2017). *The boy who was raised as a dog*. New York: Ingram Publisher Services.

Petersen, I. T., Bates, J. E., D'Onofrio, B. M., Coyne, C. A., Lansford, J. E., Dodge, K. A., & Van Hulle, C. A. (2013). Language ability predicts the development of behavior problems in children. *Journal of Abnormal Psychology*, 122(2), 542–557.

Rieffe, C., & Wiefferink, C. H. (2017). Happy faces, sad faces: Emotion understanding in toddlers and preschoolers with language impairments. *Research in Developmental Disabilities*, 62, 40–49.

Romeo, R. R., Leonard, J. A., Robinson, S. T., West, M. R., Mackey, A. P., Rowe, M. L., & Gabrieli, J. D. E. (2018). Beyond the 30-million-word gap: Children's conversational exposure is associated with language-related brain function. *Psychological Science*, doi:10.1177/0956797617742720.

Roulstone, S., Wren, Y., Bakopoulou, I., & Lindsay, G. (2012). *Exploring interventions for children and young people with speech, language and communication needs: A study of practice*. London: DfE.

Salmon, K., O'Kearney, R., Reese, E., & Fortune, C.-A. (2016). The role of language skill in child psychopathology: Implications for intervention in the early years. *Clinical Child and Family Psychology Review*, 19(4), 352–367.

Seigneuric, A., Megherbi, H., Bueno, S., Lebahar, J., & Bianco, M. (2016). Children's comprehension skill and the understanding of nominal metaphors. *Journal of Experimental Child Psychology*, 150, 346–363.

Siegel, D. J. (2014). *The developing mind second edition how relationships and the brain interact to shape who we are*. New York: Guilford Press.

Slaughter, V., Imuta, K., Peterson, C. C., & Henry, J. D. (2015). Meta-analysis of theory of mind and peer popularity in the preschool and early school years. *Child Development*, 86(4), 1159–1174.

Snow, P. C., & Powell, M. B. (2005). What's the story? An exploration of narrative language abilities in male juvenile offenders. *Psychology, Crime & Law*, 11(3), 239–253.

Tamir, M. (2011). The maturing field of emotion regulation. *Emotion Review*, 3(1), 3–7.

Torre, J. B., & Lieberman, M. D. (2018). Putting feelings into words: Affect labeling as implicit emotion regulation. *Emotion Review*, 10(2), 116–124.

van den Bedem, N. P., Dockrell, J. E., van Alphen, P. M., de Rooij, M., Samson, A. C., Harjunen, E. L., & Rieffe, C. (2018a). Depressive symptoms and emotion regulation strategies in children with and without developmental language disorder: A longitudinal study. *International Journal of Language & Communication Disorders*, 53(6), 1110–1123.

van den Bedem, N. P., Dockrell, J. E., van Alphen, P. M., Kalicharan, S. V., & Rieffe, C. (2018b). Victimization, bullying, and emotional competence: Longitudinal associations in (pre)adolescents with and without developmental language disorder. *Journal of Speech, Language, and Hearing Research*, 61(8), 2028–2044.

Westrupp, E. M., Reilly, S., McKean, C., Law, J., Mensah, F., & Nicholson, J. M. (2020). Vocabulary development and trajectories of behavioral and emotional difficulties via academic ability and peer problems. *Child Development*, 91(2), e365–e382.

Winstanley, M., Webb, R., & Conti-Ramsden, G. (2017). More or less likely to offend? Young adults with a history of developmental language disorders. *International Journal of Language and Communication Disorders*, March–April, 53(2), 256–270.

Wolters, N., Knoors, H., Cillessen, A. H. N., & Verhoeven, L. (2014). Behavioral, personality, and communicative predictors of acceptance and popularity in early adolescence. *The Journal of Early Adolescence*, 34(5), 585–605.

Further reading

Cross, M. (2011). *Children with social emotional and behavioural difficulties and communication problems: There is always a reason* (2nd edition). London: Jessica Kingsley Publishers.

Hagen, Å. M., Melby-Lervåg, M., & Lervåg, A. (2017). Improving language comprehension in preschool children with language difficulties: A cluster randomized trial. *Journal of Child Psychology and Psychiatry*, 58(10), 1132–1140.

Kim, Y.-S. G., & Phillips, B. (2016). Five minutes a day to improve comprehension monitoring in oral language contexts. *Topics in Language Disorders*, 36(4), 356–367.

Leitão, S., Claessen, M., & Kane, R. (2018). A randomized controlled trial of an oral inferential comprehension intervention for young children with developmental language disorder. *Child Language Teaching and Therapy*, 35(1), 39–54.

Levickis, P., Sciberras, E., McKean, C., Conway, L., Pezic, A., Mensah, F. K., . . . Reilly, S. (2018). Language and social-emotional and behavioural wellbeing from 4 to 7 years: a community-based study. *European Child & Adolescent Psychiatry*, 27(7), 849–859.

Spencer, Sara (ed.). (2018). *Supporting adolescents with language disorders*. Guildford: J&R Press.

Ukrainetz, T. (2015). Improving text comprehension: Scaffolding adolescents into strategic reading. *Seminars in Speech and Language*, 36(1), 17–30.

Yaghoub Zadeh, Z., Im-Bolter, N., & Cohen, N. J. (2007). Social cognition and externalizing psychopathology: An investigation of the mediating role of language. *Journal of Abnormal Child Psychology*, 35(2), 141–152.

Additional resources

Video Interaction Guidance website www.videointeractionguidance.net

The Royal College of Speech and Language Therapists (RCSLT) have a number of fact sheets which can be found here, https://www.rcslt.org/policy/uk-wide/fact-sheets-on-speech-and-language-therapy, including ones on:

Looked After Children www.rcslt.org/-/media/Project/RCSLT/rcslt-looked-after-children-factsheet.pdf

Social, Emotional and Mental Health and Wellbeing https://www.rcslt.org/-/media/docs/RCSLT_SEMH_A4_2019_Web_Singles.pdf?la=en&hash=1DDE04F06D86CCA9C3A4E537EEA96468A5632767

Behaviour and Communication https://www.rcslt.org/-/media/docs/RCSLT_

The Five Good Communication Standards help settings become 'communication friendly'; there are guidelines for looked after children https://www.rcslt.org/-/media/Project/RCSLT/5-good-standards-a4-2019.pdf

The RCSLT also has Clinical Guidelines for working with SEMH www.rcslt.org/speech-and-language-therapy/clinical-information/social-emotional-and-mental-health and Social Communication Disorder www.rcslt.org/speech-and-language-therapy/clinical-information/social-communication-disorder

See also the Social Communication Intervention Programme http://research.bmh.manchester.ac.uk/scip/ and Supporting children and young people's mental health services https://www.rcslt.org/-/media/docs/RCSLTCYPMHSA4Digital.pdf?la=en&hash=ADEF0D30638C3E9623E151BC96FDD9BBCA532ADC

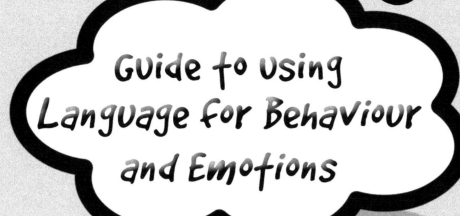

Guide to using Language for Behaviour and Emotions

Young people with SLCN and SEMH benefit from a cohesive, coordinated team approach, with everyone who comes into contact with the young person having a role to play. The *LFBE* approach can be used flexibly by the team who support each young person individually within a communication and emotion friendly environment.

The *LFBE* approach

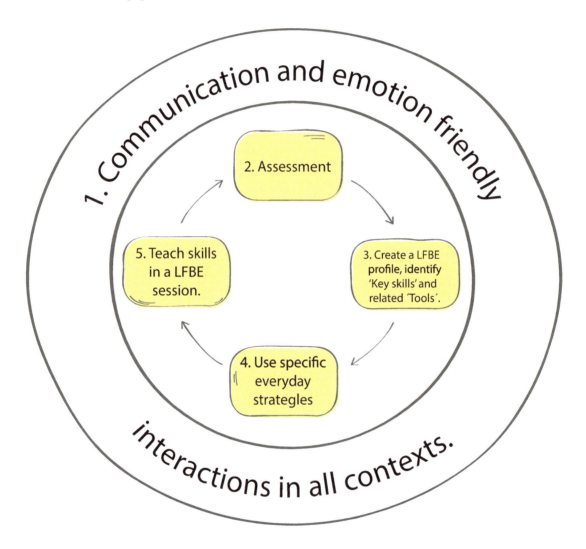

As shown previously, the *LFBE* approach starts with ensuring interactions with young people are communication and emotion friendly. The assessment informs greater understanding of the young person's needs. Targets and tools are then selected so that the daily communication environment can be specifically modified and then an individual skill development programme implemented. After an appropriate time, progress can be measured and the programme adapted accordingly. Thus, the cycle continues.

1 Creating a communication and emotion friendly environment

The daily interactions that young people experience are a key part of the development of communication and emotional skills. It is important for adults to reflect on their own interaction skills, perhaps with the support of peers or a professional such as a speech and language therapist (speech-language pathologist) who can help them build on current strengths. The skills required to interact in a constructive manner with young people with SLCN and SEMH are very particular, and even the most skilled practitioners benefit from reflection and fine-tuning of their skills.

Young people learn about communication, language, emotions and thinking skills simultaneously via positive supportive interactions. Therefore, work with *LFBE* needs to start with, and the success of it depends upon, building supportive relationships and environments as detailed next.

Building strong interpersonal relationships

Build strong relationships by being:

- Playful: relax, be genuine and enjoy the interaction.
- Accepting: everyone has a voice and a valid perspective.
- Curious: be interested in the young person and what they have to say.
- Empathic: try to see it from the other person's point of view.
- Patient: give others time.

There are three strands to creating a communication and emotion friendly environment.

1 **Communication strategies**

2 **Emotional coaching strategies**

3 **Using talk to extend young people's thinking**

These are detailed next. With colleagues, reflect on these strategies. Come back to them from time to time to remind yourselves. In a busy work schedule, fundamentals such as patience and giving time can feel like luxuries, so occasionally everyone needs reminding about how important these are.

Creating a communication and emotion friendly environment

Communication strategies

Non-verbal communication	• Be aware of your body language and tone of voice and make it calm, open and friendly. • Show you are listening with eye contact, nodding and quiet 'hmm' or 'uh-huh'. • Keep background noise and other distractions to a minimum, changing rooms if necessary.
Listening	• Listen with your full attention. Sometimes that is all that is needed. • Give time for the young person to speak. • If you need to interrupt then do so gently, asking 'is it OK if I come in here?' • In simple terms, tell the young person what you have understood.
'Listen' to body language as well	• If needed, talk about what the young person's non-verbal communication is saying about how they might be feeling e.g. 'you look a bit confused to me. Is that right?'
Language	• Keep it short. Don't say too much at one time. • Talk in short, simple sentences. • Use simple everyday vocabulary. Avoid jargon. • Pause after you speak, to allow extra time for the young person to think about what has been said. • Model language they could use e.g.: 'I agree/ disagree because. . .'
Visual support	• Use visual images as well as speech whenever you can, and especially for important information. • Use quick drawings to help explain what you are saying or to check you have understood. For example, hand-drawn stick people with thought, feeling and speech bubbles.

Checking understanding	• Do not presume a young person understands well, just because they talk a lot. • Check understanding by saying 'tell me what you need to do' or 'tell me what I said in your own words' but avoid asking 'do you understand?'

Creating a communication and emotion friendly environment

Emotional coaching strategies

Create an environment where it feels comfortable to talk	• Establish a safe space where it is OK to talk about emotions, but where there is no pressure to do so. • Set aside time to talk about emotions, but also respond in the moment. • Acknowledge how the young person feels and be empathic e.g. 'That's a big worry. I get it,' or 'You're upset. I would be too.' • Be a facilitator who gently ponders and invites responses, recognising that there is no right answer. • Try to understand the young person's perspective *before* sharing yours. • Explain your thinking, but leave the young person to do their own thinking. They need to come up with their own solutions. • Set clear boundaries about the work you are doing and your relationship.
Accept emotions	• Acknowledge that all feelings are important and there for a reason. • How we express emotions matters because how we express them can have an impact on us and others.
Build body awareness	• Help the young person to recognise body cues that are related to emotions e.g. 'What does sadness feel like in your body?', 'Does your neck feel tight or tingly? Perhaps you're stressed?'
Recognise, label and explore emotions	• Discuss emotions in context, as they happen. • Look out for emotional cues in themselves or others, also when reading books or watching films and when talking about the *LFBE* scenarios. • Point out clues which indicate how someone might be feeling e.g. 'I don't think she ever expected that to happen! I bet she was amazed' or 'look at that frown, is he confused or angry?'

	• Help the young person to label their emotions and refine and extend their understanding and use of words, e.g. 'were you annoyed or livid?' • Make sure suggestions are tentative, **always** check if you have got it right e.g. 'I wonder if you're feeling let down?' • Point out others' perspectives. • Reflect on complex or conflicted emotions. Acknowledge that it is possible to feel very different feelings at the same time e.g. You can feel loved and annoyed at the same time, or have many feelings about one event.
Don't get too attached to your feelings	• Remember that your feelings are not you, they come and go. You have a choice about what to do about them and how to react.

Creating a communication and emotion friendly environment

Using talk to extend young people's thinking

- Have a 'to and fro' conversation which allows one speaker to build on what the previous speaker has said.
- Do not allow anyone, including adults, to dominate the conversation. In one to one conversations aim for 50:50.
- Adults should guide the conversation by facilitating and modelling, not telling or directing.
- Respond to the young people's ideas with encouragement, for example, 'tell me more about that' rather than opinions or answers.
- Ground rules should be clear: have explicit agreements about listening, turn taking and respecting others' views. Everyone has a voice and their views are equally valid.
- Use words that talk about what's going on inside people's heads, such as 'think, know, believe, remember, reflect, and consider.'
- Use open questions like 'what do you think she's feeling?', rather than closed questions e.g. 'is she sad?'
- Encourage self-reflection by asking questions like 'how well did you do?' 'how did you solve that problem?' 'what helped you?'
- Aim for improvement by asking 'what would you do better or differently next time?'
- Generalise the learning away from this conversation: 'where can you apply what you learnt today?' 'Who can you tell about what you learnt? What will you say?'

2 Assessment

The communication and emotion friendly environment is essential, but assessment will enable the young person's support to be more specifically tailored to their needs. The different types of assessment provided within the *LFBE* book are outlined in the following table. The Starter Assessment is required for all young people before they start the scenario intervention. It only provides basic information, so the Complete *LFBE* Assessment is recommended. The Complete Assessment is made up of a further eight short assessments. These may be used flexibly by skilled practitioners to build a more complete profile of the young person's communication. Individual practitioners may also make the decision to undertake further assessment, particularly as none of the *LFBE* assessments are standardised. The more information that is known about a young person, the more tailored the intervention can be. Although comparatively time-consuming in the short term, thorough assessment is more likely to lead to positive impacts and time savings in the long term. The assessments can then also be used to measure progress.

1 Starter assessment		
Assessment tools provided	**Page**	**Information gathered**
In order to start the *LFBE* programme all young people **must have** completed **Assessment Scenario 1.** (For older young people, practitioners may choose to use Assessment Scenario 2 as the baseline.)	54	• Language Level to start the intervention. • Very basic information about the young person's communication from their and from an adult's perspective. This includes: saying when they do not understand, talking about feelings, telling a story and solving people problems verbally. • Information about how the young person views their support from adults.
Young person's view of their own communication.	74	
How well does the adult help me?	77	
Adults' views of young person's communication skills checklist.	79	

2 Complete *LFBE* assessment

In **addition** to the starter assessment listed on the previous page, the Complete *LFBE* Assessment provides a range of measures which may be used in their entirety or at the practitioner's discretion.

Assessment tools provided		Page	Information gathered
	Comprehension monitoring assessment	83	Ability to use comprehension monitoring strategies.
	Behaviour vocabulary assessment	91	Knowledge of the words that are used to discuss behaviour. Ability to define words.
	Crazy phrases assessment	95	Understanding of common idioms/figures of speech related to behaviour.
	Sarcasm and implied meaning assessment	100	Understanding of basic exaggeration, implied meaning, sarcasm and 'white lies'.
	Emotion words assessment	106	Understanding of a range of emotion vocabulary.
	Narrative assessment	110	Ability to structure stories.
	Solving people problems assessment	117	Ability to verbally problem-solve real-life interpersonal situations.

3 Creating a *LFBE* profile, identifying key skills and related tools

Once the assessment has been completed, the results may then be collated using the '*Language for Behaviour and Emotions* Profile' (page 126). Record the *LFBE* Language Level on the form and analyse the profile and identify which key skills to target first. Tools to teach the key skills can then be selected.

Key skills

1 What to do when things don't make sense (understanding language).
   ○ Saying when you don't understand (comprehension monitoring).
   ○ Understanding words (vocabulary).
   ○ When people don't say what they mean (figurative language).
2 Talking about feelings (emotional literacy).
   ○ What's that feeling called? (naming emotions).
   ○ Dealing with feelings (emotional regulation).
3 Finding clues and explaining your thinking (inference and verbal reasoning).
4 The story (narrative).
5 Bringing it all together and solving people problems.

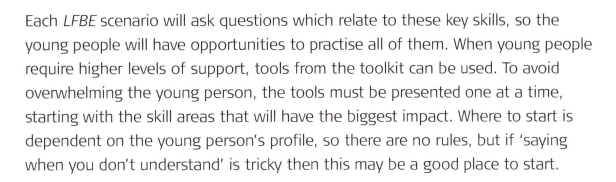

Each *LFBE* scenario will ask questions which relate to these key skills, so the young people will have opportunities to practise all of them. When young people require higher levels of support, tools from the toolkit can be used. To avoid overwhelming the young person, the tools must be presented one at a time, starting with the skill areas that will have the biggest impact. Where to start is dependent on the young person's profile, so there are no rules, but if 'saying when you don't understand' is tricky then this may be a good place to start.

When working one to one with a young person: look at the *LFBE* profile with the young person, their family and professionals and collaborate to identify which key skills are a priority. Look through the relevant tools and choose which ones are to be used. The '*LFBE* action plan' (page 131) and '*LFBE* action plan summary' (page 138) can be used to summarise the intervention and be shared with the young person, family and team members.

When working with a group: identify one key skill at a time for the whole group to focus on. Involve the young people and discuss which skills are a

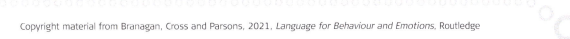

priority for them. Look through the relevant tools as a group and select the most useful ones.

- Identify one key skill to start with (choose from the key skills listed earlier).
- Look at the relevant tools for that key skill and identify the ones that are most appropriate for the young people you are working with.

Once the young people are familiar with the tools and are starting to internalise the skills, additional tools targeting another key skill can be introduced.

Use the 'Attendance sheet' (page 260) to record the key skill that will be the focus of the intervention.

Toolkit to develop the key skills

Each section of the toolkit has a simple social story to explain why these skills are important to young people, the tools themselves as well as an introduction for adults.

	Key skill	Tools in the toolkit
	Saying when you don't understand (comprehension monitoring)	• Introduction to comprehension monitoring (page 264). • Why it's important to say when things don't make sense (page 267). • Self-awareness rating (page 270). • How to check it makes sense (page 271). • What to say when you don't understand (page 273). • How to let someone know I don't understand (page 274).
	Understanding words (vocabulary)	• Introduction to developing vocabulary (page 276). • Why it's important to learn new words (page 282) • Tricky words: definitions and symbols (page 282). • Word Wizard (page 295).

	Key skill	Tools in the toolkit
		• 10 steps to learning words independently (page 296). • Behaviour vocabulary list and definitions (page 297).
	When people don't say what they mean. Crazy phrases (figures of speech/idioms), implied meaning and sarcasm	• Introduction to 'When people don't say what they mean' (page 299). • Why it's important to know when people don't say what they mean (page 301). • Definitions of crazy phrases used in the assessment (page 303). • Definitions of crazy phrases used in the scenarios (page 305). • Learning crazy phrases (page 308).
	What's that feeling called? (naming emotions)	• Introduction to talking about feelings (page 309). • Why it's important to talk about feelings (page 313). • Where do I feel that emotion? (page 314). • Grouping feelings (page 315). • Grouping feelings short version (page 325). • What's that feeling called? (page 328). • How strong is that emotion? (page 348). • What is the main feeling in the story? (page 350).
	How can we change (or remember) that feeling? (emotion regulation)	• Accepting feelings (page 356). • If you **LIKE** a feeling you can. . . (page 357). • If you **DON'T LIKE** a feeling you can. . . (page 358).
	Finding clues and explaining your thinking (inference and verbal reasoning)	• Why it's important to find clues and explain thinking. (page 361). • Scenarios (pages 140–261).

	Key skill	Tools in the toolkit
	The story (narrative)	• Narrative tools from page 363
	Solving people problems	• Solving people problem tools available from page 379.

4 Specific everyday strategies

Group or individual interventions will help to build a skill, but young people need everyone who works with them (professionals, support workers, carers and family etc.) to be aware of their needs and to be implementing specific strategies every day to have an impact. These can be identified by analysing the skill profile and using the '*LFBE* action plan' (page 131) to select strategies that will support skill development in everyday situations. By receiving support in real contexts, the young person can learn how to apply the skill, and over time do so naturally. This works best when the practitioner who is leading the intervention is in close communication with other team members and the teaching of specific skills is working in tandem with the teaching of specific strategies for daily interactions. In addition to the strategies listed next, tools from the toolkit may be implemented in the class or other learning settings. The '*LFBE* action plan' can be useful in the process of identifying specific everyday strategies and tools from the toolkit to use. They will often be beneficial to the young person's peers also.

	Key skills	Specific everyday strategies
	Saying when you don't understand (comprehension monitoring)	• Use the 'Self-awareness rating' (page 270) in class or in one to one sessions to check understanding. Ensure that adults respond when young people indicate that they do not understand. • Model strategies: saying when *you* don't understand.

	Key skills	Specific everyday strategies
		• Praise young people when they say that they do not understand. • Encourage specific strategies e.g. 'I got that bit. The bit I didn't understand was . . .'
	Understanding words (vocabulary)	• Regularly teach vocabulary to the whole class (Use *Word Aware*, Parsons & Branagan, 2021). • Use targeted vocabulary identified and taught in the group. • Use the words in context and explain their meaning.
	When people don't say what they mean. Crazy phrases (figures of speech/idioms), implied meaning and sarcasm	• Be aware of the crazy phrases (idioms) you use. • Encourage young people to identify when crazy phrases (idioms) are used or encountered in reading. • Discuss the meaning of crazy phrases (idioms) that are used. • Keep track by displaying the crazy phrases (idioms) or writing them in a book.
	What's that feeling called? (naming emotions)	• Use 'Emotional coaching strategies' (page 30) to reflect on emotions. In particular: • Set aside time to talk about emotions, but also respond in the moment. • Help the young person to label their emotions, and refine and extend their understanding and use of words, e.g. 'were you annoyed or livid?' • Look out for emotional cues in themselves or others, when reading books or watching films and when talking about the *LFBE* scenarios. • Keep track of the emotions discussed either via displays or journals.

	Key skills	Specific everyday strategies
	How can we change (or remember) that feeling? (emotion regulation)	• Use these tools to reflect on challenges/ positive experiences as they occur: • Accepting feelings (page 356). • 'If you **LIKE** a feeling you can . . .' (page 357). • 'If you **DON'T LIKE** a feeling you can . . .' (page 358). • Model use of the strategies.
	Finding clues and explaining your thinking (inference and verbal reasoning)	• Young people need language at the right level. Aim to focus questions at the level identified via the assessment. This is particularly important when reflecting on incidents and emotions are running high.
	The story (narrative)	• Use the 'Story frames' (page 368) when creating stories or when explaining what has happened, thus modelling their use.
	Bringing it all together and solving people problems	• Use the 'Problem-solving frames' (page 382) to reflect upon real problems, but be cautious when emotions are running high.

5 Teaching skills in a *LFBE* session

The specific everyday strategies are crucial, but to complement this *LFBE*, sessions can be implemented to target specific skills as highlighted via the assessment process. The sessions are built around picture-based social scenarios, 60 of which are provided in from page 140. These scenarios can be used in a number of different ways:

• One to one sessions: as part of a tailored intervention programme, individual sessions allow very specific skill development and facilitation.

• Small groups: group members take turns answering questions and offering alternative views. This facilitates the understanding of others' perspectives and provides a more real experience than one to one sessions. Group participants **must** have all had individual assessments using Assessment

Scenario 1 or 2 (page 54 or 58) prior to the group sessions. The young people attending the group can be at different *LFBE* Language Levels.

- Larger group or whole class: project the image and use it as a basis for drama, debate or social skills programmes. This method can also be used to help students generalise their learning from individual or small group settings into the classroom. It is not usually feasible to have completed individual *LFBE* Language Level assessments, but teachers/ group leaders should take care to pitch the questions at the right level.

General guide for a small group

Session frequency	Twice per week is recommended

Before the session	Complete individual assessment and '*LFBE* profile' (page 126) in order to:
	• Identify the '*LFBE* Language Level' for each young person (**B**, **C** or **D**).
	• Identify one key skill to target. Choose from:
	  ○ Saying when you don't understand
	  ○ Understanding words
	  ○ When people don't say what they mean
	  ○ Talking about feelings
	  ○ The story
	  ○ Solving people problems
	• Identify and photocopy the selected tools which support the key skill.

Very first session	• As with any group, set ground rules: have explicit agreements about listening, turn taking and respecting others' views. Everyone has a voice and their views are equally valid. • Explain the purpose of the group: use the 'Finding clues and explaining thinking' introductory story provided on page 361. • Introduce one tool from the toolkit in the first session. • **Start at scenario 1 and work through them in order.** If Assessment Scenario 2 has been used to establish the baseline, then start the intervention at Scenario 21 on page 180.

Starting subsequent sessions	• Review key learning from the last session and how the young people have applied that to the wider context. • Remind the young people about the strategies they are learning and associated tools. • Introduce chosen tools from the toolkit. Focus on one key skill area at a time.
Using the scenarios	• Present the picture. Adults or young people may read the story. • Select questions at the right level and **take turns** to ask and answer questions. Aim for equal turns in talking throughout. • **Both adults and young people should both ask and answer questions.** The aim is to have a conversation, with the young people hearing adult models. • **Most questions should be at the young person's *LFBE* Language Level or below (B, C or D).** • The questions are designed to be asked in horizontal order, left to right. If a question is marked '←'then the lower level question must be asked first. • Focus on having a discussion about the issues raised rather than trying to get a 'right' answer. If multiple answers are possible then open up the discussion and ask others' views. • Model the process of answering a question. Where does the information come from? What clues do you look at? What options do you look at? How do you decide which is best? Draw or write this process so young people can then use it as a model for their own thinking. • **Do not write down what the young people say**. This interferes with interaction. Monitoring should be via assessments and attendance only.

Using the tools from the toolkit	• Each member of the group will have a *LFBE* profile which will help to identify the key skill to focus on. **Pick one key skill for the group as a whole to focus on.**
	Key skills:
	  ◦ Saying when you don't understand
	  ◦ Understanding words

	<ul><li>When people don't say what they mean</li><li>Talking about feelings</li><li>The story</li><li>Solving people problems</li></ul><ul><li>Once you have identified which key skill for the group to focus on, look at the tools and find the tools that are most suitable for your young people.</li><li>Only introduce one tool per session. Do not introduce any new tools until the last one has been understood and is being used productively, so it may take several sessions for some skills to get to this level.</li><li>Take care explaining how each tool can be used. Provide examples.</li><li>Model how the tool can be useful in the group and in other contexts.</li><li>Gradually reduce the amount of support so that the young people become more independent in their application of the strategies.<ul><li>Model how to use the tool.</li><li>Talk through how the young people can use the tool.</li><li>Present the tool and occasionally prompt.</li><li>Have the tool visible but only use it if requested.</li><li>Use the strategies without the tool.</li></ul></li><li>Provide feedback on their use of the tool, or opportunities when it could have been used.</li></ul>
Helping every young person succeed	<ul><li>The aim is that the young people succeed with most of the questions but are gently challenged, so they develop new skills. However, they may occasionally struggle with particular questions.</li><li>Do NOT alter the wording of the questions.</li><li>Useful strategies include:<ul><li>Repeat the question.</li><li>Repeat the story or part of the story.</li><li>Draw attention to key parts of the picture or text.</li><li>Ask a question from an easier Language Level.</li></ul></li></ul>

	○ Ask other group members, and then ask the original young person again. ○ Select a relevant tool from the toolkit and go through the steps. Then re-ask the question.
End of the session	• Answer the last question which links the main point of the scenario back to the young people's lives. The adults and young people should all talk about their experiences. • Recap the learning and ask the group participants to think about how this applies to their lives. • Discuss how skills used might be generalised into class and home. • Encourage self-reflection by asking questions, such as, 'How well did you do?' 'What was easy or hard?' 'What helped you?'
After the session	Support generalisation. • Make sure that everyone (families and professionals) who interacts with the young person knows the skills being targeted so they can notice when the young person uses these skills and praise them. Specific praise is most useful e.g.: 'I like the way you worked out about . . .' or 'you had some great ideas about changing feelings, such as . . .' Other generalisation ideas: • The young person takes a photocopy of the scenario and talks about it with others. • The learning is written on a sticky note and given to a teacher. • A 'learning journal' is established for group participants to write in each week. • Text messages or notes are sent to families with key tasks to practise.

Note: this structure is easily adaptable for individual interventions.

6 Reassessment

Reassessment should be completed every 20 scenarios, by using another assessment scenario and by asking the young person to reflect on their skills using the 'How well did I do' assessment (page 123). This will allow monitoring of their progress and further tailoring of the intervention. The assessment scenarios increase in length and complexity. The table following outlines which assessment to use.

	Assessment scenario	**Young person's views**
After scenarios 1–20 are complete	Assessment scenario 2	How well did I do?
After scenarios 21–40 are complete	Assessment scenario 3	How well did I do?
After scenarios 41–60 are complete	Assessment scenario 4	How well did I do?

If a young person is not making progress then effort should be made to pinpoint the factors that are hindering this. If not already completed, a complete *LFBE* assessment should be conducted. If major concerns persist then referral to specialists is recommended.

Assessment

General assessment administration guidelines

Ensure you are familiar with each assessment before starting with a young person. Role play with a colleague if necessary. The purpose of the assessment is to find out what the young person is able to do independently. Therefore, you should be generally encouraging and supportive, but don't prompt them. For instance, you may say things: such as 'well done, good effort, keep trying' or 'tell me more' but <u>do not</u> to ask follow up questions that are not listed.

Exceptions

- In the 'assessment scenario' and 'comprehension monitoring' assessments there are follow up questions to ask, but these are specified.

- The 'Young person's views of their own communication' and 'how well does the adult help me?' are about capturing the young person's personal opinion, so prompting is permitted as long as it does not influence the young person's view unduly.

Record as much detail as possible without interrupting the flow too much. At times, audio recording may be required (with consent).

Language for Behaviour and Emotions assessment overview

	Sources of information	Information gathered
1 Understanding What to do when things don't make sense		
1a Comprehension monitoring Saying when you don't understand	Starter assessment Assessment scenario Adults' views of young person's communication Young Person's views of their own communication	Starter assessment gathers information about Spontaneous use of comprehension monitoring strategies (e.g.: asking about the meaning of words/phrases or asking for repeats) Adults' and young person's views
	Additional elements for Complete *LFBE* Assessment Comprehension monitoring assessment	Additional assessment adds further information about Use of comprehension monitoring strategies (e.g.: asking about meaning or for a repeat)

	Sources of information	Information gathered
1b Understanding words (vocabulary)	<u>Starter assessment</u> Adults' views of young person's communication: one question only	<u>Starter assessment gathers information about</u> Adults' views of young person's understanding of vocabulary (one question only)
	<u>Additional elements for Complete LFBE Assessment</u> Behaviour vocabulary assessment	<u>Additional assessment adds further information about</u> Knowledge of behaviour-related vocabulary Ability to define words
1c Figurative language When people don't say what they mean	<u>Starter assessment</u> Adults' views of young person's communication: one question each about idioms, sarcasm and implied meaning	<u>Starter assessment gathers information about</u> Adults' views of young person's understanding of idioms, sarcasm and implied meaning (one question for each only)
	<u>Additional elements for Complete LFBE Assessment</u> Crazy phrases assessment Sarcasm and implied meaning assessment	<u>Additional assessment adds further information about</u> Understanding of common idioms related to behaviour Understanding of sarcasm, idioms, implied meaning and 'white lies'

2 Talking about feelings

		Starter assessment	Starter assessment gathers information about
	2a Naming emotions What's that feeling called?	**Starter assessment** Assessment scenario Adults' views of young person's communication Young person's views of their own communication	**Starter assessment gathers information about** Capacity to label main character's emotion appropriately Capacity to apply emotion accurately to own experience Adults' and young person's views of ability to use emotion vocabulary
		Additional elements for Complete *LFBE* Assessment Emotion words assessment	**Additional assessment adds further information about** Understanding of emotion vocabulary
	2b Emotional regulation Dealing with feelings	**Starter assessment** Assessment scenario Adults' views of young person's communication Young person's views of their own communication	**Starter assessment gathers information about** At least one example per scenario for talking about how main character could manage own emotions. Adults' and young person's views of ability to manage emotions
		Additional elements for Complete *LFBE* Assessment No additional assessment for this dimension	N/A

COMPANION @ WEBSITE

	Sources of information	Information gathered
3 Inference and verbal reasoning Finding clues and explaining thinking	Starter assessment Assessment scenario	Starter assessment gathers information about Ability to understand questions, infer and verbally reason. Level of questions to target during intervention
	Additional elements for Complete *LFBE* Assessment No additional assessment for this dimension	N/A
4 Narrative The story	Starter assessment Assessment scenario Adults' views of young person's communication Young person's views of their own communication	Starter assessment gathers information about Ability to retell a story and generate an ending. Adults' and young person's views of ability to generate stories
	Additional elements for Complete *LFBE* Assessment Narrative assessment	Starter assessment gathers information about Ability to structure narrative on more detailed retell task

5 Bringing it all together and solving people problems	<u>Starter assessment</u> Assessment scenario Adults' views of young person's communication Young Person's views of their own communication	<u>Starter assessment gathers information about</u> Ability to talk through steps logically to come up with an answer with minimal prompting. Adults' and young person's views of ability to solve people problems with words
	<u>Additional elements for Complete</u> *LFBE* Assessment Solving people problems assessment	<u>Starter assessment gathers information about</u> Ability to apply verbal problem-solving to real life situations

Assessment record sheet: Scenario 1

Assessment record sheet: Scenario 1

To be completed prior to commencing the *Language for Behaviour and Emotions* programme.

Name:	Date:

1 Present the accompanying picture. Read this story to the young person.

Diego was really good at football and so he had been selected to go to training at the new football club after school. Diego had been told that the coach was really good and that the facilities were unparalleled. Diego didn't know anyone else who was going to be there and he had never met the coach before. He wanted his dad to come in with him.

2 During/after reading the story observe if the young person . . .

Spontaneously asked if they did not know the meaning of a word or phrase	☐ Yes	☐ No
Spontaneously asked for repeats of parts that they were not sure about/cannot remember	☐ Yes	☐ No

3 After the story ask the young person . . .

How well did you understand the story?	☐ Didn't really understand it	☐ Understood some of it	☐ Understood it
Is there anything I could do to help you understand the story better? (If the answer is yes, go to 4)			

4 Implement the strategy that the young person suggested and tick the relevant strategy used.

☐ Reread the story ☐ Discussed unfamiliar vocabulary ☐ Discussed unfamiliar phrases ☐ Other: _____

5 Ask all of these questions. Do not miss any out. Provide general encouragement but do not prompt. Record the young person's answer exactly as they say it. Write on the reverse of photocopied sheet, as required

Question	Young person's answer	Language level			
		A	B	C	D
1 Where is Diego going?					
2 Finish this sentence: 'Diego had been told that the coach . . .'					
3 Who does Diego want to come into the training with him?					
4 How does Diego feel?					
5 What could Diego say to his Dad?					
6 What else could Diego do or say that might be even better?					
7 What does 'coach' mean?					
8 Who is someone who is not going to football training with Diego?					
9 Why does it bother Diego that he has to go to the training session alone?					
10 What could Diego do that will make himself feel a little better?					
11 Retell this story and add your own ending to show what happens next.					
12 What would be the consequences if Diego refused to go to training? (Tell me 3 things)					

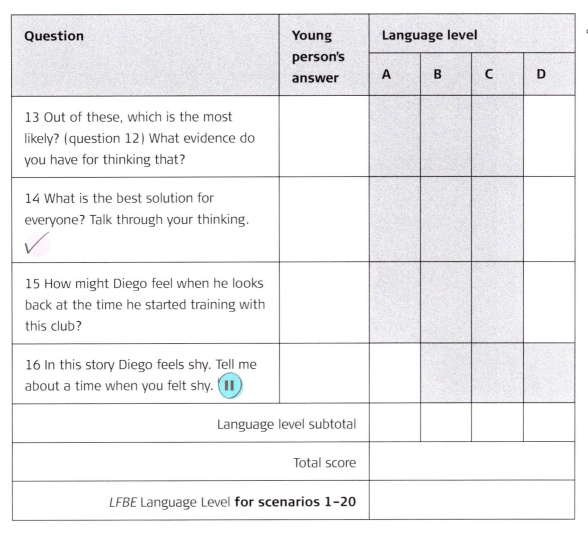

Question	Young person's answer	Language level			
		A	B	C	D
13 Out of these, which is the most likely? (question 12) What evidence do you have for thinking that?					
14 What is the best solution for everyone? Talk through your thinking. ✓					
15 How might Diego feel when he looks back at the time he started training with this club?					
16 In this story Diego feels shy. Tell me about a time when you felt shy. ❙❙					
Language level subtotal					
Total score					
LFBE Language Level **for scenarios 1–20**					

See scoring guidance on page 70 and further analysis on page 72.

Assessment record sheet: Scenario 2

Assessment record sheet: Scenario 2

To be administered after completing scenarios 1–20 and before commencing scenarios 21–40. It may be appropriate for some older young people to omit scenarios 1–20. In which case this assessment scenario may be used as their starting point.

Name:	Date:

1 Present the accompanying picture. Read the story to the young person.

Chantelle had a conundrum. Yesterday, when her sister brought home a drawing from nursery, Chantelle's mum went on and on about how wonderful and beautiful the picture was. Chantelle couldn't remember a time when her mum made such a fuss about her work. So, Chantelle made a plan. After school she got out her pens and pencils and spent a very long time drawing the best picture she could. As soon as she had finished, Chantelle stuck her own picture on the fridge so that everyone could see it. Now all she had to do was wait.

2 During/after reading the story observe if the young person. . .

Spontaneously asked if they did not know the meaning of a word or phrase	☐ Yes	☐ No
Spontaneously asked for repeats of parts that they were not sure about/cannot remember	☐ Yes	☐ No

3 After the story ask the young person. . .

How well did you understand the story?	☐ Didn't really understand it	☐ Understood some of it	☐ Understood it
Is there anything I could do to help you understand the story better? (If the answer is yes, go to 4)			

4 Implement the strategy that the young person suggested and tick relevant strategy used.

☐ Reread the story ☐ Discussed unfamiliar vocabulary ☐ Discussed unfamiliar phrases ☐ Other: _____

5 Ask all of these questions. Do not omit any. Provide general encouragement but do not prompt. Record the young person's answer exactly as they said it. Write on the reverse of photocopied sheet, as required.

Question	Young person's answer	Language level			
		A	B	C	D
1 Who is this story about?					
2 Finish this sentence: 'Yesterday, when her sister brought home a drawing. . .'					
3 Where did Chantelle put her picture?					
4 How does Chantelle feel about her sister?					
5 What does 'plan' mean?					
6 What was Chantelle's plan?					
7 What might happen next?					
8 Why might Chantelle's Mum not notice that Chantelle has a problem?					
9 Is Chantelle's plan a good plan? (yes/no) Why/why not?					
10 What could Chantelle do to make herself feel better? (without drawing a picture)					
11 Retell this story, and add your own ending to show what happens next.					
12 What is Chantelle's motive for putting her picture on the fridge?					

Question	Young person's answer	Language level			
		A	B	C	D
13 What can you infer from this story about Chantelle's age?					
14 What is the best solution for everyone? Talk through your thinking. ✓					
15 What are the consequences of that? (question 14)					
16 In this story, Chantelle felt jealous. Tell me about a time when you felt jealous. ⏸					
Language level subtotal					
Total score					
LFBE Language Level **for scenarios 21–40**					

See scoring guidance on page 70 and further analysis on page 72.

Assessment record sheet: Scenario 3

Assessment record sheet: Scenario 3

To be administered before commencing scenarios 41–60.

Name:	Date:

1 Present the accompanying picture. Read the story to the young person.

Freddie always thought that his teacher was a dragon who didn't like him, but today she had chosen him to take this important envelope to the school office. Freddie knew that if he got caught taking a peek inside, he would get into trouble, but he really couldn't understand why his teacher had chosen him, and why the envelope was so paramount. He thought that if he stopped somewhere quiet where no one could see him, perhaps he could take a look. Freddie slowed his pace as he went downstairs, but before he got to take a look, some children appeared on the landing. He waited until they had passed, but as he opened the envelope a voice boomed from the top of the stairs, 'Freddie!'

2 During/after reading the story observe if the young person. . .

Spontaneously asked if they did not know the meaning of a word or phrase	☐ Yes	☐ No
Spontaneously asked for repeats of parts that they were not sure about/cannot remember	☐ Yes	☐ No

3 After the story ask the young person. . .

How well did you understand the story?	☐ Didn't really understand it	☐ Understood some of it	☐ Understood it
Is there anything I could do to help you understand the story better? (If the answer is yes, go to 4)			

4 Implement the strategy that the young person suggested and tick the relevant strategy used.

☐ Reread the story ☐ Discussed unfamiliar vocabulary ☐ Discussed unfamiliar phrases ☐ Other: _____

5 Ask all of these questions. Do not omit any. Provide general encouragement but do not prompt. Record the young person's answer exactly as they said it. Write on the reverse of photocopied sheet, as required.

Question	Young person's answer	Language level			
		A	B	C	D
1 What has Freddie been given?					
2 Where has Freddie been asked to go?					
3 Who did Freddie see on the landing?					
4 How is Freddie feeling when he is carrying the envelope?					
5 How do Freddie's feelings change when he hears his name called?					
6 Who could it be on the stairs calling his name?					
7 What does 'peek' mean?					
8 Why did Freddie slow his pace on the stairs?					
9 What does 'his teacher was a dragon' mean?					
10 When Freddie hears his name being called, you said he felt . . . how could he make himself feel a bit better?					
11 Put this story into your own words, and add your own ending to show what happens next.					

Question	Young person's answer	Language level			
		A	**B**	**C**	**D**
12 What is Freddie's motive for looking in the envelope?					
13 What might be the consequences of Freddie looking in the envelope?					
14 What's a solution that everyone involved would be satisfied with? Talk through your thinking. ✓					
15 If you found out that it was Freddie's birthday today, would that change how you thought about this story? (yes/no) How?					
16 Freddie was being nosy. Tell me about a time when you were nosy. ⏸					
Language level subtotal					
Total score					
LFBE Language Level **for scenarios 41–60**					

See scoring guidance on page 70 and further analysis on page 72.

Assessment record sheet: Scenario 4

Assessment record sheet: Scenario 4

To be administered after completing the *Language for Behaviour and Emotions* programme.

Name:	Date:

1 Present the accompanying picture. Read the story to the young person.

Layla had a brand-new phone and was showing everyone at school. Several students were jostling and by the time Nathan got to look at the phone, half the class had already seen it. Nathan only had it for a few seconds when he was pushed and although he tried to hold onto the phone, it fell on the ground. Layla wasn't looking as Max picked up the phone. Then Max shouted 'Bianca just broke Layla's phone! Bianca just broke Layla's phone!' Layla spun around and scrutinised her phone, which now had a big scratch across the screen, and she got really upset. Max whispered to Nathan, 'It was me who pushed you, but if you say anything about this to anyone, you'll get it in the neck.' Although Layla was his friend and she looked sad for the rest of the day, Nathan didn't go and speak to her about what happened. He knew he should, but still he couldn't speak to her.

2 During/after reading the story observe if the young person. . .

Spontaneously asked if they did not know the meaning of a word or phrase	☐ Yes	☐ No
Spontaneously asked for repeats of parts that they were not sure about/cannot remember	☐ Yes	☐ No

3 After the story ask the young person. . .

How well did you understand the story?	☐ Didn't really understand it	☐ Understood some of it	☐ Understood it
Is there anything I could do to help you understand the story better? (If the answer is yes, go to 4)			

4 Implement the strategy that the young person suggested and tick relevant strategy used

☐ Reread the story ☐ Discussed unfamiliar vocabulary ☐ Discussed unfamiliar phrases ☐ Other: _____

5 Ask all of these questions. Do not omit any. Provide general encouragement but do not prompt. Record the young person's answer exactly as they said it. Write on the reverse of photocopied sheet, as required.

Question	Young person's answer	Language level			
		A	B	C	D
1 Where does this story take place?					
2 What did Layla bring to school?					
3 What happened?					
4 How does Nathan feel?					
5 What does 'jostling' mean?					
6 Who has been affected by this incident?					
7. What's the main issue here?					
8 Why doesn't Max speak to Layla?					
9 What does 'get it in the neck' mean?					
10 Nathan is feeling pretty bad right now. How can he make himself feel a little better?					
11 Put this story into your own words, and add your own ending to show what happens next.					
12 Tell me this story from Layla's perspective.					

Question	Young person's answer	Language level			
		A	B	C	D
13 What makes this a difficult problem for Nathan to solve?					
14 What is the best solution to this problem and why? ✓					
15 How might Layla feel when she looks back on this incident?					
16 In this story Nathan feels guilty. Tell me about a time when you felt guilty. ⏸					
Language level subtotal					
Total score					
LFBE Language Level					

See scoring guidance on page 70 and further analysis on page 72.

Scoring guidelines

3 points	The young person has understood the question and has given a relevant and appropriate answer. Longer answers are well structured and easy to follow. The answer is accurate and does not require the listener to interpret further. There may be minor grammatical errors but these do not affect the meaning conveyed.
2 points	The young person's response gives a clear indication that they have understood the question. The response is plausible but it requires the listener to interpret a little. Longer answers may lack a bit of structure or be missing minor elements. Grammatical errors may mildly affect the meaning conveyed.
1 point	The young person's response shows possible understanding of the question. The answer has some relation to the question, but it is ambiguous. It is possible, but less plausible. Longer answers may be rambling and lack clarity, or too brief and omitting key information. The listener needs to interpret the young person's answer. A young person can score a maximum of 1 if they point without speaking.
0 points	Here the answer is incorrect, inaccurate and tangential to the question or no response is given.

Note: The complexity and length of the story increases with each assessment scenario and this may impact on the Language Level achieved. For some young people as the story complexity increases, they may find it harder to answer the same level of questions.

Allocation of Language Level following assessment

0–18	Do not start the programme. The young person is more suited to *Language for Thinking* (Parsons and Branagan, 2016) which has simpler stories and targets the foundation skills for *LFBE*. Use 'Solving people problems *LFBE* Language Level A' (page 379) to support day-to-day problems.

19–25	Language Level B. Also consider using *Language for Thinking* as above to establish foundation skills
26–34	Language Level C
35–44	Language Level D
44+	This section of the programme is complete. Repeat assessment with next assessment scenario. If this score is achieved for assessment Scenario 4 then there is no need to continue with this programme unless the LFBE complete assessment indicates other areas of need.

Scenario assessment further analysis

Tick the relevant box and comment as required. Information can then be added to the *LFBE* profile.

Theme	Questions	Guide	Not needed	Really tricky	A bit tricky	No problem
Comprehension monitoring	B, C, D	• Spontaneously using strategies (asking about meaning or for information to be repeated). • Able to use strategies when prompted.	Doesn't use strategies but clearly understood text and questions.	Did not understand all of the text, but did not use strategies.	Used strategies when prompted.	Spontaneously uses strategies.

Scenario assessment further analysis

Score all of the scenario questions using 'Scoring guidelines' on page 70. Maximum score for each question is 3.

Theme	Question	Guide	Comments	Really tricky Score 0–1	A bit tricky Score 2	No problem Score 3
Emotion vocabulary	4	Label's main character's emotion appropriately				
	16	Applies emotion accurately to own experience.				
Emotion regulation	10	Able to generate a strategy that the main character could use.				
Narrative	11	Does story have clear structure? Is it easy to follow?				
Problem-solving	14	Ability to talk through steps logically to come up with an answer, with minimal prompting.				

Young person's view of their own communication

Name:	Date:

Discuss each question in turn. The 'How do you find it?' rating scale (page 270) will provide support.

		Really tricky	Tricky sometimes	Easy
When things don't make sense	1 How easy or tricky is it to ask questions if things don't make sense?			
	2 What's it like when people use long/ complex words?			
	3 How easy or tricky is it to work out if someone is being sarcastic?			
Talking about feelings: What's that feeling called?	4 How easy or tricky is it for you to work out how you are feeling?			
	5 How easy or tricky is it to understand what others are thinking or feeling?			
	6 How easy or tricky is it to put into words how you are feeling?			

		Really tricky	Tricky sometimes	Easy
Talking about feelings: Dealing with feelings	7 If you are feeling bad, how easy or tricky is it for you to make yourself feel better? e.g. If you are feeling really angry, can you get yourself to calm down?			
	8 If you feel good, how easy or tricky is it for you to try and remember that feeling?			
Finding clues and explaining your thinking	9 How easy or tricky is it for you to answer questions and explain things?			
The story	10 How easy or tricky is it to tell someone (who wasn't there) all the details about something that happened?			

		Really tricky	Tricky sometimes	Easy
Solving people problems ✓	11 When you disagree or argue with friends, how easy or tricky is it for you to talk about it and make it better?			
	12 When you disagree or argue with other people at school, how easy or tricky is it for you to talk about it and make it better?			
	13 When you disagree or argue with your family/ people you live with, how easy or tricky is it for you talk about it and make it better?			

Comments

How well does the adult help me?

Young person's name:	Date:

Think about one adult who works with you. It could be a teacher, a teaching assistant or anyone else. How well do they help you communicate? Are there any ways that they could help you more? Don't tell me who you are thinking of. You don't need to say their name. The 'How well does the adult help me?' rating scale (page 270) will provide support.

	How well does the adult help you communicate by doing these things?			Does this help you? Would it help if the adult did this more?		
	Not great	OK sometimes	They are great at this	OK as it is. It doesn't really matter	They are great at this and it helps me	Would like the adult to do this more often
Listening to me						
Helping me to put my thoughts into words						
Explaining things so that I can understand						

	How well does the adult help you communicate by doing these things?			Does this help you? Would it help if the adult did this more?		
	Not great	OK sometimes	They are great at this	OK as it is. It doesn't really matter	They are great at this and it helps me	Would like the adult to do this more often
Encouraging me to ask questions when I don't understand						
Helping me to understand my feelings						
Helping me to calm down or feel better						
Helping me to use words to solve problems with other people						

What other things do people do that really help you?

Are there other things that people could do to help you? Things that they might not be doing now?

Adults' views of the young person's communication

Young person's name:	Date:
Adult(s) completing this form:	

This checklist is best completed by family members or practitioners who know the young person well. If there are questions you cannot answer, it would be useful to spend some time observing the young person or talking to other people who know them to gather this information. *LFBE* will be most effective if it addresses real issues, so this information is important.

	Don't know	Really tricky	Tricky sometimes	No problem
1 How tricky is it for the young person to ask for clarification, such as: • 'What does that mean?' • 'I don't get that?' • 'Can you say that again?'				
2 How tricky is it for the young person to understand complex words and jargon that adults use?				
3 How tricky is it for the young person to understand 'crazy phrases' (figures of speech/idioms) e.g. 'Get a grip'.				

	Don't know	Really tricky	Tricky sometimes	No problem
4 How tricky is it for the young person to understand sarcasm?				
5 How tricky is it for the young person to understand when people use implied meaning? (e.g. 'I wouldn't take my shoes off now' meaning 'Don't take your shoes off.')				
6 How tricky is it for the young person to describe how someone is feeling using basic words e.g. 'confused, cross, happy, sad'?				
7 When talking about feelings, how tricky is it for the young person to use more complex terms e.g. 'disappointed, irritated, stubborn'?				
8 How tricky is it for the young person to spontaneously talk about their own feelings?				
9 How tricky is it for the young person to talk about why they, or someone else, might feel the way they do?				
10 How tricky is it for the young person to work out what others are thinking or feeling? (Without being told)				

11 How tricky is it for the young person to manage their emotions when things aren't going as they expected? E.g. if they didn't get to do the things they want or they try something and it doesn't work.					
12 Does the young person have any strategies for changing a negative emotion? E.g. they are feeling cross but are able to calm themselves down.					
13 How tricky is it for the young person to answer questions and explain things?					
14 How tricky is it for the young person to clearly describe an event to someone who wasn't there?					
15 When relaying events, how tricky is it for the young person to give enough detail so that the listener is able to easily follow what they are saying?					
16 When their explanation is not clear, how tricky is it for the young person to respond to questions and fill in the missing gaps?					

	Don't know	Really tricky	Tricky sometimes	No problem
17 If the young person has a problem with other people, how tricky is it for them to try and sort it out by talking about it?				
18 Is the young person able to think of a variety of ways of solving a problem?				
19 How tricky is it for the young person to spontaneously consider the consequences of different actions? (e.g. If I do X, Y is likely to happen)				
20 How tricky is it for the young person to talk about or acknowledge the other person's point of view?				

Summary/comments

Once completed, transfer responses to the *LFBE* profile.

Comprehension monitoring assessment

Name:	Date:

This assessment is designed to find out if the young person:

- Recognises when they have not understood or remembered all of the information.

- Is able to suggest comprehension monitoring strategies that would help them understand more.

The stories aim to stretch most young people's ability to understand by using some longer stories, some complex vocabulary and crazy phrases (idioms/figures of speech), thus providing them with opportunities to use comprehension monitoring strategies.

Instructions

- Say 'I am going to read you some very short stories and then ask you about them. Most people find these stories a bit tricky.'

- Read the first story. Pause for a moment to allow the young person a chance to spontaneously comment or show confusion. Record if they show any indication. After the pause, ask 'Did you understand the story?' Record the yes/no response.

- Next ask 'Is there anything I could do to help you understand this story better?' Record their response by ticking the corresponding box.

- Implement the strategies suggested by the young person e.g. If the young person asks you to explain what a word means, do so.

- Finally say to the young person 'Tell me the main facts about this story, using your own words.' Tick any relevant information they can tell you. If they use the underlined words, ask them if there is another way that they could say that. Only tick the main facts given if they can say it in their own words.

- If they do not give all the information ask 'anything else?' but only say this once per question.

- Record the strategies suggested and used (on the following page).

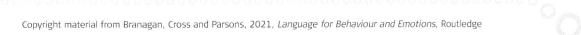

Extension

- The purpose of the additional two items is to analyse the impact of increased support. This will be particularly useful when the young person has not understood some or all of the paragraphs and/or not suggested strategies themselves.

- Follow the same instructions as above, but instead of asking 'is there anything I could do to help you understand this story better?' offer the suggested strategies. Record the young person's choice and then implement the strategy. If the young person does not choose a strategy, select one and trial it.

Again, ask the young person to tell you the key facts of the story and record these. If any of the underlined words are used, ask the young person to express it in their own words.

Comprehension monitoring assessment

Read the story to the young person	'Did you understand the story?'		'Is there anything I could do to help you understand this story better?'	Provide support strategies as requested and then instruct: 'Tell me the main facts about this story, using your own words.' If they use the underlined words, ask them if there is another way that they could say that. Shows understanding of the main facts:
	yes	no		
1 Paige was a diehard Comic Con fan. She went whenever she could. Her pièce de résistance was her Wonder Woman outfit.			☐ Don't know/no response/can't ask for what help they need. ☐ No, I understand it. ☐ Tells you what help they need.	☐ Paige was very keen on going to events about comic books/characters. ☐ Her most amazing costume was Wonder Woman.
2 Usually our science teacher Mr Columbus could look so stern it was unnerving. When he talked about geocaching though, he really came alive and showed his more likeable personality.			☐ Don't know/no response/can't ask for what help they need. ☐ No, I understand it. ☐ Tells you what help they need.	☐ Mr Columbus looked rather serious. ☐ He enjoyed talking about his special hobby.

Read the story to the young person	'Did you understand the story?'		'Is there anything I could do to help you understand this story better?'	Provide support strategies as requested and then instruct: 'Tell me the main facts about this story, using your own words.' If they use the underlined words, ask them if there is another way that they could say that. Shows understanding of the main facts:
	yes	no		
3 Connor had not seen his grandparents since they emigrated a number of years ago. He felt particularly fretful as he waited for them. Dad had said that Grandad was now rotund and that Nana was now quite frail.			☐ Don't know/no response/can't ask for what help they need. ☐ No, I understand it. ☐ tells you what help they need.	☐ Grandparents had moved to another country a few years ago. ☐ Connor was worrying as he waited. ☐ Grandad was fat. ☐ Nana was weak.
4 Miss Luddon was a sprightly old lady who lived in a very old house on our street. She was happy to chat to people about just about anything, especially her prestigious academic career. However, her age was a card she kept close to her chest.			☐ Don't know/no response/can't ask for what help they need ☐ No, I understand it. ☐ Tells you what help they need.	☐ Miss Luddon was active and talkative. ☐ She didn't tell people her age. ☐ She used to work at universities/colleges. ☐ She was well thought of.

Q 1–4. Note spontaneous strategies suggested by the young person (accompanies pages 85–86)

☐ Reread/say it again

☐ Asked about unfamiliar vocabulary

☐ Asked about unfamiliar phrases

☐ Say it in shorter sentences

☐ I didn't get the bit about . . . .

☐ Other (please specify)

Extension items

Read the story to the young person	'Did you understand the story?'		If no, 'to help you understand this better I could . . . .' 1. Say it again 2. Explain some of the tricky words/phrases 3. Say it in shorter sentences Which one would you like me to do?	Provide support strategies and then instruct: 'Tell me the main facts about this story, using your own words.' If they use the underlined words, ask them if there is another way that they could say that. Shows understanding of the main facts:
	yes	no		

5. Troy had never met an entomologist before, but when he saw his new neighbour's collection he was transfixed. The highlight was definitely the arachnids.	☐ Don't know. ☐ Say it again. ☐ Explain some of the tricky words/phrases. ☐ Say it in shorter sentences. ☐ Other. . .	☐ Troy had never met an insect/spider collector. ☐ He was amazed at the collection. ☐ He particularly liked the spiders.
6 Despite feeling morose, Keesha reminded herself that the exam results were not the end of the world, but she would have to work hard to rectify her situation.	☐ Don't know. ☐ Say it again. ☐ Explain some of the tricky words/phrases. ☐ Say it in shorter sentences. ☐ Other. . .	☐ Keesha was feeling sad. ☐ Her exam results were not the worst thing that could happen. ☐ To improve, she would need to work hard.

Interpreting the comprehension monitoring assessment

Level	Use of strategies to promote understanding	The effectiveness of the strategies to support understanding	Interpretation	Action
Really Tricky	Frequently unable to suggest strategies to support their own understanding. Limited use of suggested strategies.	Missing out key facts of many of the short stories even after opportunities to apply strategies have been provided.	Has few or no effective strategies to enable them to understand.	• Use the tools in the 'Saying when you don't understand' section of the toolkit on page 264 to discuss and prompt for effective strategies. • Before starting each scenario, emphasise the comprehension monitoring strategies that will be used. • Spend time making sure the young person has retained the story by asking them to retell it. • Together identify any missing information. • Encourage use of strategies in everyday situations.
Tricky Sometimes	Sometimes able to suggest strategies that support their own understanding. May use a limited range of strategies.	When given opportunities to apply strategies, occasionally leaves out key facts from a few of the stories.	Is developing comprehension monitoring skills and strategies but applying them inconsistently.	

Level	Use of strategies to promote understanding	The effectiveness of the strategies to support understanding	Interpretation	Action
No Problem	Consistently able to suggest strategies that support their understanding.	Able to provide key facts after requested strategies were implemented.	Good use of comprehension monitoring strategies.	Monitor and encourage use of comprehension monitoring strategies in less-structured settings.
	Identified the key facts without support.	Identified the key facts without support, so strategies not required.	Clarification strategies were not necessary as reliably relayed key information.	

'Really tricky', 'Tricky sometimes' and 'No problem' indicate an ability to understand and respond to this task and are linked to the actions that need to be taken. There are no age norms, thus this indicator does not show whether the skill is age-appropriate or not.

Behaviour vocabulary assessment

Name:	Date:

Ask the young person to rate themselves on how well they know each word. Use the 'Understanding of words or phrases' (on page 270) as needed. If the young person indicates that they know the word, then ask them to use the word in a sentence or explain its meaning. By their very nature, some of these words are abstract, which makes them hard to explain. The explanations do not need to be perfect, but enough information needs to be provided for the listener to be sure that the young person has a basic understanding. Can they explain the word so that someone who had never heard it before would understand? Rate the young person's responses. You can refer to p. 297, Definitions of words connected with behaviour, to help with rating.

Stop if five consecutive words are unknown.

	Young person self-assessment			If they say that they know what it means, ask the young person to use the word in a sentence or to explain its meaning.		
	Never heard of it	Heard of it but not sure what it means	Know what it means	Nothing relevant	Partial infor-mation	Clearly shows under-standing
1 Time out						
2 Calm down						
3 Choice						
4 Disagree						
5 Positive						
6 Point of view						

	Young person self-assessment			If they say that they know what it means, ask the young person to use the word in a sentence or to explain its meaning.		
	Never heard of it	Heard of it but not sure what it means	Know what it means	Nothing relevant	Partial infor-mation	Clearly shows under-standing
7 Reward						
8 Cooperate						
9 Unacceptable						
10 Respond						
11 Inappropriate						
12 Responsibility						
13 Consequence						
14 Expectations						
15 Negotiate						
16 Compromise						
17 Resolve						
18 Empathy						
19 Perspective						
20 Excluded						

Interpreting the behaviour vocabulary assessment

	Score	Interpretation	Action
Really tricky	Shows understanding of 7 or fewer words by explaining or using in context.	The young person may experience significant misunderstandings about behaviour management due to vocabulary knowledge. They are likely to have wider vocabulary needs.	• Explain expectations in very simple language. • Use symbols to support rules and expectations. • Teach meanings of key behaviour-related vocabulary (Definitions of words connected to behaviour (page 297)). • Be aware that the young person is likely to have wider vocabulary needs.
Tricky sometimes	Shows understanding of 8–16 words by explaining or using in context.	There are likely to be misunderstandings about behaviour due to vocabulary knowledge.	• Teach meanings of key behaviour related vocabulary (Definitions of words connected to behaviour (page 297)).

	Score	Interpretation	Action
			• Develop comprehension monitoring strategies. (see the 'Saying when you don't understand' section of the toolkit (page 264)). • Monitor understanding of wider vocabulary.
No problem	Shows understanding of 17–20 words by explaining or using in context.	Good knowledge of behaviour-related vocabulary.	• Continue to expose to rich vocabulary. • Monitor understanding of wider vocabulary.

'Really tricky', 'Tricky sometimes' and 'No problem' indicate an ability to understand and respond to this task and are linked to the actions that need to be taken. There are no age norms, thus this indicator does not show whether the skill is age-appropriate or not.

Crazy phrases assessment (idioms/ figures of speech)

Name:	Date:

A young person needs to be working at least at *LFBE* **Language Level C** in order to complete this assessment. If you do not know the young person's Language Level, complete Assessment Scenario 1 on page 54. The Crazy Phrases Assessment is **UK specific** and so will need adapting for non-UK populations as idioms vary significantly from one country to another.

Ask the young person to rate themselves on how well they know each phrase. The 'Understanding of words or phrases' rating scale (on page 270) will be a useful support at this point. If the young person indicates that they know what the phrase means, then ask them to explain it or think of a situation when it would be used. By their very nature, these phrases are complex and hard to explain. The explanations do not need to be perfect, but enough information needs to be provided for the listener to be sure that the young person has a basic understanding. Can they explain it so that someone who had never heard it before would understand? Rate the young person's responses. You can refer to the Definitions of crazy phrases used in assessment (page 303) to help with rating.

Stop if five consecutive phrases are unknown.

	Young person self-assessment			If the young person says that they know what the phrase means, ask them to explain it or think of a situation when it would be used.		
	Never heard of it	Heard of it but not sure what it means	Knows what it means	Nothing relevant	Partial infor-mation	Clearly shows under-standing
1 Get a move on!						
2 Winding someone up						

	Young person self-assessment			If the young person says that they know what the phrase means, ask them to explain it or think of a situation when it would be used.		
	Never heard of it	Heard of it but not sure what it means	Knows what it means	Nothing relevant	Partial infor- mation	Clearly shows under- standing
3 Get on my nerves						
4 Get cracking						
5 I don't have a clue						
6 Pack it in						
7 Have a go at someone						
8 Button it						
9 Create a scene						
10 Don't lose your cool						
11 Get it in the neck						
12 Get a grip						
13 Call it quits						
14 It will all end in tears						
15 We must get to the bottom of this						
16 Out of order						

	Young person self-assessment			If the young person says that they know what the phrase means, ask them to explain it or think of a situation when it would be used.		
	Never heard of it	Heard of it but not sure what it means	Knows what it means	Nothing relevant	Partial infor-mation	Clearly shows under-standing
17 Clean up your act						
18 In the dog house						
19 Let the side down						
20 Up to your neck						
21 Let's start with a clean sheet						
22 Turn over a new leaf						
23 Watch your mouth						
24 Going through a sticky patch						
25 Shoot your mouth off						
Total						

Note: This assessment provides a brief 'snapshot' of young people's knowledge of crazy phrases (idioms). It should not be used as a list of what to teach.

Interpreting the crazy phrases assessment (idioms/ figures of speech)

	Score	Interpretation	Action
Really tricky	Shows understanding of 8 or fewer phrases by explaining or using in context.	This young person may be taking language too literally. This is likely to be causing them considerable difficulties and misunderstand-ings.	• Avoid using crazy phrases in everyday situations. • Explain all that are used to them. • Aim to develop understanding of crazy phrases in a structured way (see 'When people don't say what they mean' section of the toolkit (page 299)).
Tricky sometimes	Shows understanding of 9–18 phrases by explaining or using in context.	This young person may be confused when these crazy phrases are used.	• Be aware when you and other people use crazy phrases. • When you use crazy phrases, check that the young person has understood. • Allocate time to develop understanding of crazy phrases as part of teaching (see 'When people don't say what they mean' section of the toolkit (page 299)).

	Score	Interpretation	Action
No problem	Shows understanding of 19–25 phrases by explaining or using in context.	Has a good understanding of these crazy phrases.	• Talk about any unfamiliar crazy phrases as they come up, either spoken or written. Have fun exploring their meaning as part of a rich language experience.

'Really tricky', 'Tricky sometimes' and 'No problem' indicate an ability to understand and respond to this task and are linked to the actions that need to be taken. There are no age norms, thus this indicator does not show whether the skill is age-appropriate or not.

Sarcasm and implied meaning assessment (includes exaggeration and white lies)

Name:	Date:

Use with assessment pictures on page 105. Administer all items.

Please note: some of these statements are true and some are untrue.

Instructions

Say, 'I am going to read you some very short stories that go with these pictures and ask you questions about them.'

1 Dylan went for lunch at Chloe's house. He looked at the table, 'Wow, there is enough food to feed the whole street.'
Is what Dylan says true?　❒ Yes　❒ No　❒ Don't know
Why did Dylan say 'Wow, there is enough food to feed the whole street'?

2 Mohamed knocked over his tea. Tyler said 'Well, that was clever.'
Is what Tyler said true?　❒ Yes　❒ No　❒ Don't know
Why did Tyler say 'Well, that was clever'?

3 Suzy came in from the garden and left the back door open. Dad said, 'Suzy, it's cold in here.'
Is what Dad said true?　❒ Yes　❒ No　❒ Don't know
Why did Dad say 'Suzy, it's cold in here'?

4 Tom's mum answered the door. It was Tom's friend, Declan. When she called him, Tom didn't look up from his phone. Tom's mum said, 'Take your time Tom, Declan's got all day.'

Is what Tom's mum said true?   ❏ Yes   ❏ No   ❏ Don't know

Why did Tom's mum say 'Take your time Tom, Declan's got all day?'

5 Chelsea loves her Nan even though she gives terrible presents. This birthday was no different. Nan gave Chelsea an ugly brown T-shirt. When Nan gave her the present, Chelsea said, 'Thanks Nan, that's lovely.'

Is what Chelsea said true?   ❏ Yes   ❏ No   ❏ Don't know

Why did Chelsea say 'Thanks Nan, that's lovely?'

6 Dad walked into the kitchen. There were cups and plates all over the counter. He started clearing them up saying, 'That's fine. I will tidy everything up. I have nothing else to do.'

Is what Dad said true?   ❏ Yes   ❏ No   ❏ Some of it   ❏ Don't know

Why did Dad say 'That's fine. I will tidy everything up. I have nothing else to do.'?

7 Chantelle was having a bad day. Nothing had gone well. Riley came up to her and said, 'You alright?' Chantelle replied. 'Yes, fine thank you.' Riley then disappeared with his mates. Chantelle's best friend Jodie asked Chantelle, 'You OK?' Chantelle replied, 'No, it's been a terrible day so far!'

Is what Chantelle said to Riley true?   ❏ Yes   ❏ No   ❏ Don't know

Why did she say 'Yes, fine thank you' to Riley?

Why did she give a different answer to her friend Jodie?

8 Kate had been shopping. Her boyfriend Harrison was on the sofa. Kate came in with the shopping and said 'These are really heavy.'
Is what Kate said true?   ❒ Yes   ❒ No   ❒ Don't know
Why did Kate say 'These are really heavy'?

Key

	Type		Type
Q1	Exaggeration/ joke	Q5	White Lie
Q2	Sarcasm	Q6	Implied meaning/ sarcasm
Q3	Implied meaning	Q7	White lie/social reply
Q4	Sarcasm	Q8	Implied meaning

Source: Adapted from *The Strange Stories Test* N. Kaland et al, 2005.

Interpreting the sarcasm and implied meaning assessment (includes exaggeration and white lies)

	Score	Interpretation	Action
Really tricky	Could identify information that is true or untrue and explain why characters said what they did for **3 or fewer questions**.	Likely to have significant mis-understandings when non-literal language is used.	• Language used should be simple, direct and literal avoiding exaggeration, implied meaning, sarcasm and white lies. • Use strategies in the 'Introduction to When people don't say what they mean' (page 299).

	Score	Interpretation	Action
Tricky sometimes	Could identify information that is true or untrue and explain why characters said what they did for **4–6 questions**.	Likely to have some misun-derstandings when non-literal language is used.	• Look at the key (page 103) to further analyse error type. • Use 'Introduction to When people don't say what they mean' (page 299).
No problem	Could identify information that is true or untrue and explain why characters said what they did for **7–8 questions.**	Is able to understand basic non-literal language.	• Expose to rich language. • Be mindful as they may struggle with more complex non-literal language. These assessment stories are very simple.

'Really tricky', 'Tricky sometimes' and 'No problem' indicate an ability to understand and respond to this task and are linked to the actions that need to be taken. There are no age norms, thus this indicator does not show whether the skill is age-appropriate or not.

When people don't say what they mean

Sarcasm and implied meaning pictures

Emotion words assessment

Name:	Date:

Instructions

Ask the young person to rate themselves on how well they know the word. The 'Understanding of words or phrases' rating scale (on page 270) will be a useful support at this point. If the young person indicates that they know the word, then ask them to talk about a time they felt this way, give an example or explain what it means. By their very nature, emotion words may be abstract which makes them hard to explain. The explanations do not need to be perfect, but enough information needs to be provided for the listener to be sure that the young person has a basic understanding. Can they explain it well enough so that someone who had never heard the word before would understand? For words with more than one meaning the definition provided must relate to an emotion. Prompt if a different term is defined. You can refer to the 'whats that feeing called?' list of definitions (p.329) to help with rating

Stop if five consecutive words are unknown.

	Young person self-assessment			If they say that they know what it means, say 'talk about a time you felt this way, give an example or explain what it means.'		
	Never heard of it	Heard of it but not sure what it means	Knows what it means	Nothing relevant	Partial informa-tion	Clearly shows under-standing
1 Safe						
2 Lonely						
3 Annoyed						
4 Cheerful						

	Young person self-assessment			If they say that they know what it means, say 'talk about a time you felt this way, give an example or explain what it means.'		
	Never heard of it	Heard of it but not sure what it means	Knows what it means	Nothing relevant	Partial information	Clearly shows under-standing
5 Hopeful						
6 Uncomfortable						
7 Generous						
8 Protective						
9 Frustrated						
10 Inspired						
11 Argumentative						
12 Devious						
13 Grief						
14 Eager						
15 Vain						
Total						

Interpreting emotion word assessment

	Score	Interpretation	Action
Really tricky	Shows understanding of **6 or fewer** words by talking about a time they felt this way, giving an example or explaining what it means.	Finds defining emotions vocabulary very tricky. May have reduced knowledge of emotions vocabulary.	• Explain all emotions in simple terms. • Use the 'What's that feeling called?' section of the tool kit (p. 328). • See the 'Emotional coaching strategies' in the guide (on page 30).
Tricky sometimes	Shows understanding of **7–11** words by talking about a time they felt this way, giving an example or explaining what it means.	Developing the ability to define emotions vocabulary, but still some gaps.	• Use the 'What's that feeling called?' section of the tool kit (p. 328). • See the 'Emotional coaching strategies' in the guide (on page 30).

	Score	Interpretation	Action
No problem	Shows understanding of **12–15** words by talking about a time they felt this way, giving an example or explaining what it means.	Good ability to define emotions vocabulary.	• Continue to expose them to emotional vocabulary and extend emotional vocabulary via reading and discussions. • Ask them to explain terms to others.

'Really tricky', 'Tricky sometimes' and 'No problem' indicate an ability to understand and respond to this task and are linked to the actions that need to be taken. There are no age norms, thus this indicator does not show whether the skill is age appropriate or not.

Narrative assessment

Instructions

- This assessment uses the picture on the following page. Please note that this is the same picture used for Scenario 34, but the accompanying story is different.

- Say 'I am going to tell you a story. Listen carefully because then it will be your turn to tell me the story.' Then read the Narrative assessment text.

- After you have finished, ask the young person if they would like you to read the story again before they retell the story in their own words. The young person may also read the story themselves. If the young person reads the story themselves, the text should then be removed from view when they retell it.

- Use the **Narrative analysis** sheet on page 113. As the young person tells the story, tick the elements that they include. Recording the narrative for later analysis will be more accurate, but it is also more time consuming. If you have time and permission, it is recommended that the narrative is recorded and analysed later.

- Encourage the retelling by giving as much eye contact as possible, smiling, nodding and saying 'mmm.'

- If a young person stops mid-story, encourage him/her to continue by repeating back the last part of the story or saying 'tell me more.' Do not provide specific prompting.

- If the young person omits particular components of the story, wait for him/her to finish the whole story before asking specific questions. DO NOT INTERRUPT the story telling.

- After the storytelling is complete, ask specific questions about any missing components such as 'where did this happen?' or 'how do you think she felt about that?' This information goes in the 'Elicited with specific questions' column on the Narrative analysis sheet.

Narrative assessment picture

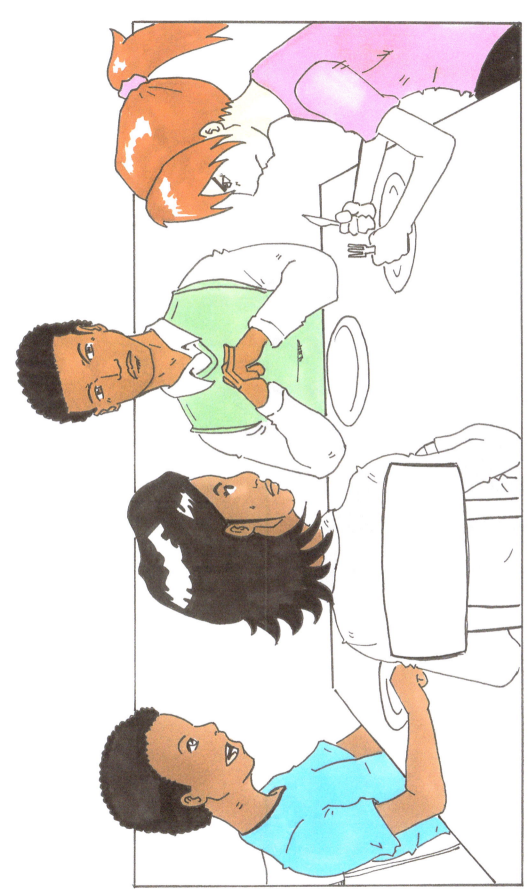

111

Narrative assessment text

One day after school, Candice went to Lucky's house to have a meal with his family. The food was delicious, and Candice was really enjoying herself until Lucky started talking about something that happened in school. He told his parents that she had laughed at a new student in their class. He made it sound like it was just her, but the whole class had laughed when the boy had slipped as the head teacher brought him into class. Their teacher had told them all off.

Candice felt herself getting angrier and angrier. She didn't know how to explain herself calmly, so she sat at the table glaring at Lucky. She decided that she would have a serious talk with Lucky later when he was on his own.

On the way home, Candice questioned Lucky about what he had said. He said it was just for a laugh, but Candice was still not sure that he was being truthful. She didn't trust him any more.

Instructions

Say, 'I can read it again if you want me to, or you can read it.'

After re-reading: 'Now it's your turn to retell the story in your own words.'

Narrative analysis

Name:		Date:	
Story components	**Included in narrative**	**Elicited with specific questions**	
Character: Who?	❑ Candice/girl. ❑ Lucky/boy. ❑ Parents/mum and dad.		
Setting: Where? and When?	❑ Lucky's house. ❑ After school/mealtime.		
Initiating event: When did the trouble start?	❑ Lucky told a story about the new student slipping in class.		
Internal response: How did Candice feel and react?	❑ Felt herself getting angrier and angrier. ❑ Could not explain it calmly. ❑ Glared at Lucky.		
Plan: What did Candice think she would do?	❑ Talk to Lucky when he was on his own.		
Attempt: What did Candice do?	❑ Spoke to Lucky on the way home.		
Consequence: How did it end?	❑ Candice no longer trusts Lucky.		
Use of connectives	❑ And ❑ As Others: ❑ But ❑ So ❑ Until ❑ When		

Source: Narrative components from Gillam and Gillam, 2016

Other skills	**Really tricky**	**Tricky sometimes**	**No problem**
Non-verbals: Did the speaker use appropriate eye contact and tone of voice?	❒ No or limited eye contact. ❒ Flat and monotone.	❒ Some eye contact. ❒ Some variation in tone of voice.	❒ Good eye contact. ❒ Variation in tone of voice.
Coherence: Was the story easy to follow?	❒ Really hard to follow.	❒ Occasionally hard to follow.	❒ Easy to follow.
Grammar: Were the sentences grammatically correct?	❒ Significant errors.	❒ Occasional errors.	❒ No errors noticed.

Narrative assessment interpretation guide

	Score	Interpretation	Action
Really tricky	Many of the story components are missing. The young person struggles to fill in the missing details when asked. The story is hard to follow.	Narrative skills are insufficient to tell a coherent story, has difficulties recalling the story or the young person has not engaged fully with the task. They may struggle to tell their side of a story.	• When working through the *LFBE* scenarios, whenever you see the book symbol make sure you use the tools on page 364 to help. • Follow guidance in 'Introduction to narrative' (see page 363). • A structured narrative intervention in addition to *LFBE* may be required (also detailed in the 'Introduction to narrative' (see page 363)).
Tricky sometimes	A few story components are missing. The young person may not be able to fill in all the missing details.	Developing narrative skills, but inconsistent. They might find it hard to consistently tell their side of a story.	• When working through the *LFBE* scenarios, whenever you see the book symbol make sure you use the resources on page 364 to help. • Follow guidance in 'Introduction to narrative' (see page 363).

	Score	Interpretation	Action
No problem	The initial retell gives almost all of the story components. The story is easy to follow. Any elements missing are easily provided when questioned.	Narrative skills are developed enough to tell a simple story.	• Continue to provide opportunities to tell longer, more elaborate spoken stories and also to write stories.

'Really tricky', 'Tricky sometimes' and 'No problem' indicate an ability to understand and respond to this task and are linked to the actions that need to be taken. There are no age norms, thus this indicator does not show whether the skill is age appropriate or not.

Solving people problems assessment

Name:	Date:

Read this story to the young person

Mason and Liam had arranged to go to the cinema on Saturday. When Saturday came, Mason decided that he was too tired to go. His phone was out of charge, but he saw another friend, Tyler, so Mason asked Tyler to pass on a message to Liam. Tyler forgot to pass on the message. Liam waited for Mason at the bus stop but he never showed up. Liam also tried to call Mason, but because he was on his phone, Liam did not see the bus coming and so didn't make it to the cinema.

Repeat the story and check that the young person knows who did what. Use the pictures on page 120 to help.

Then ask these questions and write down the answers

1 What happened?

2 How did Mason feel? (The one who was too tired to go)

How did Liam feel? (The one who was left waiting)

How did Tyler feel? (The one who forgot to pass on the message)

3 Why might each person see it differently?

4 Tell me three solutions to this problem.

5 Find one solution that works best for all three people.

6 What are the possible consequences of this solution?

Tyler

Liam

Solving people problem pictures

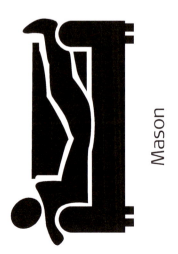

Mason

Interpreting the solving people problems assessment

Level of concern	Score	Interpreta-tion	Action
Really Tricky	Answers **3 or fewer** questions fully (with incomplete or no response to the remaining).	Is likely to struggle to reflect and use language to solve interpersonal problems.	• Use 'Why it is important to learn how to solve people problems (page 381). • Use Solving People Problems frame *LFBE* Language Level A or B (see page 382–387). • Develop understanding of key vocabulary around problem-solving e.g. solution, consequences. Use the tools in Understanding words (vocabulary) page 282–294.
Tricky sometimes	Answers **4–5** questions fully (with incomplete or no response to the remaining).	Developing the ability to use language to solve interpersonal problems.	• Develop problem-solving skills (using the tools in the 'Solving people problems' section on page 379). • Check/develop understanding of key vocabulary around problem-solving e.g. solution, consequences. Use the tools in Understanding words (vocabulary) page 282–294.
No problem	Answers **all 6** questions fully	Has the basic skills to ver-bally reflect on solving interpersonal problems.	• Provide opportunities to solve people problems more independently.

'Really tricky', 'Tricky sometimes' and 'No problem' indicate an ability to understand and respond to this task and are linked to the actions that need to be taken. There are no age norms, thus this indicator does not show whether the skill is age appropriate or not.

How well did I do?

Name:	Date:

To be used to collect the young person's views.

	How easy or tricky was it to. . .
	. . . to ask when it didn't make sense? Really tricky/didn't do it I can do it sometimes Easy 1_____2_____3_____4_____5
	What helped?
	. . . work out what the feeling was called? Really tricky/didn't do it I can do it sometimes Easy 1_____2_____3_____4_____5 **. . . think of how to change (or remember) the feeling?** Really tricky/didn't do it I had one idea I could think of several things to do 1_____2_____3_____4_____5
	What helped?
	. . . answer this sort of questions . . . **Who was involved?** (A) Really tricky/didn't do it I can do it sometimes Easy 1_____2_____3_____4_____5 **What's going to happen next?** (B) Really tricky/didn't do it I can do it sometimes Easy 1_____2_____3_____4_____5 **What were they trying to do?** (C) Really tricky/didn't do it I can do it sometimes Easy 1_____2_____3_____4_____5 **What are the consequences of that?** (D) Really tricky/didn't do it I can do it sometimes Easy 1_____2_____3_____4_____5
	What helped?

How easy or tricky was it to. . .
. . . retell the story or tell your own version clearly? Really tricky/didn't do it   I missed some bits out   Easy 1_____2_____3_____4_____5
What helped?
. . . think of a way to solve the problem that would make everyone happy? Really tricky/didn't do it   I could solve it for one person   Easy 1_____2_____3_____4_____5
What helped?

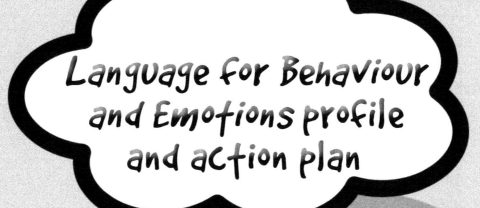

Language for Behaviour and Emotions profile and action plan

LFBE profile

Name:	Date:

Assessment components:

GREEN = Assessment scenario

PURPLE = Young person's view of their own communication

BLUE = Adults' views of young person's communication.

BLACK = Complete *LFBE* Assessment.

Areas assessed	Information gathered	*LFBE* Language Level (Please circle)
Finding clues and explaining your thinking	*LFBE* Assessment Scenario	**B C D**

Areas assessed	Information gathered	Really tricky	Tricky sometimes	No problem
'Saying when you don't understand'	'Assessment scenario': Did they ask for clarification when needed? (page 55)			
	'Young person's view of their own communication' Q1: Asking when they do not understand (page 74).			
	'Adults' views of young person's communication' Q1: Does the young person ask for clarification? (page 79)			
	'Comprehension monitoring assessment' (page 83).			
	Overall summary of 'Saying when you don't understand'.			

Areas assessed	Information gathered	Really tricky	Tricky sometimes	No problem
'Understanding words'	'Young Person's view of their own communication' Q2 Understanding long/complex words (page 74).			
	'Adults' views of young person's communication' Q2 Understanding long/complex words (page 79).			
	'Behaviour vocabulary assessment': understanding of words associated with behaviour (page 91).			
	Overall summary of 'Understanding words'.			
'When people don't say what they mean'	'Young Person's view of their own communication' Q3. Understanding sarcasm (page 74).			
	'Adults' views of young person's communication' Q3–5. Understanding of crazy phrases, sarcasm and implied meaning (page 79).	.		
	Crazy phrases assessment (page 95).			
'When people don't say what they mean'	Sarcasm and implied meaning assessment (includes exaggeration and white lies) (page 100).			
	Overall summary of 'Saying when you don't understand'.			

Areas assessed	Information gathered	Really tricky	Tricky sometimes	No problem
Talking about feelings: What's that feeling called?	'Assessment scenario' Q4, Q10. (page 55).			
	'Young Person's view of their own communication' Q4–8. Talking about feelings and dealing with feelings (page 74).			
Dealing with feelings	'Adults' views of young person's communication' Q6–12. Are they able to talk about feelings and deal with their feelings (page 79).			
	Emotion words assessment. Understanding of a range of emotions. (page 106).			
	Overall summary of 'Talking about feelings'.			
Finding clues and explaining your thinking	'Young person's view of their own communication' Q9. Ability to answer questions and explain things. (page 74).			
	'Adults' views of young person's communication' Q13. Ability to answer questions and explain things. (page 79).			
	Overall summary of 'Finding clues and explaining your thinking'.			
The story (narrative)	Assessment scenario Q11 (page 55).			

Areas assessed	Information gathered	Really tricky	Tricky sometimes	No problem
	'Young person's view of their own communication' Q10. Ability to provide details about what has happened. (page 74).			
	'Adults' views of young person's communication' Q14–16. Ability to explain an event clearly (page 79).			
	LFBE 'Narrative assessment' (page 113).			
	Overall summary of 'The story'.			
Solving people problems ✓	Assessment scenario Q14 (page 55).			
	'Young person's view of their own communication' Q11–13. Solving problems verbally (page 74).			
	'Adults' views of young person's communication' Q17–20. Ability to solve problems with words (page 79).			
	'Solving people problems assessment' (page 117).			
	Overall summary of 'Solving people problems'.			

'Really tricky', 'Tricky sometimes' and 'No problem' indicate an ability to understand and respond to this task and are linked to the actions that need to be taken. There are no age norms, so this indicator does not show whether the skill is age appropriate or not.

Language for Behaviour and Emotions

Strategies the young person has identified as helpful. From 'How well does the adult help me?' on page 77.

❒ Listening to me. ❒ Helping me to put my thoughts into words. ❒ Explaining things so that I can understand. ❒ Encouraging me to ask questions when I don't understand. ❒ Helping me to understand my feelings.	❒ Helping me to calm down or feel better. ❒ Helping me to use words to solve problems with other people. ❒ Other:

LFBE action plan

Name	DOB	Date of assessment	Date of feedback

Summary of skills	Area to work on x/✓	Support tools: Tick which tools are going to be used	Specific strategies for daily interactions
Saying when you don't understand		❏ Why it's important to say when things don't make sense (page 267). ❏ Self-awareness rating (page 270). ❏ How to check it makes sense (page 271). ❏ What to say when you don't understand (page 273). ❏ How to let someone know that you don't understand (page 274).	**Be aware** • The young person may not understand what you say and so needs small amounts of information at a time. • Watch for signs of not understanding. **Teaching points** • No one understands everything all of the time. • There is no shame in saying 'I don't know.' • Comprehension monitoring is a skill, and, like all skills, it needs practice. **Specific everyday strategies** • Use the 'Self-awareness rating' (page 270) in class or in one to one sessions to check understanding. Ensure that adults respond when the young person indicates that they do not understand. • Model strategies: saying when *you* don't understand.

Summary of skills	Area to work on x/✓	Support tools: Tick which tools are going to be used	Specific strategies for daily interactions
			• Praise the young person when they say that they do not understand. • Encourage specific strategies e.g. 'I got that bit. The bit I didn't understand was. . .'
Understanding Words		❏ Why it's important to learn new words (page 282). ❏ Tricky words: definitions and symbols (page 282). ❏ Word Wizard (page 295). ❏ 10 steps to learning words independently (page 296). ❏ Definitions of words connected to behaviour (page 297).	**Be aware** • The young person is likely to have wider vocabulary needs. • Explain expectations using very simple words. • Use symbols/pictures to support rules and expectations. **Teaching points** • Important words: choose words carefully and teach methodically within context. • Word learning strategies are important. • Use visual supports and simple definitions as part of this process. **Specific everyday strategies** • Regularly teach vocabulary to the whole class (Use 'Word Aware 1', Parsons & Branagan, 2021). • Use targeted vocabulary identified and taught in the group. Use the words in context and explain their meaning.

Summary of skills	Area to work on x/✓	Support tools: Tick which tools are going to be used	Specific strategies for daily interactions
When people don't say what they mean		❏ Why it's important to know when people don't say what they mean (page 301). ❏ Definitions of crazy phrases used in the assessment (page 303). ❏ Definitions of crazy phrases used in the scenarios (page 305). ❏ Learning crazy phrases (page 308).	**Be aware** • Language used should be simple, direct and literal, avoiding exaggeration, implied meaning, sarcasm and white lies. **Teaching points** • Specifically teach crazy phrases (idioms) as part of literacy. • Discuss crazy phrases as they arise. • Celebrate and enjoy crazy phrases. Some of them are crazy! **Specific everyday strategies** • Be aware of the crazy phrases (idioms) you use. • Encourage young people to identify when crazy phrases (idioms) are used or encountered in reading. • Discuss the meaning of crazy phrases (idioms) that are used. • Keep track by displaying the crazy phrases (idioms) or writing them in a book.

Summary of skills	Area to work on x/✓	Support tools: Tick which tools are going to be used	Specific strategies for daily interactions
Talking about feelings (emotional literacy)		**What's that feeling called?** ❚❚ ❒ Why it's important to talk about feelings (page 313). ❒ Where do I feel that emotion? (page 314) ❒ Grouping feelings (page 315). ❒ Grouping feelings short version (page 325). ❒ What's that feeling called? (page 328) ❒ How strong is that emotion? (page 348) ❒ What is the main feeling in the story? (page 350) **Dealing with feelings** ❒ Accepting feelings (page 356). ❒ If you **LIKE** a feeling you can. . . (page 357)	**Be aware** • The young person's identification of emotions in self and/or others is limited. • The young person's understanding of emotions vocabulary is limited. • Explicitly label emotions in daily interactions. **Teaching points** • Expose them to a range of emotion words via personal experiences, literature and discussion. • Teach specific emotions vocabulary. • Help them to identify emotions in others. **Specific everyday strategies** • Keep track of emotions discussed either via displays or journals. Use these tools to reflect on challenges/positive experiences as they occur. • Use 'Emotional coaching strategies' (guide page 30) to reflect on emotions. In particular: • Set aside time to talk about emotions, but also respond in the moment.

Summary of skills	Area to work on x/✓	Support tools: Tick which tools are going to be used	Specific strategies for daily interactions
		❒ If you **DON'T LIKE** a feeling you can. . . (page 358)	• Help the young person to label their emotions and refine and extend their understanding and use of words, e.g. 'were you annoyed or livid?' • Encourage the young person to look out for emotional cues in themselves or others when reading books or watching films and when talking about the *LFBE* scenarios.
Finding clues and explaining your thinking (inference and verbal reasoning)		❒ Why it's important to find clues and explain thinking (page 361). ❒ Scenarios (page 139).	**Be aware** • Keep the young person's Language Level in mind and keep questions at or below this level. • Only ask harder questions if the young person is very familiar with the topic being discussed. • When emotions are running high, keep questions as simple as possible or say nothing till things calm down. **Teaching points** • How to answer questions, via modelling, opportunities for structured talk.

Summary of skills	Area to work on x/✓	Support tools: Tick which tools are going to be used	Specific strategies for daily interactions
			Specific everyday strategies: • This is particularly important when reflecting on incidents. Use the right 'problem solving frames' (from page 379) and 'Story frames' (page 368) to help.
The story (narrative) 📖		❒ Why it's important to be able to tell stories (page 367). ❒ Story frame *LFBE* Language Level A (page 368). ❒ Story frame *LFBE* Language Level B (page 369). ❒ Story frame *LFBE* Language Level C/D (page 371).	**Be aware** • Stories/narrative are problematic, so if the information is important ask for short responses. • Provide visual support for stories/narrative. • Re-tell what you have understood from what the young person has said. **Teaching points** • How stories/narrative are structured. • Give extra time to formulate longer responses. **Specific everyday strategies** • Use the 'Story frames' (page 368) when creating stories or when explaining what has happened.

Summary of skills	Area to work on x/✓	Support tools: Tick which tools are going to be used	Specific strategies for daily interactions
Solving people problems ✓		❐ Why it's important to learn how to solve people problems (page 381). ❐ Problem solving frame *LFBE* Language Level A (page 382). ❐ Problem solving frame *LFBE* Language Level B (page 384). ❐ Problem solving frame *LFBE* Language Level C/D (page 386).	**Be aware** • Verbally solving incidents with peers is challenging. • Avoid problem-solving when the young person is angry or upset. **Teaching points** • Positive outcomes can be achieved via words. • Practise with less emotional events first. **Specific everyday strategies** • Use the 'Problem-solving frames' (from page 382) to reflect upon real problems, but be cautious when emotions are running high.

Information from the action plan may be summarised on to the '*LFBE* action plan summary' on the following page.

LFBE action plan summary

Name	DOB	Date of assessment	Date of feedback

The skills I will be learning:	
Target:	
Strategies to support my learning in the classroom:	
Group or individual session timings:	
When:	
Who will support me:	
Tools I will be using:	

Scenarios

1. Granny's house

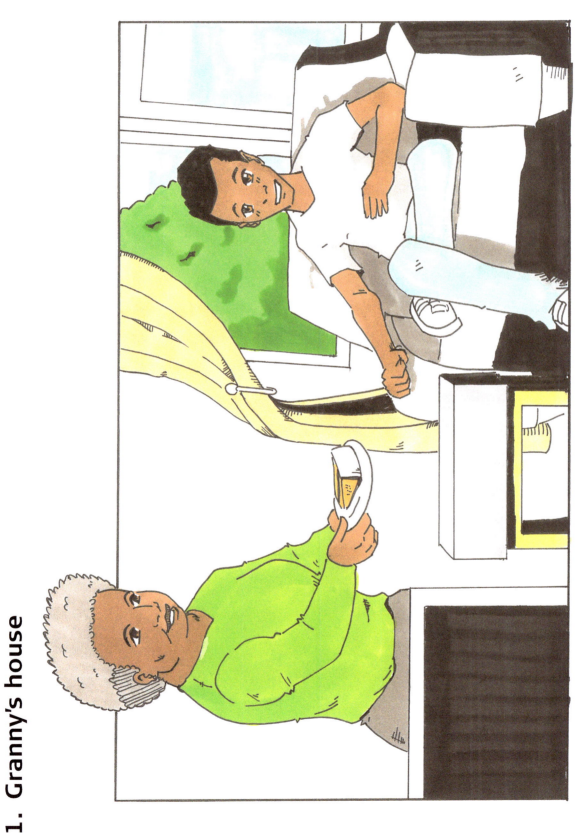

Caleb liked going to Granny's house. He'd liked it ever since he was very little. Granny's house was a bit cramped and the furniture was so old that Caleb had to sit carefully on the chairs in case he broke them. But Caleb knew that Granny would always make a fuss of him and give him lots of his favourite cake and biscuits. The only time Granny raised her voice was when Caleb forgot to wash his hands before eating.

1. Granny's house

NB: all adults and young people to take turns asking and answering questions as part of a conversation

A	B	C	D
Where does Caleb like going?	How does Caleb feel when he goes to Granny's house?	← What is another word that could describe how Caleb feels about going to Granny's house?	Do you think Caleb might behave differently at Granny's house from how he behaves at home? Why might he be different?
Describe Caleb's granny's house.	Is Granny rich?	← How do you know?	← How sure can you be of your opinion? (What supports your view?)
Finish this sentence: 'The only time Granny raised her voice was when Caleb. . .'	How does Granny feel when she tells Caleb off?	What does 'raised her voice' mean?	How could they sort things out if Granny found out that Caleb had lied about washing his hands?
In this story, Caleb feels comfortable being at Granny's house. Tell me about a time when you felt comfortable being with someone.	Talk about this story using the word 'comfortable'.	What is the opposite of feeling comfortable? When might you feel like that?	If you were feeling uncomfortable and wanted to feel more comfortable what could you say or do?
Do you ever go and visit people? What happens? (Adults should also talk about their experiences.)			

← ask the question to the left first

Use resources from the toolkit to help think through these specific questions or as needed:

pages 264–308   pages 309–355   pages 356–360   pages 363–378   pages 379–391

2. New home

Jake, his mum and his brother had all moved to a new house. It was in a new town and a long way away from everyone that Jake knew. He liked the new house though. The house was much bigger than the old one, and, best of all, he now had his own room. Jake had heard his Mum lock the front door, but he checked the window lock again.

2. New home

NB: all adults and young people to take turns asking and answering questions as part of a conversation

A	B	C	D
Where is Jake?	How does Jake feel about his new room?	What other emotions could Jake be feeling?	↳ What evidence do you have for your view?
What does Jake like best about the new house?	↳ Why?	Why might Jake be finding it a little bit hard having his own room?	↳ What suggests that?
What did Jake do with the window?	Finish this sentence: 'Jake checked the window lock again because he was feeling. . .'	↳ What else could he do to make himself feel better?	↳ What do you suspect is the action that will help him most? Why?
How far away is Jake's new house from his old house?	How could Jake get from his new house to his old house?	↳ Jake's mum doesn't want him to go back to his old house that way. Why might she not want this?	How could Jake and his mum come to an agreement about how he gets back to visit his old friends? (Talk through the steps.)

Have you ever moved to a new house? Did you want to move? How did you cope with living in a new place? (Adults should also talk about their experiences.)

↳ ask the question to the left first

Use resources from the toolkit to help think through these specific questions or as needed:

pages 264–308   pages 309–355   pages 356–360   pages 363–378   pages 379–391

3. Cute new puppy

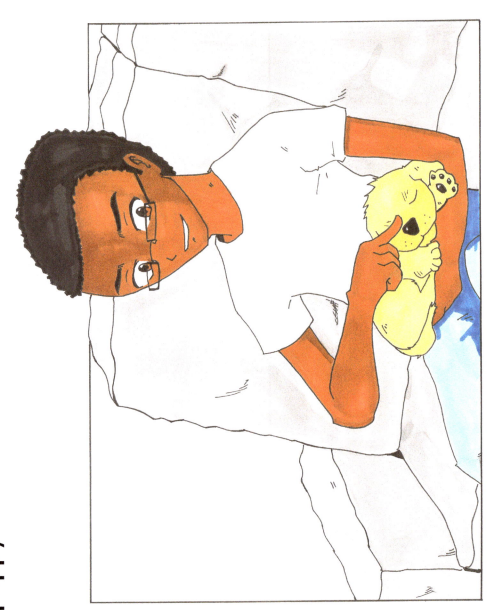

Jacobo had chosen his new puppy eight weeks ago and now he was here! Bip was very cuddly, but also very energetic. Jacobo played with him for ages, as Bip explored his new home. When Bip wanted to sleep, he curled up on Jacobo's lap and started to close his eyes. Jacobo looked at Bip's cute face and couldn't stop smiling, so he poked the puppy's nose to wake him up.

3. Cute new puppy

NB: all adults and young people to take turns asking and answering questions as part of a conversation

A	B	C	D
What was the puppy called?	How did Jacobo feel when Bip arrived?	What could Jacobo do to remember this feeling?	What can you you infer about Jacobo from this story?
Where was Bip trying to sleep?	How might Bip feel about being poked?	Why shouldn't Jacobo try to wake Bip up?	What is Jacobo's motivation for waking Bip up?
What did Bip and Jacobo do together?	Why did Bip need to sleep?	Retell this story in your own words and with your own ending.	How might Jacobo feel when he looks back on this day?
Who poked the puppy?	What's the problem with Jacobo being excited?	Why might Jacobo think it is ok to poke Bip?	Think about what Jacobo wants and what Bip needs. What is the best solution?
How do you feel when an animal comes up to you? How do you react? (Adults should also talk about their experiences.)			

← ask the question to the left first

Use these resources to help think through these specific questions or as needed:

pages 264–308   pages 309–355   pages 356–360   pages 363–378   pages 379–391

4. Runny nose

Abe was particularly excited as today Dad had said they could go to his favourite fast-food restaurant. Once they got to the restaurant, Abe ordered something to eat. As he was waiting to collect his food, Abe noticed the server sneeze loudly. The server wiped his nose with his hand and then wiped his hand on his trousers. Abe didn't want the food any more.

4. Runny nose

NB: all adults and young people to take turns asking and answering questions as part of a conversation

A	B	C	D
Who is in this story?	What could Abe do in this situation?	What would be the most sensible thing for Abe to do?	← Justify your decision.
What did the server do?	What should the server do in this situation?	The server knows he should wash his hands, but he didn't. Why not?	What is the server's motive in this situation?
Finish this sentence: 'Today Abe felt particularly . . .'	How did Abe feel when he saw the server sneeze and wipe his nose with his hand?	After Abe saw the server sneeze and wipe his nose with his hand, does he still feel excited? Why/why not?	What might be Abe's motivation for saying nothing?
In this story, Abe is disgusted when he sees the server sneeze and wipe his nose with his hand. Tell me about a time you felt disgusted.	Talk about this story using the word 'disgusted'.	Can you think of a word that is a bit like 'disgusted'? How is your word different from 'disgusted'?	If you were feeling disgusted and wanted to feel better, what could you say or do?
Do you ever go out to eat? What's it like? Has someone in your family every sneezed when they were serving food? What happened? (Adults should also talk about their experiences.)			

← ask the question to the left first

Use these resources to help think through these specific questions or as needed:

pages 264–308   pages 309–355   pages 356–360   pages 363–378   pages 379–391

5. Long holidays

It was the summer holidays and all of Mila's friends were away on holiday, leaving her with no one to play with but her baby brother. When Mila complained, her mum said 'Keep busy and you'll miss your friends less.' So Mila had got really good at inventing games to play on her own at home. Mila couldn't wait to chat with her friends in person again. They would all hang out and swap stories.

5. Long holidays

NB: all adults and young people to take turns asking and answering questions as part of a conversation

A	B	C	D
Make a face like Mila's.	How does Mila feel?	Can you think of another word for how she might feel? How is that word different from sad?	How might Mila feel when she looks back at the school holidays?
Where are Mila's friends?	What is a holiday?	Are holidays always fun? Why/why not?	↵ If someone else disagreed with your point of view, how would you defend it?
What did Mila's mum say?	How did Mila react to what Mum said?	↵ What did Mila learn from this?	What kind of person do you think Mila is? How did you come to that conclusion?
In this story, Mila is lonely as all of her friends have gone away. Tell me about a time when you felt lonely.	Talk about this story using the word 'lonely'.	What else could Mila do to make herself feel better?	↵ Sometimes the solution Mila thought of involved help from her mum. How could Mila convince her mum that it would be worth it?

If you were feeling lonely and wanted to feel better, what could you say or do?
How do you feel if you can't see your friends? How long do you go without seeing them? (Adults should also talk about their experiences.)

↵ ask the question to the left first

Use these resources to help think through these specific questions or as needed:

pages 264–308   pages 309–355   pages 356–360   pages 363–378   pages 379–391

6. Boring game

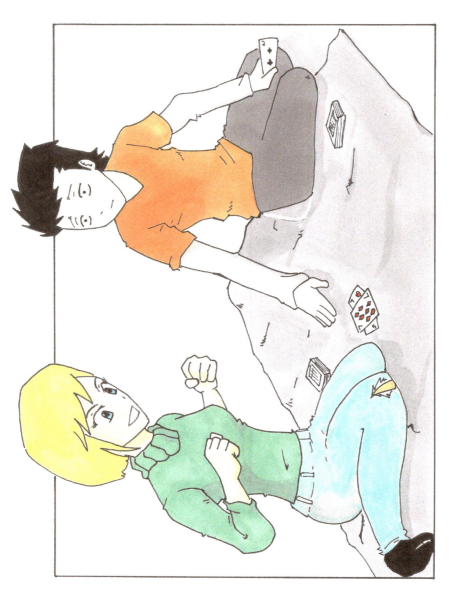

Today Charlotte beamed as she played her new card game with one of her best friends, Tenzin. She liked it so much that she could keep playing it for ages, but she saw that Tenzin was getting bored. She made a joke about how boring the game was and suggested they play something else. Tenzin was relieved even though he knew how much Charlotte enjoyed this game.

6. Boring game

NB: all adults and young people to take turns asking and answering questions as part of a conversation

A	B	C	D
Finish this sentence: 'Today Charlotte beamed as. . .'	How did Charlotte feel?	Not all days are as good as this, so what could Charlotte do to remember this feeling on bad days?	How easy was it for Charlotte to stop playing a game she liked? What evidence supports your view?
Apart from Charlotte, who else was in the story?	In this story what's the problem?	How might Charlotte have worked out that Tenzin was bored?	What does Charlotte think is more important: playing the game she likes or making sure Tenzin plays what he wants? How do you know?
What did Charlotte and Tenzin do?	What does 'relieved' mean?	Retell this story, but add your own ending.	What might the consequences be if Tenzin just said 'This game is boring'?
Tell me about a time when you were bored by a game.	What could Tenzin have said?	Why might Tenzin have decided to keep playing?	What is the best solution for both Tenzin and Charlotte? Talk through the steps.
Charlotte was 'beaming'. How might other people describe you when you are happy? Can you remember a time like that? (Adults should also talk about their experiences.)			

← ask the question to the left first

Use these resources to help think through these specific questions or as needed:

pages 264–308   pages 309–355   pages 356–360   pages 363–378   pages 379–391

7. Picnic

One weekend Jade and Dwaine went to the park with their families for a picnic. Dwaine was reaching for the sausage rolls when he knocked over the ketchup. It went all over Jade's dress. It was her favourite. Even though Dwaine said, 'sorry', Jade got really cross and didn't speak to Dwaine or look at him either. After a while Jade realised that Dwaine had just made a mistake, so she went to speak to Dwaine.

7. Picnic

NB: all adults and young people to take turns asking and answering questions as part of a conversation

A	B	C	D
Who spilt the ketchup?	As well as 'sorry' what else could Dwaine have said?	Why might Dwaine be confused about Jade not speaking to him?	Tell me this story from Dwaine's perspective
What did Jade do after Dwaine spilt the ketchup?	How did Jade feel at the end of the story?	How do Jade's feelings change during this story?	How might Jade feel about this incident when she looks back on it?
What was Dwaine doing when he knocked over the ketchup?	What might Jade say to Dwaine at the end of the story?	After the ketchup was spilt, what might Jade have done to help herself feel better?	What is Jade's motive for forgiving Dwayne?
By the end of the story Jade feels forgiving. Tell me about a time when you felt forgiving.	Tell me about this story using the word 'forgiving'.	Retell this story with Jade <u>not</u> being forgiving.	How can you be sure when someone has forgiven you?
What happens when someone does something bad to you? Maybe by accident. How do you respond? Why is it hard sometimes to do the right thing? (Adults should also talk about their experiences.)			

← ask the question to the left first

Use these resources to help think through these specific questions or as needed:

pages 264–308   pages 309–355   pages 356–360   pages 363–378   pages 379–391

8. The storm

Ava and her mum were driving home after visiting relatives. It had been a long day and Ava was feeling tired. The announcer on the radio said that there were storms coming. Just as they heard the word 'storms', they heard the first crack of thunder. A few seconds later lightning struck the field right next to the road, causing Ava to sit bolt upright. Mum tried to sound calm. 'Lightning never hits a moving car. We will be fine.'

8. The storm

NB: all adults and young people to take turns asking and answering questions as part of a conversation

A	B	C	D
Where had Ava and her mum been?	Why was Ava tired?	Why can it be tiring when you go to see relatives?	What are the pros and cons of visiting relatives?
What sound did they hear?	How did Ava feel when the lightning struck?	What things could Ava do to make herself feel better, if she needed to?	Out of those things, which would be the best action for Ava to take? Why?
Mum said 'Lightning never hits . . .'	It isn't true that lightning never hits a moving car. Why then did mum say that?	Sometimes when people are trying to be nice or polite, they say things that aren't true. Think of a time when it is OK for you to do this.	What was mum's motivation for saying 'Lightning never hits a moving car'?
Where did the lightning strike?	How do you think mum was feeling?	Retell this story right from the start, until they get home.	Ava was cross about her mum lying about lightning never hitting a moving car. How could they understand each other better?

What things have made you feel scared? How did you try and feel better? (Adults should also talk about their experiences.)

← ask the question to the left first

Use these resources to help think through these specific questions or as needed:

pages 264–308   pages 309–355   pages 356–360   pages 363–378   pages 379–391

9. Motocross

As Alfie was waiting to go back to class, he heard Liam and Jacob talking. They had both been away that weekend to a motocross event. They'd both recently got small motorbikes and they'd raced them around a dirt track. It sounded like it was a long way away as they had taken Jacob's family's camper van and stayed for the weekend. Liam had even won a race. Alfie had never even heard of motocross before, but he listened in even closer as they went into class.

9. Motocross

NB: all adults and young people to take turns asking and answering questions as part of a conversation

A	B	C	D
What were Liam and Jacob talking about?	What does Alfie feel about motocross?	How could Alfie manage his interest/feelings so he doesn't come across as too nosy?	If someone else said 'Motocross is boring', how would you convince them to change their mind?
Who was talking?	Why were Liam and Jacob talking just to each other?	Is it OK to listen to other people's conversations? Why/why not?	What might be a justification for listening in to a conversation?
Who had won a race?	What could Alfie do to find out more about motocross?	Do you think Liam and Jacob are likely to want Alfie to join their conversation? Why/why not?	How well do Liam and Jacob know each other? What is your evidence for this?
What are you interested in? What do you like to do or talk about?	Talk about this story using the word 'interested'.	Retell this story as if it was you listening in to the conversation. Add your own ending.	If Liam and Jacob got annoyed about Alfie trying to listen to them, how could they sort things out?
What happens when you are more interested in a topic of conversation than another person? (Adults should also talk about their experiences.)			

← ask the question to the left first

Use these resources to help think through these specific questions or as needed:

pages 264–308   pages 309–355   pages 356–360   pages 363–378   pages 379–391

10. Mrs Mad Head

Edith had just moved to a new school and she was aware that she looked different from the others. For a start her hair was very big. When she first walked into her new classroom, everyone stared at her. A group of girls decided to call her 'Mrs Mad Head' as a joke. Before they said that, Edith had wanted to be friends with them. Because she didn't like what they called her, she walked off.

10. Mrs Mad Head

NB: all adults and young people to take turns asking and answering questions as part of a conversation

A	B	C	D
Who was called 'Mrs Mad Head'?	How did Edith feel when she was called 'Mrs Mad Head'?	What things could Edith do to make herself feel better?	← From these options, what is the best thing that Edith could do to make herself feel better? Why did you choose that one?
Where did this happen?	What is the problem here?	Why might the girls think that calling Edith 'Mrs Mad Head' is an OK thing to do?	What was the girls' motive for calling Edith 'Mrs Mad Head'?
Did Edith like her nickname?	Think of several things that Edith could do next.	← Which of these is the best option? Why?	How could the girls and Edith understand each other better? Talk through the steps.
What did Edith do at the end?	Tell me about this story in one sentence.	Retell this story with your own ending.	What might the consequences be if Edith and the girls don't talk to each other about this?

Have you ever called someone a silly name? What did you think about it? (Adults should also talk about their experiences.)

← ask the question to the left first

Use these resources to help think through these specific questions or as needed:

pages 264–308   pages 309–355   pages 356–360   pages 363–378   pages 379–391

11. Late home

TJ and Jack were in the park one day when it started to rain. TJ asked Jack, 'Do you want to come back to mine?' Jack thought that would be better than going home, and so he agreed. As they walked into the house, TJ's Mum said abruptly, 'Why are you so late? You said that you would come straight home.' TJ immediately shouted back 'What do you care?!' And then to Jack, 'Come on let's play a game.' TJ's Mum stood in his way and shouted back, 'No you're not! You've got homework to do!'

11. Late home

NB: all adults and young people to take turns asking and answering questions as part of a conversation

A	B	C	D
Who was in the park?	Why did they leave the park?	Give three reasons why a young person would like to go to a friend's house rather than go home straight away.	TJ might give justifications for being late. Which ones might TJ's Mum listen to?
Whose house did they go to?	What do you think they were doing in the park?	Is it better to do homework before or after TV/computer time? Why?	Parents and young people often disagree about homework. Why is this a difficult problem to solve?
What did the boys want to do at TJ's house?	How was TJ's mum feeling?	← What could TJ do next time, so his Mum wouldn't feel like this?	What is the best solution for everyone? Talk about the different options.
What makes you feel angry?	Talk about this story using the word 'angry'.	Can you think of any other words for angry? How are they different?	What do you surmise about TJ and his Mum's relationship?

If you were feeling angry what could you say or do to feel better?
Tell me about a time when you were late, and someone was not happy with you. (Adults should also talk about their experiences.)

← ask the question to the left first

Use these resources to help think through these specific questions or as needed:

pages 264–308   pages 309–355   pages 356–360   pages 363–378   pages 379–391

12. Fishing

Mason had always enjoyed fishing. He started going with his grandad, but now he was old enough to go on his own. He really enjoyed going down to the pond when there was no one else around. Mason would sit and listen to the sounds of the wind in the trees and watch the fish occasionally break the surface of the water. When the rest of his life was busy, Mason could sit by the pond for hours and didn't really mind if he didn't catch any fish.

12. Fishing

NB: all adults and young people to take turns asking and answering questions as part of a conversation

A	B	C	D
Who is in this story?	How does Mason feel?	Why does Mason like to go to fishing?	What are the consequences of having quiet time by himself?
Where does Mason like to go?	Describe the pond.	Why doesn't Mason mind if he doesn't catch any fish?	What can you infer about how Mason feels about his life?
Who did Mason start going fishing with?	Who do you think taught Mason to fish?	Mason likes fishing on his own. How could he make sure his grandad doesn't feel upset?	Why is it especially important to be tactful with your grandparents?
In this story, Mason feels calm when he is by the pond. Tell me about a time when you felt calm.	Tell me about this story using the word 'calm'.	Mason wants to be calm, but he can't go fishing today. What other things could he do that would make himself feel calm?	What might be the consequences if Mason wasn't able to go fishing?
What things do you do that make you calm? (Adults should also talk about their experiences.)			

← ask the question to the left first

Use these resources to help think through these specific questions or as needed:

pages 264–308   pages 309–355   pages 356–360   pages 363–378   pages 379–391

13. A sudden soaking

When Jemil and Lu set off on their hike around the lake that morning, it was sunny and warm. So warm, that they were soon soaked in sweat and needing to take a detour to get more drinking water. Just after lunch, when they still had miles to go, there was a sudden crack of thunder and it began to rain heavily. Jemil huffed as he ran to the nearest tree, regretting that he didn't have a jacket with him. Meanwhile Lu squealed and ran about jumping in the puddles that soon formed.

13. A sudden soaking

NB: all adults and young people to take turns asking and answering questions as part of a conversation

A	B	C	D
Where are Jemil and Lu?	Why did Jemil go under the tree?	Why did Lu and Jemil behave differently?	In the future, why might Lu and Jemil remember their hiking trip differently?
What did Jemil and Lu hear?	How did Jemil feel when the rain started?	How do you know that Lu and Jemil did not anticipate that it would rain?	↤ What further evidence do you have for your view?
Who jumped in puddles?	Why did Lu squeal?	What could Lu do to calm down?	Jamil and Lu don't agree on what to do next. Think about it from different viewpoints. How can they agree on what to do?
What time of day was it when the storm came?	What might happen next?	Retell this story from Jemil's perspective.	↤ Now retell the story from Lu's perspective.
What things have happened to you without you expecting it? (Adults should also talk about their experiences.)			

↤ ask the question to the left first

Use these resources to help think through these specific questions or as needed:

pages 264–308   pages 309–355   pages 356–360   pages 363–378   pages 379–391

14. New school

Mia was feeling scared. She had only been to visit the school once, so she didn't know where anything was. She had felt safe at her old school, which was small and familiar. But this new school was huge and so busy. Mia only knew one other boy from her old school who was also coming here, and she hadn't seen him yet. Everyone else seemed to know each other. Just as Mia felt like she was about to cry, a girl came over and said, 'Hi, I'm Amy.' Mia and Amy chatted about their old schools, before Amy asked Mia to meet her friends. The friends all smiled as Amy and Mia approached.

14. New school

NB: all adults and young people to take turns asking and answering questions as part of a conversation

A	B	C	D
How did Mia feel at the start?	Why was Mia feeling scared?	What could she do to make herself feel better?	In this story, why is it significant that Mia previously went to a small school?
What did Amy say to Mia?	How would you describe how Amy was with Mia?	← You said Amy was 'X'. How might that impact on how Mia felt?	What was Amy's motive for coming to talk to Mia?
What did Amy and Mia chat about?	What do you think Amy, Mia and Amy's friends could talk about?	Retell this story and add your own ending.	← What are the consequences of your chosen ending?
Who did Mia know who would also be attending the new school?	Why might Mia not have seen the boy from her old school?	If Amy hadn't come to talk to Mia, what could Mia have done?	What are the pros and cons of knowing lots of people when you start a new school?
Have you ever started a new school? What was it like? How did you feel? If you haven't, what do you imagine it might be like? (Adults should also talk about their experiences.)			

← ask the question to the left first

Use these resources to help think through these specific questions or as needed:

pages 264–308   pages 309–355   pages 356–360   pages 363–378   pages 379–391

15. After the match

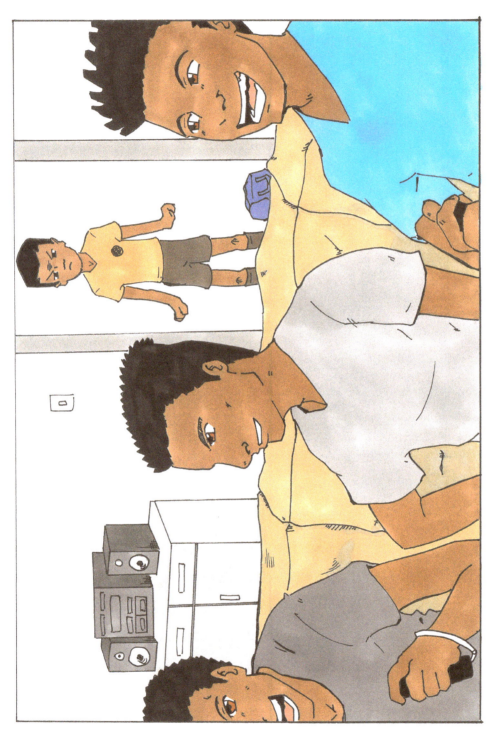

At the weekend, Jackson had been in a tournament. He had a really great time as he had played well, and his team had won all their matches. He was, however, looking forward to going home and collapsing on the sofa with a drink and a snack and just watching TV for a bit. As he threw his bag inside the door, Jackson saw that his brother Jamie had four of his mates over. The game console was plugged into the TV, and as the music was so loud, all of them were shouting.

15. After the match

NB: all adults and young people to take turns asking and answering questions as part of a conversation

A	B	C	D
Who had been playing in the tournament?	How did Jackson feel after playing in the tournament?	How did his feelings change as he got home? Why?	What led you to this conclusion?
Who had friends over?	What is the problem?	What should happen if two people want to do different things in the same room?	When two people have different views, how do they negotiate? Talk through the steps.
What were Jamie and his friends doing?	What could Jackson say to his brother?	Would you expect Jackson to come in and shout at his brother's friends? Why?/why not?	What might be the consequences if Jackson unplugs the game?
What did Jackson want to do when he got home?	What do you think Jackson is thinking as he arrives back home?	Retell this story as if you were Jackson. What happens in the end?	Do you think Jackson would have been diplomatic? Why/why not?
What do you want to do when you are exhausted? What do you do to make yourself feel better? What do you do to help think through these specific questions or as needed? (Adults should also talk about their experiences.)			

← ask the question to the left first

Use these resources to help think through these specific questions or as needed:

pages 264–308   pages 309–355   pages 356–360   pages 363–378   pages 379–391

16. The party

Olivia gave Katy her party invitation as they walked into school. All of their friends were invited. The plan was to go bowling and then for a pizza afterwards. All day everyone was talking about Olivia's party. After school Katy rushed out to tell her mum about the party, but Mum said, 'Sorry love, but that is Nan's 70th birthday, so you can't go to Oliva's party.' Katy moaned, 'Why do I have to go? It will be so boring, and Olivia will think I don't want to be her friend anymore!'

16. The party

NB: all adults and young people to take turns asking and answering questions as part of a conversation

A	B	C	D
Who invited Katy to a party?	How did Katy feel about getting Olivia's party invitation?	Katy was disappointed about not being allowed to go to Olivia's party. What could she do to make herself feel better?	What is Katy's mum's motivation for saying 'no' to Katy's request to go to Olivia's party?
What are they going to do at Olivia's party?	What is the main issue here?	What could Katy have said instead of what she did say?	How could Katy have been more tactful?
What are they planning to eat after bowling?	What is Katy worried about?	Retell this story with your own ending.	Why is this a challenging problem to solve?
How did Katy feel at the end of the story?	Why did Katy moan?	Why did Katy react the way she did?	What is a solution everyone will be satisfied with?
Have you ever been looking forward to something and then you couldn't do it? What happened? (Adults should also talk about their experiences.)			

← ask the question to the left first

Use these resources to help think through these specific questions or as needed:

pages 264–308   pages 309–355   pages 356–360   pages 363–378   pages 379–391

17. Holiday birthday

At the start of the year, Riley's teacher looked at the list of birthdays and marked them all on the calendar. The teacher explained that when it was each class member's birthday, they would have a celebration, just for them, so they could feel special. Riley noticed that there were eight children's birthdays in the summer holidays, so she asked her teacher, 'When will I have my own special celebration?' The teacher said that they would have one big party at the end of the school year for all eight children. Riley frowned and shook her head.

17. Holiday birthday

NB: all adults and young people to take turns asking and answering questions as part of a conversation

A	B	C	D
Who frowned and shook her head?	How does Riley feel?	How do you know that Riley is not happy?	What do you suspect that Riley is thinking?
Who wrote the children's names on the calendar?	Why did the teacher write the children's names on the calendar?	Why is Riley not happy with the plans for the birthday celebrations?	← What led you to this conclusion?
What did Riley ask the teacher?	What could Riley have said to the teacher about having to share her party with other children?	Why wouldn't just crying be the best thing for Riley to do?	What is the teacher's intention here?
In this story Riley feels cheated, because she does not get to have her own party. Tell me about a time when you felt cheated out of something.	Tell me about this story using the word 'cheated'.	What could Riley do to make herself feel better?	What is the best solution for everyone? How can everyone feel happy about the birthday celebrations?
Do you ever feel that things aren't fair? What do you do about it? (Adults should also talk about their experiences.)			

← ask the question to the left first

Use these resources to help think through these specific questions or as needed:

pages 264–308   pages 309–355   pages 356–360   pages 363–378   pages 379–391

18. Peppermint thief

Rihanna knew they shouldn't go into the school secretary's unoccupied office, but Malachi convinced her it would be exciting to get a peppermint from the secretary's desk. Rihanna followed Malachi in as he opened the desk drawer, but refused to take the sweet he offered. He ran off quickly, but she was still in the office when the secretary came back. Rihanna looked at the floor and tried not to cry as she was told off, but she didn't say anything about Malachi being involved.

18. Peppermint thief

NB: all adults and young people to take turns asking and answering questions as part of a conversation

A	B	C	D
Where did the story happen?	What was the problem here?	Why didn't Rihanna say that it was Malachi's idea?	What do you suspect about Malachi?
What did Malachi want to get?	How did Rihanna feel when she was being told off?	What could Rihanna do to make herself feel better?	Why do you think Rihanna went into the office even though she knew she shouldn't?
Who did <u>not</u> take a peppermint?	What could Rihanna have said to the secretary?	In your own words, retell this story with your own ending.	Do you suspect Rihanna will do anything different next time? Why/why not?
What did the school secretary do at the end of the story?	What might Rihanna do next?	Why didn't Rihanna want to cry?	What is the best solution for both Rihanna and Malachi? Talk through the steps.
Have you ever done something just because a friend wanted to? Why is it sometimes hard to say 'no' to friends? (Adults should also talk about their experiences.)			

← ask the question to the left first

Use these resources to help think through these specific questions or as needed:

pages 264–308   pages 309–355   pages 356–360   pages 363–378   pages 379–391

19. Street tree

Jamal could remember the day a tree was planted on the street outside his house. It had been a surprise, but since that day he had enjoyed watching the tree grow bigger. He had watered it in the Summer and swept up the leaves in the Autumn. Jamal had even convinced his dad to put up a nesting box to attract birds. Every day Jamal watched carefully so that he could see any birds that flew in and out. Coming home from school one day, Jamal couldn't believe his eyes when he saw that some workers had cut down the tree.

19. Street tree

NB: all adults and young people to take turns asking and answering questions as part of a conversation

A	B	C	D
Tell me two things that Jamal does to look after the tree.	When the tree was growing, how did Jamal feel about the tree?	← How do you know?	What in particular made you realise that Jamal cares for the tree?
What did the workers do?	How might the workers cut down the tree?	Why might the workers cut down the tree?	Cutting down street trees is sometimes controversial, why?
Finish this sentence: 'Jamal couldn't believe his eyes when . . .'	How did Jamal feel when he saw that the tree had been cut down?	After the tree was cut down, what could Jamal do to make himself feel better?	Jamal's neighbour was pleased that the tree was cut down. How could they talk about it without getting upset with each other?
In this story, Jamal shows that he cares about the tree. Tell me about a time you cared.	Talk about this story using the word 'cared'.	How do Jamal's feelings change during this story?	If you were feeling caring, what would others notice about you?
What things do you care about? How do you show that you are caring? (Adults should also talk about their experiences.)			

← ask the question to the left first

Use these resources to help think through these specific questions or as needed:

pages 264–308   pages 309–355   pages 356–360   pages 363–378   pages 379–391

20. Present from Dad

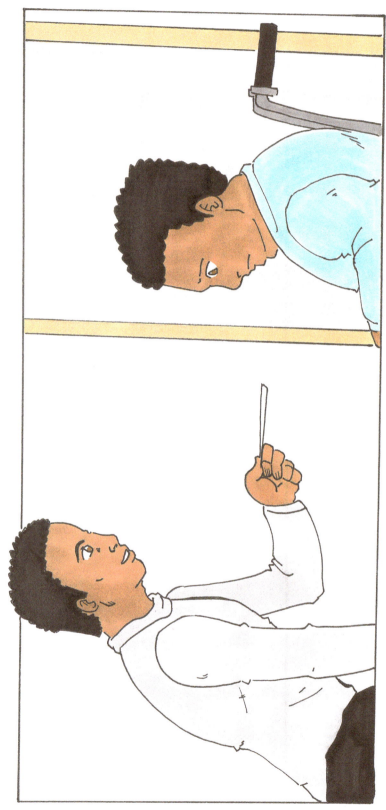

It was Brooklyn's birthday, and he was going paintballing with his friends, but first his Dad was coming around to give him his present. Brooklyn didn't see his Dad very often, but when he did come, he brought the best presents. This year Brooklyn had been hoping for a new phone, so he'd been dropping hints and he really thought his Dad would get him one. The doorbell rang, Brooklyn rushed to the door and there was his Dad. His Dad said 'Happy Birthday!' as he handed Brooklyn an envelope. Brooklyn's face fell. His Dad's smile faded, but he said nothing.

20. Present from Dad

NB: all adults and young people to take turns asking and answering questions as part of a conversation

A	B	C	D
Whose birthday is it?	How did Brooklyn feel when he saw his present from Dad? Can you think of another word for it?	What could Brooklyn do to make himself feel better?	What are the motives for giving presents?
Who was Brooklyn waiting for?	What might Brooklyn's friends give him for presents?	How could Brooklyn have handled this situation differently?	How might Brooklyn feel when he looks back on this?
What did Brooklyn want for his birthday?	Would his friends give him a phone? Why/why not?	Retell this story adding your own ending.	Retell this story from Brooklyn's Dad's perspective.
What was Brooklyn's Dad holding?	What could be in the envelope?	Brooklyn's Dad wanted to buy him a phone but he didn't. Think of two reasons why that might have happened.	What is the best solution for everyone? Talk through the steps.

Have you ever been given a present you were disappointed with? What did you do? (Adults can also talk about their experiences.)

← ask the question to the left first

Use these resources to help think through these specific questions or as needed:

pages 264–308   pages 309–355   pages 356–360   pages 363–378   pages 379–391

21. End of year

It was the end of the year and everyone was excited about the next step, but it was also the last time that they would see some of their friends. Emma had been thinking about what she could give her classmates, as she had made some great friends. She bought eight big bags of sweets to give out, so everyone in her class would get loads of sweets each. She felt a bit like Father Christmas as she walked into school with her bag bulging.

21. End of year

NB: all adults and young people to take turns asking and answering questions as part of a conversation

A	B	C	D
What was everyone excited about?	What time of year do you think it is in this story?	Why was it the last time they would see some of their friends?	What is significant about what Emma is doing?
What was Emma going to give out?	How does Emma feel? Can you think of another word for it?	← What could Emma do to remember that feeling?	What was Emma's motivation for giving out the sweets?
How many bags of sweets did Emma bring to school?	Why was her bag bulging?	Is everyone going to be pleased with that many sweets? Why/why not?	If someone objects to Emma giving out sweets, how could she convince them to change their mind?
Finish this sentence: 'She felt a bit like . . .'	Talk about this story using the word 'generous'.	Retell this story with your own ending.	Her teacher does not want Emma to give out the sweets. How could they reach an agreement that both are happy with? Talk through the steps.
Can you ever have too many sweets or presents? Have you ever had too many? (Adults should also talk about their experiences.)			

← ask the question to the left first

Use these resources to help think through these specific questions or as needed:

pages 264–308   pages 309–355   pages 356–360   pages 363–378   pages 379–391

22. Artwork

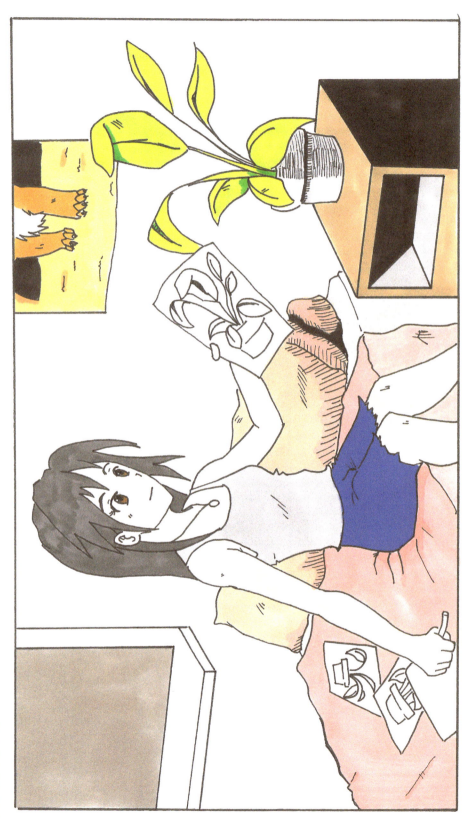

When Priya had heard Miss Maddox tell the class that their art homework was to draw a houseplant, she immediately felt down in the dumps. She knew that she wasn't very good at drawing and the detail required to draw a houseplant was particularly challenging. She could imagine everyone laughing next week in class when they compared her drawings to theirs. After a whole weekend of drawing, Priya threw down her pencil and screamed. Not one of her pictures was perfect. It was late, so rather than attempt another drawing, she decided to choose one that was pretty much OK. Pausing and looking at it, she realised it wasn't too bad.

22. Artwork

NB: all adults and young people to take turns asking and answering questions as part of a conversation

A	B	C	D
Where is Priya and what is she doing?	How does Priya feel when she throws down her pencil? Can you think of another word for it?	What did Priya do to make herself feel better?	← Why might this solution be useful?
What was the art homework?	How did Priya feel when she was given her homework?	What does 'down in the dumps' mean?	← Why say 'down in the dumps' instead of miserable?
What did Priya imagine would happen in school?	Why might her classmates laugh at her picture?	← Why wouldn't some of her classmates laugh?	← What do you suspect might happen when Priya takes her homework into school?
Finish this sentence: 'It was getting late so . . .'	What does 'satisfied' mean?	Retell this story with your own ending that solves Priya's problem.	← Why is the ending you chose a good solution?
What things do you feel satisfied with when they are finished? (Adults should also talk about their experiences.)			

← ask the question to the left first

Use these resources to help think through these specific questions or as needed:

pages 264–308   pages 309–355   pages 356–360   pages 363–378   pages 379–391

23. Favourite band

Ella couldn't believe her eyes when she opened the message from her friend. The old cinema in her own town was going to be converted into a live music venue. And it got even better, because the opening act was going to be their favourite band, 'The Midnight Climbers.' Ella screamed, as this was the band she listened to every day and all her friends loved. In Ella's mind she was their number one fan. She really wanted tickets, but she also knew that lots of other people would want them too.

23. Favourite band

NB: all adults and young people to take turns asking and answering questions as part of a conversation

A	B	C	D
How did Ella first hear about the concert?	How does Ella feel when she hears the news? Can you think of another word for it?	What could Ella do to remember this feeling?	← What evidence tells you that Ella is feeling like this?
Who is the opening act at the new music venue?	Why is Ella very excited?	What does 'couldn't believe her eyes' mean?	What can you infer from how Ella feels when you read 'couldn't believe her eyes'?
Finish this sentence: 'Ella also knew . . .'	What will Ella do next?	Use your own words to retell this story. Also add your own ending.	Ella's mum thinks the tickets are too expensive. How can Ella convince her mum to buy the tickets?
Who does Ella think is 'The Midnight Climbers' number one fan?	Tell me this story using the word 'desperate'.	How do Ella's feelings change when she starts to think about the tickets?	What's a solution Ella and her mum will be satisfied with? Talk through the steps.
Have you ever been desperate to do something? (Adults should also talk about their experiences.)			

← ask the question to the left first

Use these resources to help think through these specific questions or as needed:

pages 264–308   pages 309–355   pages 356–360   pages 363–378   pages 379–391

24. Fetch!

Rhys and Daniel had been out for most of the day, and they were now bored. They were in the park when they saw a dog, but they couldn't see an owner. The boys found a stick, and they threw it for the dog. The dog chased the stick and brought it back, but the next time Rhys threw it the stick hit the dog on the head. Daniel thought this was funny. The dog didn't seem to mind and still brought the stick back. Daniel threw the stick, and it hit the dog again. This time it nearly hit his eye. Daniel laughed again, this time louder, and picked up the stick again aiming it at the dog.

24. Fetch!

NB: all adults and young people to take turns asking and answering questions as part of a conversation

A	B	C	D
Who was in the park?	Why were the boys bored?	Why shouldn't you play with someone else's dog when the owner is not there?	What might be the consequences of playing with someone else's dog?
Finish this sentence: 'The stick hit the dog on the head. Daniel thought this was. . .'	How did Daniel feel when the stick hit the dog?	Do we know how Rhys felt when the dog was hit by the stick? Why don't we know?	What evidence would you need before you make a decision about how Rhys feels?
How many times did the stick hit the dog?	What might Rhys say to Daniel?	What would happen if the dog's owner came along and saw the boys?	Why might it be hard for Rhys to challenge Daniel about the stick hitting the dog?
Where on the body did the stick hit the dog?	Talk about this story using the word 'cruel'.	Was it cruel for the dog to be hit by mistake? When does it become cruel?	Rhys thinks Daniel is being cruel to the dog. What is the best solution to the problem?
Have you ever thrown a stick for someone else's dog? Have you ever witnessed anyone being cruel to an animal? (Adults should also talk about their experiences.)			

← ask the question to the left first

Use these resources to help think through these specific questions or as needed:

pages 264–308   pages 309–355   pages 356–360   pages 363–378   pages 379–391

25. New trainers

Shanayde couldn't wait to go to school because at the weekend she had bought some new trainers. Her old ones had got embarrassing, because they were so worn out. The new ones were amazing. She never thought that she would be able to get trainers that looked as brilliant as these. The sales assistant had said that Shanayde would be the envy of all her classmates, as they were the latest style. At school the next day, Kyle took one look at her trainers and said 'Did you get those from the charity shop?' Everyone turned and looked at her trainers. Shanayde felt hot and her skin prickled with sweat.

25. New trainers

NB: all adults and young people to take turns asking and answering questions as part of a conversation

A	B	C	D
What did Shanayde buy?	Why was Shanayde excited to go to school with her new trainers?	What reaction had Shanayde expected when she got to school?	↓ What evidence supports your view?
What were Shanayde's old trainers like?	How are the new trainers better than the old ones?	Why shouldn't Kyle have said what he said?	What is Kyle's motivation for saying what he said?
Finish this sentence: 'Shanayde felt hot and. . .'	Why does Shanayde's skin 'prickle with heat'?	Retell this story with your own ending.	↓ What are the consequences of the ending you chose?
What did Kyle say about the trainers?	↓ How did Shanayde feel when Kyle said that? Can you think of another word for it?	What could Shanayde do to make herself feel better?	What is the best way for Shanayde to solve her problem? What can she do that would be OK for Kyle too? Talk through the steps.
Has anybody ever been mean about something of yours? (Adults should also talk about their experiences.)			

↓ ask the question to the left first

Use these resources to help think through these specific questions or as needed:

pages 264–308   pages 309–355   pages 356–360   pages 363–378   pages 379–391

26. Bus ride betrayal

On Sunday afternoon, Samuel went to the cinema with several of his friends. It was the first time that he was permitted to go with the group, as he was a year younger than the others. Coming home they all caught the bus together and Jonathan, the oldest in the group, said, 'I think this is your stop, Samuel,' with a smirk. Samuel jumped off the bus quickly without looking where he was. It was only when he'd waved goodbye to his friends that Samuel realised that he didn't know where he was. It was getting dark and he knew that his phone had run out of charge.

26. Bus ride betrayal

NB: all adults and young people to take turns asking and answering questions as part of a conversation

A	B	C	D
Where is Samuel at the end of the story?	How does Samuel feel after he'd waved goodbye? Think of another word for how he feels.	What could Samuel do to make himself feel better?	How might Jonathan feel when he looks back on this?
Where did Samuel go with his friends?	How did Samuel feel when he was on the bus?	Why did Jonathan say 'This is your stop, Samuel'?	What was Jonathan's motive for what he did? Why do you think that?
When did this story take place?	Tell me this story in your own words.	Retell this story and add your own ending.	← What might be the consequences of that ending? Justify your thinking
Finish this sentence: 'Samuel's phone had . . .'	What could Samuel do next?	What could Samuel do next time to ensure this doesn't happen again?	What is the best solution for everyone? Think about what needs to be done now and what needs to happen the next day. Talk through the steps.

Have your friends ever played a trick on you? How mean was it? What did you do? (Adults can also talk about their experiences.)

← ask the question to the left first

Use these resources to help think through these specific questions or as needed:

Pages 264–308   pages 309–355   pages 356–360   pages 363–378   pages 379–391

27. Frustrating French

Connor dreaded French lessons, as each lesson felt like a perpetual fog. He never seemed to understand the grammar rules and kept getting the words in the wrong order. It felt like he would never be able to get the basics right. Did the teacher think that his long repetitive explanations helped? The more Mr Strongman talked, the less Connor seemed to grasp. It obviously helped Dylan though, as he looked as if he understood everything. He always had his hand up asking questions. Looking up from his work, Connor could tell when Mr Strongman was marking his test, as he sighed and looked glum.

27. Frustrating French

NB: all adults and young people to take turns asking and answering questions as part of a conversation

A	B	C	D
What lesson was Connor in?	How does Connor feel about learning French? Think of another word for it.	What could Connor do to make himself feel better?	How could Dylan convince Connor that French is OK?
What is Connor's teacher's name?	What could Connor do to be less confused about French?	What is a solution to this problem that everyone would be satisfied with?	What might be the consequences of Connor doing nothing?
Finish this sentence: 'He never seemed . . .'	Why is it useful to learn another language?	If Dylan looks as if he understands everything, why does he ask questions?	What might be Dylan's motive for listening and asking questions in French lessons?
What lessons do you sometimes find confusing?	Talk about this story using the word 'confused'.	Retell this story but with your own ending.	If Connor went to France on holiday, might he change his mind about French lessons? Why/why not?
If you are struggling to follow something in class, what should you do? Who is more responsible for student learning, teachers or students? (Adults should also talk about their experiences.)			

 ask the question to the left first

Use these resources to help think through these specific questions or as needed:

pages 264–308   pages 309–355   pages 356–360   pages 363–378   pages 379–391

28. The forgotten washing up

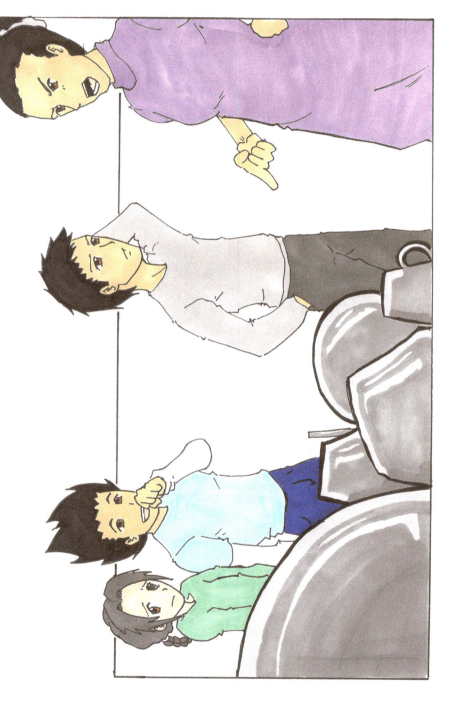

Mum asked Krish and Raj to wash up while she was out, but Krish's friend unexpectedly came around and they went out together. Raj felt left out until he remembered he had a new game, so he sat and played it. The washing up got forgotten. When Mum got back, Raj got into trouble and they were still arguing when Krish came home with his friend. Krish said Raj was going to do the washing up, but Raj disagreed. Krish really believed that he hadn't done anything wrong. This sort of thing kept happening and although Raj understood that Krish was forgetful, he'd had enough.

28. The forgotten washing up

NB: all adults and young people to take turns asking and answering questions as part of a conversation

A	B	C	D
Who did Mum ask to wash up?	Who forgot something?	Why might Krish say Raj was going to do the washing up?	Did Krish behave differently because his friend was with him? Why do you think that?
Where did this happen?	What's the problem here?	Explain what happened here and what you think will happen next.	Retell this from Mum's perspective.
What did Krish do?	How did Raj feel when Krish came back? Can you think of another word for it?	What could Raj do to make himself feel better?	Why might this be a difficult problem for Raj to solve?
Who has had enough?	How does Mum feel?	Why does the washing up not being done bother Mum?	What is the best solution for everyone? Talk through the steps.
Do you ever forget to do what your mum/dad/carer asks you to do? Do you sometimes 'forget' on purpose? (Adults should also talk about their experiences.)			

← ask the question to the left first

Use these resources to help think through these specific questions or as needed:

pages 264–308   pages 309–355   pages 356–360   pages 363–378   pages 379–391

29. One step at a time

Emily had been looking forward to the end of year trip and was so excited to finally be at the camp. On the first morning, she got up early so she could have breakfast first and have plenty of time to get ready. She had her coat on and was first outside raring to go, but she had no idea which activity would come first. Emily felt a lump in her throat when the instructor told the class what they were about to do. She listened hard to the instructions, but found it hard to remember. She wasn't particularly scared, but she didn't like the idea of falling, so she volunteered to go first and went across the high ropes like a snail.

29. One step at a time

NB: all adults and young people to take turns asking and answering questions as part of a conversation

A	B	C	D
Who was on the trip?	How did Emily feel when she started the activity? Think of another word for it.	What could Emily do to make herself feel better?	If you were the instructor, what could you do to convince Emily that she doesn't need to be so cautious?
How was Emily feeling before the trip?	How did Emily's feelings change when she heard what she was going to do today?	What does 'lump in her throat' mean?	What evidence do you have that this is an activity camp?
Who gave the instructions?	Talk about this story using the word 'cautious'.	Retell this story with your own ending.	What are the pros and cons of being cautious?
Talk about a time when you have been cautious?	What might other people say when Emily is being slow?	← Why might that bother Emily?	What is the best solution here for everyone?
Have you ever done something that scared you a bit? How did you feel afterwards? (Adults should also talk about their experiences.)			

← ask the question to the left first

Use these resources to help think through these specific questions or as needed:

pages 264–308   pages 309–355   pages 356–360   pages 363–378   pages 379–391

30. Broken bike

Sofia was riding her bike home from school one day when part way home her chain came off. Sofia tried several times to put it back on, but it just wouldn't go. She was just about to start pushing her bike home when Reza, a boy from her class, came along and offered to help. Sofia wasn't convinced that he'd be able to fix it. Reza tried several times to get the chain back on but without any luck. 'I think we can do it if we do it together,' suggested Sofia. And within a moment it worked! The chain slotted into place, and Sofia's bike was fixed again. They high-fived and Sofia rode off home.

30. Broken bike

NB: all adults and young people to take turns asking and answering questions as part of a conversation

A	B	C	D
Where was Sofia going on her bike?	How did Sofia feel when she couldn't get the chain back on her bike? Think of another word for it.	At that time, what three things could Sofia do to make herself feel better?	← Out of these which is the best solution for everyone? Why?
Who came along and helped Sofia?	What's the word for working together to solve a problem, as Sofia and Reza did?	Why did Sofia suggest that they cooperate to fix the bike?	What are the consequences of cooperation?
Who fixed the bike?	What will happen next?	Retell this story with your own ending.	← What led you to this conclusion?
Finish this sentence: 'Sofia suggested, "I think we . . ." '	Tell me about this picture using the word 'cooperated'.	What were the main things that happened in this story?	Imagine you are Reza. Tell the story from his perspective.
Tell me about a time when you cooperated with someone. (Adults should also talk about their experiences.)			

← ask the question to the left first

Use these resources to help think through these specific questions or as needed:

pages 264–308   pages 309–355   pages 356–360   pages 363–378   pages 379–391

31. Class entertainment

Amber was pulling faces in class when the teacher's back was turned. Chioma copied Amber just to see if she could get away with it. Peggy thought that they were both hilarious and although she tried not to, she burst out laughing. 'My lesson is obviously very entertaining, Peggy.' The teacher wasn't pleased with her, especially when she couldn't explain what she was laughing at. She bit her lip while she was being told off and felt a bit sick. While this was happening, Chioma and Amber stood on their chairs and danced, but only Amber was fast enough to sit down before the teacher turned around.

31. Class entertainment

NB: all adults and young people to take turns asking and answering questions as part of a conversation

A	B	C	D
Where did this happen?	What could Peggy have said when she was being told off?	Why didn't Peggy say why she was laughing?	← What's your evidence for thinking that?
What was Amber doing at the start of the story?	What does 'burst out laughing' mean?	What could Peggy do to make herself feel better?	What did you realise about Amber and Chioma?
Finish this sentence: 'She bit her lip while . . .'	Why did Peggy try not to laugh?	Why did the teacher say 'My lesson is obviously very entertaining'?	In your own words, tell this story from the teacher's point of view.
Who sat down before the teacher turned round?	How did Amber and Chioma feel when they were dancing? Can you think of another word for it?	What might Peggy think about Amber and Chioma at the end?	Think about all the different people in this story. What is the best solution for everyone? Talk through the steps.

Do you try and make people laugh when you shouldn't? Do you know someone who does? (Adults should also talk about their experiences.)

← ask the question to the left first

Use these resources to help think through these specific questions or as needed:

pages 264–308   pages 309–355   pages 356–360   pages 363–378   pages 379–391

32. Lift home

Logan and Aiden were heading home from school. They usually walked together, as they lived around the corner from each other. They were grumbling because it had been a tough day and the walk seemed to take ages. A car pulled up. 'Hi Aiden, how are you doing?' Aiden took a minute to recognise the driver. 'You remember me, don't you? I'm Jason, I work with your dad.' 'Oh yes,' Aiden replied shakily. 'Hop in, I'm going your way,' the man continued. He saw the boys hesitate so he persisted, 'It's OK, your Dad wouldn't mind. He knows me.'

32. Lift home

NB: all adults and young people to take turns asking and answering questions as part of a conversation

A	B	C	D
Who was walking home?	How were the boys feeling before they met the man in the car? Can you think of another word for it?	It had been 'a hard day'. Why do you think that might have been?	What evidence is there about what good friends the two boys are?
Who was driving the car?	When the boys met Jason, how did they feel then? Did they feel different things?	Why should the boys take notice of their feelings? How might they stay calm?	What is the man's motive for giving the boys a lift? Could he have other motives?
Whose dad did Jason know?	What might be the problem about going in a car with someone you don't know well?	Retell this story with your own ending.	What might be the consequence of making the wrong decision?
Whose car do you go in?	If you didn't want a lift with someone, what could you say?	Does Aiden know this man well? How do you know?	What is the best solution for everyone? Talk through the steps.

Who would you get in a car with? Have you talked about this with your parents/carers? (Adults should also talk about their experiences.)

← ask the question to the left first

Use these resources to help think through these specific questions or as needed:

pages 264–308   pages 309–355   pages 356–360   pages 363–378   pages 379–391

33. The prom

At the school prom Zayna was with her friends, dancing and having a really good time. They were mucking around doing silly dances, and when Zayna did a funny chicken dance everyone laughed and gave her a round of high fives. Zayna was still laughing about it when she arrived home and she couldn't stop talking about it. Later that night Courtnie messaged Zayna, telling her that she loved her dancing, but that Zayna needed to look online because someone had posted a video of her chicken dance and there were lots of comments already. Zayna dreaded going to school tomorrow, as she knew what would happen.

33. The prom

NB: all adults and young people to take turns asking and answering questions as part of a conversation

A	B	C	D
Who was at the school prom?	How do you think Zayna felt when she saw her dance online? Think of another word for it.	What could Zayna do to make herself feel better?	Does everyone enjoy proms? Why/why not?
What was posted online?	What is the problem?	Why did Courtnie message Zayna about the video?	Why do you suspect the person (whoever that is) posted the video online?
What happened at the prom?	Who has been affected?	Tell this story in your own words and also add what happens next.	What is the best solution for everyone? Talk through the steps.
Finish this sentence: 'Zayna dreaded going . . .'	What does 'dread' mean?	Does Zayna really know what will happen at school tomorrow?	What suggests that this type of thing has happened before?

Tell me about a time when you dreaded something. (Adults should also talk about their experiences.)

← ask the question to the left first

Use these resources to help think through these specific questions or as needed:

pages 264–308   pages 309–355   pages 356–360   pages 363–378   pages 379–391

34. Volcanic tea

Candice was glad that Lucky had invited her for a meal with his family. The food was delicious, and she was really enjoying herself until he started talking about something that happened in school. Lucky told his parents that she had laughed at a new student in their class. She felt she could erupt like a volcano, but she didn't want to do that in front of his parents. All the children in the class had laughed when the boy had slipped as the head teacher brought him into class, and the teacher had told them all off. She didn't know how to explain this calmly, so sat at the table glaring at Lucky.

34. Volcanic tea

NB: all adults and young people to take turns asking and answering questions as part of a conversation

A	B	C	D
Who was at tea?	How did Candice feel when Lucky was talking about what happened at school? Can you think of another word for it?	What could Candice do to make herself feel better?	How might Lucky feel when he looks back on this later?
Finish this sentence: 'She was really enjoying herself until . . .?	What might Lucky's parents think of Candice?	What does 'erupt like a volcano' mean?	Why might Lucky have behaved in this way? Why do you think that?
Where did this happen?	How did Candice feel at the end?	Retell this story and add your own ending.	What's Candice's motive for not expressing her feelings in front of Lucky's parents?
What did Lucky do?	What could Candice have said?	What might happen at school the next day?	What is the best solution for everyone? Think about what Candice could do at the time and what she might do later. Talk through the steps.

Have you ever felt bad after you laughed at someone? (Adults should also talk about their experiences.)

← ask the question to the left first

Use these resources to help think through these specific questions or as needed:

pages 264–308   pages 309–355   pages 356–360   pages 363–378   pages 379–391

35. Basketball game

Down at the park on Saturday, Elijah and Yemi were playing basketball as they often did. It was rather unfair now because Yemi had grown so much that he was a good deal taller than his friend. A group of older boys approached Yemi and asked him to join their game, as they needed one more player. Yemi had watched them and seen that they were really good players. The older boys didn't want Elijah to join them, as he was too short. Yemi declined and said, 'I can't leave Elijah out, because he's my friend.' The older boys shouted 'losers' and went back to their game.

35. Basketball game

NB: all adults and young people to take turns asking and answering questions as part of a conversation

A	B	C	D
Who is playing basketball in the park?	How might Yemi feel when he is invited to play basketball by the older boys? Think of another word for it.	How might Elijah's feelings differ from Yemi's?	↓ Justify your conclusions.
What did Yemi say?	What word describes Yemi's actions?	Would you like a loyal friend? Why/why not?	What did you observe Yemi do that was loyal?
What do the older boys shout at the end of this story?	← How might that make Elijah and Yemi feel?	What could Elijah and Yemi do to make themselves feel better?	What is the best solution for everyone? Talk through the steps.
Where did this story happen?	Tell me about this story using the word 'loyal'.	Tell this story from the start and then add your own ending.	How might Elijah feel when he thinks back on this event?

Have you ever been in a situation where not everyone has been invited to join in an activity? (Adults should also talk about their experiences.)

← ask the question to the left first

Use these resources to help think through these specific questions or as needed:

pages 264–308   pages 309–355   pages 356–360   pages 363–378   pages 379–391

36. Maths breakthrough

Coyote found maths hard as he really had to concentrate. Although it didn't happen often, he liked it when he got it right. His best friend Jonah was good at maths and when they worked together Jonah always knew the answers straight away. Today Coyote wanted to get out in the sun, so he thought if he could get Jonah to do his maths homework for him, he could go out and play football. He rang his friend, but hung up before Jonah answered. He tried the maths again, and after reading the instructions carefully, he started and found his brain was on fire! Finally, he understood it, and although there was more maths to do, he put his book away grinning and rang Jonah again. He could tell Jonah about his achievement!

36. Maths breakthrough

NB: all adults and young people to take turns asking and answering questions as part of a conversation

A	B	C	D
What was Coyote trying to do?	How did Coyote feel when he understood the maths? Think of another word for it.	What could Coyote do to remember this and how it happened?	Did Coyote believe he could do the maths? What evidence do you have for your view?
Who was Coyote's best friend?	What does 'concentrate' mean?	Why did Coyote hang up the phone the first time he called Jonah?	What made you realise that Coyote had to work harder at maths than Jonah?
What did Coyote do in the end?	What will happen next in the story?	Retell this story with your own ending.	How would Coyote have felt if he'd got the answers from Jonah? Why do you think that?
Where was Coyote?	What would you do if you were Coyote?	Is there anything Coyote could have done to make maths homework easier to do?	Coyote needs to get his homework done, and he wants to get time outside to relax. Is what he does the best solution? Talk through your thinking.
What lessons do you have to work harder in? Are there any lessons you find easy? (Adults should also talk about their experiences.)			

↞ ask the question to the left first

Use these resources to help think through these specific questions or as needed:

pages 264–308   pages 309–355   pages 356–360   pages 363–378   pages 379–391

37. Who cares about football?

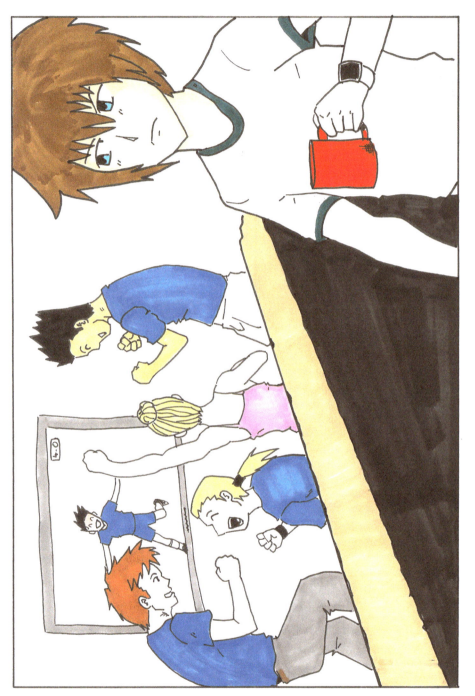

Gilson could hardly wait to see his favourite TV programme, because the last episode had ended with a cliffhanger. Rather than binge-watch, he liked to look forward to it all week. Heading home, he thought how good the action would look on the big screen. When he got home, his sister and her friends were watching football. Scarlet was shouting at the TV and didn't even notice as he came in. He asked when it was going to finish and she said, 'Not long.' He went to get a drink, and when he came back it was in extra time. He was glad they were having a great time, but he wasn't. He went upstairs and paced around, listening to them yelling downstairs and thinking 'This could go on for ages!'

37. Who cares about football?

NB: all adults and young people to take turns asking and answering questions as part of a conversation

A	B	C	D
What did Gilson want to do?	What does Gilson's pacing tell you?	What is the most likely thing to happen next?	← What led you to this conclusion?
What was Scarlet doing?	How does Gilson feel? Think of another word for it.	What could Gilson do to calm down?	What conclusions can you draw about Scarlet and her friends?
Where did this happen?	What's the main problem here?	Retell this story with your own ending.	What questions would you want to ask Gilson and Scarlet to understand them better?
What could Gilson hear from upstairs?	Who could help Gilson feel better?	Why do you think Gilson won't make a fuss in front of Scarlet's friends?	What is the best solution for everyone? Talk through the steps. Of these things, what could Gilson do now and what might he do another time?

Have you ever been looking forward to watching something and then couldn't? (Adults can also talk about their experiences.)

← ask the question to the left first

Use these resources to help think through these specific questions or as needed:

pages 264–308   pages 309–355   pages 356–360   pages 363–378   pages 379–391

38. A big fat ginger cat

Sojourn had been interested to learn more about Benjamin Zephaniah when she heard some of his poetry in school. She enjoyed reading and performing his poems in class, and her teacher, Mrs Grenyer, was pleased with her. Sojourn wasn't usually keen on homework, but she had the seed of a great idea for a poem of her own. She was about to start when her big fat ginger cat, Treak, curled up on her lap. She stroked him gently while looking at his sweet face, his contentedness was contagious. After a while, she realised it was nearly bedtime and she hadn't done any homework. Her stomach lurched, but Treak was such a cuddly fluffball.

38. A big fat ginger cat

NB: all adults and young people to take turns asking and answering questions as part of a conversation

A	B	C	D
Who are the main characters in the story?	How does Sojourn feel towards Treak? Can you think of another word for it?	Does Sojourn generally care what her teacher thinks of her?	What evidence supports your thinking?
What had Sojourn enjoyed doing in school?	How does Sojourn feel about not doing any homework?	What could Sojourn do to make herself feel better about not doing the homework?	What might the consequences be if she doesn't do her homework, for her and for Mrs Grenyer?
Finish this sentence: 'Sojourn wasn't usually keen on. . .'	Why was Mrs Grenyer pleased with Sojourn?	Retell this story with your own ending.	Retell this story from Mrs Grenyer's perspective.
What did the cat do?	What do you think will happen at school the next day?	What does 'the seed of a great idea' mean?	What could Sojourn do to solve this problem? Is there any way for Sojourn to justify not doing her homework?

← ask the question to the left first

Have you ever been distracted by something? Did it stop you doing what you were supposed to? (Adults can also talk about their experiences.)

Use these resources to help think through these specific questions or as needed:

pages 264–308   pages 309–355   pages 356–360   pages 363–378   pages 379–391

39. Bus trip

The annual trip to the seaside had been so much fun. Bobbi-Jo's class had been permitted to take more money than the younger pupils, so they had played in the arcades and also eaten ice cream and candy floss. They were all heading back to the bus when Bobbi-Jo noticed that she didn't have her new hat. Not again! Her mum would be so angry, so she ran back to the arcade where she last recalled seeing it. She crossed her fingers as she entered the arcade, but it was nowhere to be seen. She approached a member of staff and asked her if she had seen an orange hat with flowers on it. The lady went away and came back smiling as she handed Bobbi-Jo her hat. Bobbi-Jo ran back to the bus as fast as she could, again with her fingers crossed.

39. Bus trip

NB: all adults and young people to take turns asking and answering questions as part of a conversation

A	B	C	D
Where did Bobbi-Jo go with her class?	What does 'permitted' mean?	Why might older pupils be permitted to take more spending money than the younger children?	The younger children think the decision to permit the older children to take more money is unfair. How might the teachers justify their decision?
What did Bobbi-Jo lose?	How did Bobbi-Jo feel when she lost her hat? Think of another word for it.	What could Bobbi-Jo do to make herself feel better?	What can you surmise from the story about Bobbi-Jo losing things?
What was Bobbi-Jo doing when she noticed that she had lost her hat?	When the teacher realises that Bobbi-Jo is not with the class, how might the teacher feel?	How will the teacher's feelings change when Bobbi-Jo returns with her hat?	What are the likely consequences for Bobbi-Jo? Justify your view.
How was Bobbi-Jo getting back to the bus?	What will happen next?	Retell this story with your own ending.	What might Bobbi-Jo think when she looks back on this day?

Do you sometimes lose things? Have you ever felt relieved when you have found something? (Adults should also talk about their experiences.)

← ask the question to the left first

Use these resources to help think through these specific questions or as needed:

pages 264–308   pages 309–355   pages 356–360   pages 363–378   pages 379–391

40. Lost and found

On their way to school, Josei and Omar found a wallet. Josei picked it up, but hesitated before asking, 'Should we look inside?' Omar didn't think twice, 'Of course, how else are we going to know if there's any money in it . . . er . . . or who it belongs to?' They looked through each section very carefully, taking everything out. There was no money, but there was a credit card with a name printed on it that neither of them recognised. 'What are we going to do?' asked Josei. Omar said 'Let's take it to the school office, as we are quite close to school.' At school the receptionist looked in the wallet and said 'Mm. Mr Kempsey. I believe that's Chantelle's dad. I'll give him a call. If it's his, I expect he'll be relieved that such honest young people found his wallet.'

40. Lost and found

NB: all adults and young people to take turns asking and answering questions as part of a conversation

A	B	C	D
Who picked up the wallet?	How did Josei feel when she picked up the wallet? Think of another word for it.	At that moment, what could Josei do to make herself feel better?	If you keep something you find, is that the same as stealing? Why/why not?
Where did they find the wallet?	What does 'hesitated' mean?	Why might Josei have hesitated before looking in the wallet?	When you find something that is valuable, why might it be hard to be honest?
Who suggested taking the wallet to the school office?	What was Omar thinking when they found the wallet?	Retell this story and add your own ending.	If you hand in a wallet with lots of money in it, should you expect a reward. Why/why not?
What did the receptionist say?	Why did the receptionist think the young people had been honest?	What does it mean when Omar 'didn't think twice'?	Is what happened the best solution for everyone? Compare what happened to another option.
Have you ever found something valuable? (Adults should also talk about their experiences.). When you find something valuable that is not yours, how do you decide what to do?			

← ask the question to the left first

Use these resources to help think through these specific questions or as needed:

pages 264–308   pages 309–355   pages 356–360   pages 363–378   pages 379–391

41. Poor Ralf

Logan came home from school and the house was eerily quiet. With five children and several pets, the house was usually a hive of activity at this time of day. To ensure he got some peace and quiet, Logan usually went straight upstairs, avoiding the commotion, but today he couldn't work out what was happening. Although he wanted to stick to his usual routine, he was intrigued about what was going on, so he sidled into the living room. There in his basket lay Ralf, suspiciously still. Unusually, his nose was not even twitching. Logan's brothers and sisters were all around and no one said a word. They didn't need to, for they all had red eyes, downturned mouths and sniffling noses.

41. Poor Ralf

NB: all adults and young people to take turns asking and answering questions as part of a conversation

A	B	C	D
Who came home?	What did Logan notice immediately when he entered the house?	Why did Logan sidle into the living room?	Was Logan expecting to see what he saw? Provide evidence for your view.
Where was Ralf?	Who is Ralf?	Logan is now very upset. What could he do to make himself feel better?	What conclusions can you draw about how Ralf was viewed by the family?
Who else was in the house?	How did Logan's brothers and sisters feel?	When someone dies, people often feel grief. This is a bit like sad. How is it different from sad?	Logan's parents don't want another dog. What might be their justification for this decision?
Finish this sentence: 'Everyone had red . . .'	Talk about this story using the word 'grief'.	Retell this story with your own ending.	What might be the best solution if some of the family want another pet? Talk through the pros and cons of the different solutions

Have you ever had a pet die? Have you ever been to a funeral? (Adults should also talk about their experiences.)

← ask the question to the left first

Use these resources to help think through these specific questions or as needed:

pages 264–308   pages 309–355   pages 356–360   pages 363–378   pages 379–391

42. Exam results

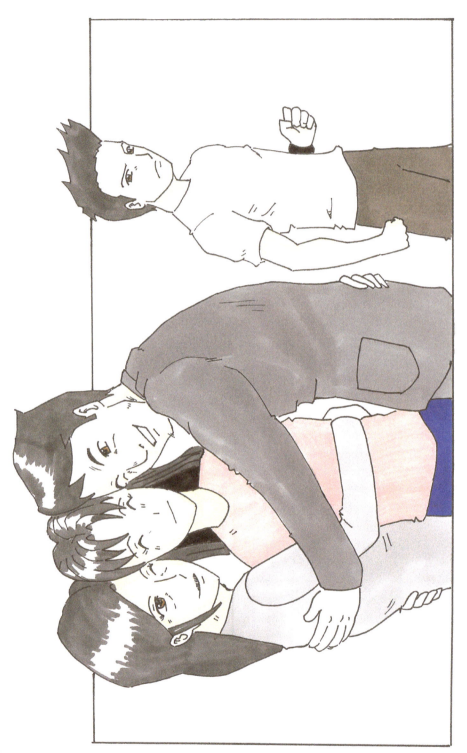

'We are so proud of you, Maria', Mum exclaimed as she hugged her. Dad stepped in too, beaming as he hugged his daughter. 'You are really clever!' he added. They all looked at Gabriel, waiting for him to join the family hug. Gabriel had to admit Maria had done well in her exams, and way better than he had. He forced a smile and mumbled his congratulations. Mum then announced that she was going to take Maria shopping as a special reward. Just the two of them, and Maria could buy something she really wanted. Gabriel shuffled backwards and frowned. Mum and Dad had never taken him shopping like that, even when he achieved good grades. He was trying to stay calm, but Gabriel realised his blood was beginning to boil.

42. Exam results

NB: all adults and young people to take turns asking and answering questions as part of a conversation

A	B	C	D
Who got hugged?	How did Gabriel feel when he 'forced a smile'?	What does 'his blood was beginning to boil' mean?	What can you infer when you heard that Gabriel 'forced a smile and mumbled his congratulations'?
What did Gabriel do when he heard about Maria and Mum going shopping?	How does Gabriel feel at the end of this story, after he has heard about Maria being taken shopping?	What could Gabriel do to make himself feel better?	What is Mum's intention when she takes Maria shopping?
Who hugged Maria?	How did Maria feel?	How aware might Maria have been of how Gabriel is feeling? Why/why not?	What evidence supports your view?
Finish this sentence: 'Mum and Dad had never . . .'	What do you think Gabriel will do next?	Retell this story, adding your own ending.	Gabriel needs to sort this out. What could he say or do to make it better? What is the best solution here for both Gabriel and Maria?

Have you ever felt really left out? Or did you ever forget about someone when you were very pleased? (Adults should also talk about their experiences.)

← ask the question to the left first

Use these resources to help think through these specific questions or as needed:

pages 264–308   pages 309–355   pages 356–360   pages 363–378   pages 379–391

43. Bad day

Today nothing anyone could do could make Levi feel any better. At break his friends tried telling him silly jokes. That didn't work. At lunchtime the cook noticed Levi was slouching and frowning and so gave him a smile, together with an extra serving of his favourite food, lasagne. That didn't work. After school Dad offered to take him to the climbing wall, which he usually really enjoyed, but not today. Mum suggested that the whole family go to see a movie, but Levi couldn't find any that he wanted to see. Even the promise of popcorn didn't make him feel any more motivated. As Granny would say, he must have 'got out of bed on the wrong side.' Eventually Levi realised that the only person who could fix this was himself.

43. Bad day

NB: all adults and young people to take turns asking and answering questions as part of a conversation

A	B	C	D
Who is the main person in this story?	How did Levi feel in this story? Think of a similar word.	Why didn't people's efforts to cheer him up work?	What do you think made Levi realise that he needed to fix things himself?
Name one person who tried to help Levi.	Why did people try to help Levi?	What could Levi do to make himself feel better?	What might be the consequences of Levi's behaviour?
What did the cook notice about Levi?	What is Levi's problem?	What might have caused this problem? Put yourself in Levi's shoes and give it your best guess.	← What's your evidence for thinking that?
What would Granny say about how Levi was feeling?	Tell me this story using the word 'glum'.	What does 'got out of bed on the wrong side' mean?	When Granny says that Levi 'got out of bed on the wrong side', does that help? Why/why not?

In this story Levi feels glum. Tell me about a time when you felt glum. (Adults should also talk about their experiences.)

← ask the question to the left first

Use these resources to help think through these specific questions or as needed:

pages 264–308   pages 309–355   pages 356–360   pages 363–378   pages 379–391

44. Little cousins

From the time they were born, Kacey couldn't remember a time when she didn't look forward to seeing her little twin cousins, Grace and Ellie. When they were very little, Kacey would help soothe whichever one was crying by stroking their hair. Now they were a little older, Kacey liked visiting even more. At bedtime they would all snuggle into a living room chair, although it was a little too small for them all, and she would read the twins a story until they both nodded off. They weren't always well behaved, however. Ellie in particular often pulled on the poor dog's fur, which he really didn't like. Consequently, Kacey had learnt that she needed to watch the twins like a hawk whenever the dog was nearby.

44. Little cousins

NB: all adults and young people to take turns asking and answering questions as part of a conversation

A	B	C	D
Who are Kacey's cousins?	How would you describe how Kacey is with her cousins?	'Affectionate' is a bit like 'nice'. How are these two words the same and different?	What can you infer from this story about Kacey 's relationship with her cousins?
Finish this sentence: 'Grace and Ellie are both . . .'	How old do you think Grace and Ellie are now?	← How do you know?	If someone else disagreed with your point of view about the age of the twins, how would you defend it?
What do the little girls sometimes do to hurt the dog?	What could Kacey do to stop the girls annoying the dog?	Why did Kacey need to watch the girls 'like a hawk' when the dog is nearby?	What might the consequences be if Kacey left her cousins alone with the dog?
Where do they sit and read a book?	Tell me this story using the word 'affectionate'.	How do you know that Kacey 's aunt trusts her with the twins?	Retell the story from Kacey 's aunt's perspective.

In this story, Kacey shows she is affectionate towards her cousins. Tell me about a time when you were affectionate. (Adults should also talk about their experiences.)

← ask the question to the left first

Use these resources to help think through these specific questions or as needed

Pages 264–308   pages 309–355   pages 356–360   pages 363–378   pages 379–391

45. Quidditch

Ajay had read most of the Harry Potter books and seen all of the films, so when Jayden invited him to watch him play Quidditch he thought he would know all about it. The players did have broomsticks, although they couldn't fly them of course, and there was also a golden snitch. That bit he understood. Just like the films and books there were 'chasers, beaters and seekers', but Ajay couldn't work out which one was which. Even though he didn't understand it, the game was entertaining, with lots of cheering from the crowd. When one of the other spectators asked Ajay about the rules, he shook his head and had to admit that he didn't have a clue. After the game, Jayden took one look at Ajay and said, 'Mate, your face is such a picture!'

45. Quidditch

NB: all adults and young people to take turns asking and answering questions as part of a conversation

A	B	C	D
Where is Ajay?	How does Ajay feel about Quidditch?	How are Ajay's feelings about Quidditch different from how he expected to feel?	← Justify your thinking.
Who asked Ajay about the rules of the game?	Why might the spectator have asked Ajay in particular?	Explain what 'didn't have a clue' means.	What in the story helps you to work out what 'didn't have a clue' means?
Who invited Ajay to the Quidditch game?	Why might Ajay have been invited to the game?	What does 'your face is a picture' mean?	What is Jayden's intention when he says to Ajay, 'your face is a picture'?
In this story, Ajay is bewildered by the rules of Quidditch. Tell me about a time when you felt bewildered.	Tell me about this story using the word 'bewildered'.	What three things could Ajay do to make himself feel better?	← Out of those, what is the best solution? Why?
Have you ever been in a situation where you didn't know as much as you thought you did? How was that for you? (Adults should also talk about their experiences.)			

Use these resources to help think through these specific questions or as needed:

pages 264–308   pages 309–355   pages 356–360   pages 363–378   pages 379–391

46. Finally!

From the time that the Christmas holiday started, it had been frantic. Every minute of it had been busy. It had been one long round of visiting relatives, meeting friends and endless eating. And of course, there was all the fun and games of Christmas day, with so much happening. Although most of this had been OK, sometimes it could be a bit much. Granny and Grandad, not before time, had gone back to their home, so now the TV could be turned down. Mum had stopped cooking and at last had turned her crazy Christmas music off. Dad had disappeared into a book, and Jamie had gone out with his mates. There was nothing to do, nowhere to go and just a few leftover chocolates. Finally!

46. Finally!

NB: all adults and young people to take turns asking and answering questions as part of a conversation

A	B	C	D
What time of year was it?	How does the person in the story feel? Think of another word for how he feels.	If all of the activity got to be too much, what could the person in the story do to make themselves feel a bit better?	What does 'not before time' imply?
Who had the family visited?	What is this person's main problem?	Someone might describe the same situation as either peaceful or boring. What changes your experience of the same situation?	How might the different family members ensure that everyone enjoys their family get-togethers?
Who had gone home?	If a group of people were being peaceful, what could they be doing?	If you were feeling peaceful, what would others notice about you?	How could you tactfully tell someone to go home?
Talk about a time when your house was peaceful.	Talk about this story using the word 'peaceful'.	Retell this story and add your own ending.	What evidence do you have that the person telling the story liked it being peaceful?
Have you ever wanted something to end that other people were enjoying? (Adults should also talk about their experiences.)			

← ask the question to the left first

Use these resources to help think through these specific questions or as needed:

pages 264–308   pages 309–355   pages 356–360   pages 363–378   pages 379–391

47. Noisy breakfast

Jana woke up feeling sluggish. 'Not again,' he thought. He had so much to do, but he didn't know where to start. He saw a whole lot of cheerful, chatty messages on his phone. People wanted him to answer questions and make arrangements, but he couldn't face it. He had worked late last night but still hadn't finished the work that was due in today. 'You are a real ray of sunshine this morning!' said Moni, who was dancing around the kitchen to some extremely loud music while Jana just looked on silently. He tried to smile for her sake, although he suspected that she had no idea about how he was feeling. She insisted he decide on their arrangements for later in the day, because she needed to plan her day. Jana thought his head might explode.

47. Noisy breakfast

NB: all adults and young people to take turns asking and answering questions as part of a conversation

A	B	C	D
Who's in this story.	How did Moni feel?	What do you think might be the best thing for Moni to do?	Why did Moni say 'You are a real ray of sunshine this morning!'? What was her motivation?
What did Jana do first?	How did Jana feel? Think of another word for how he feels.	What could Jana do to make himself feel a bit better? 	Do you suspect Jana often feels like this? (yes/no) Why do you think that?
What was Moni doing at breakfast?	What does 'sluggish' mean?	Retell this story with your own ending.	What do you surmise has happened to make Jana feel like this?
What did Jana hear?	What could Jana say to Moni?	How might Jana's friends be affected by his actions?	What could Jana do to make the situation better? What is the best solution for both Moni and Jana?
Have you ever felt this bad? Did you ever find it hard to know what to do when a friend was very sad? (Adults should also talk about their experiences.)			

← ask the question to the left first

Use these resources to help think through these specific questions or as needed:

pages 264–308   pages 309–355   pages 356–360   pages 363–378   pages 379–391

48. Phone call

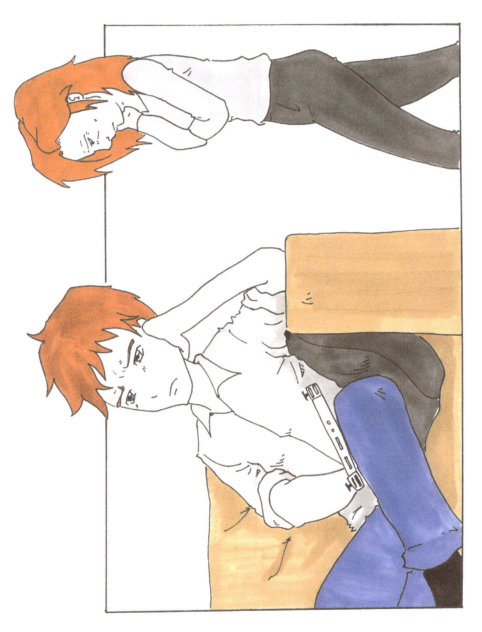

Carter knew as soon as Mum answered the phone that something was up. She was standing very still, and even when she did speak her voice was much quieter than usual. Carter held his breath as he listened in, trying to work out who she was talking to and what it was about. Although he tried to distract himself and play a game, Carter couldn't stop thinking about the phone call. His concentration was so bad that he couldn't even get past the first level of his game. As soon as he heard Mum hang up the phone, he jumped out of his chair and ran to her. Until he saw her puffy eyes, Carter hadn't realised she'd been crying. Mum wiped her eyes, cleared her throat and quietly said, 'Sit down you nosy parker. I've got some news for you.'

48. Phone call

NB: all adults and young people to take turns asking and answering questions as part of a conversation

A	B	C	D
What happened at the start of this story?	How does the phone call make Carter feel? Think of another word to describe how Carter is feeling.	← Why does he feel like this?	What made you realise that Carter was feeling the way he does?
Who listened in on the phone call?	Why did Carter listen to his Mum's conversation?	Why did Mum call Carter a 'nosy parker'?	← What justification does Mum have for thinking this?
What did Carter do to try to distract himself?	What does 'distract' mean?	While Mum was on the phone, what else could Carter have done to make himself feel better?	What evidence suggests that the news may not be good news?
Who was talking on the phone?	What is Carter's problem?	How did Carter work out that something was up?	What is Mum's motive for wanting to talk to Carter as soon as she gets off the phone?

Have you ever been desperate to find out what was going on and no one would tell you? (Adults should also talk about their experiences.)

← ask the question to the left first

Use these resources to help think through these specific questions or as needed:

pages 264–308   pages 309–355   pages 356–360   pages 363–378   pages 379–391

49. Bike chain sculpture

Lexi had worked hard on a piece for the graduation show, and she had been encouraged by her tutor Ivy, who had told her, 'You will knock 'em dead.' At the show today, when people saw what she had made out of old bike chains, they were intrigued, and lots of people asked her questions about her work. Meanwhile, Lexi was keeping an eye out for her Nan. When she finally appeared, Lexi dashed over and gave her a hug. They wandered around the show together and Nan said something complimentary about everything she saw. When they came to the bike chain sculpture, Nan laughed and said, 'it's a shame that this person didn't get a chance to finish their work!' When her Nan saw who the work was by, her face fell. She was soon relieved when she saw Lexi's smiling face. Their laughing got louder and louder and attracted lots of attention.

49. Bike chain sculpture

NB: all adults and young people to take turns asking and answering questions as part of a conversation

A	B	C	D
What happened in this story?	How did Lexi feel when her Nan commented on her work?	← What could Lexi do to remember these feelings?	What can you infer about Lexi and Nan's relationship? What evidence do you have?
Who was at the graduation show?	How does Lexi feel about her Nan?	Why did Lexi's Nan try to say nice things about all of the work?	Did Lexi's Nan mean to be rude about the sculpture? (yes/no) What evidence do you have for your view?
What did Ivy say?	Why is it good for a tutor to be encouraging?	What does 'knock 'em dead' mean?	What was Ivy's motivation when she encouraged Lexi?
What was Lexi's sculpture piece made of?	How would you feel if someone was rude about something you worked hard at?	What do you think is most likely to happen next? Why?	If Lexi hadn't smiled, how could they have sorted things out between them?
Have you ever overheard someone saying something bad about you? (Adults should also talk about their experiences.)			

← ask the question to the left first

Use these resources to help think through these specific questions or as needed:

pages 264–308   pages 309–355   pages 356–360   pages 363–378   pages 379–391

50. Answering back

During History, the class had been set the task of making a model of an Egyptian pyramid, but most of the students were messing about or just talking. Especially Tracey, who was gossiping non-stop about her sister's new pierced ears. Mrs Philips approached and sharply interrupted. 'Come on, you've only got half an hour to finish your work.' Tracey huffed, 'We were only talking.' 'Well, you need to stop talking and start working,' responded Mrs Philips in an effort to move them on. Then Tracey replied, 'We weren't the only ones talking. You're always telling us off.' Mrs Philips let out a quick breath before replying sternly, 'Tracey that is enough. Get down to work.' Tracey wouldn't let it lie and responded again, 'I don't know why you're picking on me.' Mrs Philips raised her voice further and barked, 'For once young lady, you've got to understand the impact of your behaviour.'

50. Answering back

NB: all adults and young people to take turns asking and answering questions as part of a conversation

A	B	C	D
Who was gossiping non-stop?	How was Mrs Philips feeling when she said 'Come on, you've only got half an hour.'	← What could Tracey have done at this point to stop the situation getting worse?	← What do you know about Tracey that indicates that she might find that difficult?
What is the teacher's name?	Why was the teacher cross at the end of the story?	What might have made Tracey feel argumentative?	← What are the consequences of being argumentative?
What were most of the students doing?	How might the other pupils feel about what is happening in class?	Should any of the students say something to Tracey? Why/why not?	What might be a pupil's motivation for saying something to Tracey?
Finish this sentence: 'The class had been set the task of . . .'	Summarise what happened in this story.	Tell this story from another student's perspective.	Think about all the people involved in this situation. What is the best solution here, for everyone?
Have you ever felt like you were being picked on by a teacher? Did you deserve it? (Adults should also talk about their experiences.)			

← ask the question to the left first

Use these resources to help think through these specific questions or as needed:

pages 264–308   pages 309–355   pages 356–360   pages 363–378   pages 379–391

51. Ice skating

Amy and Charlie had been friends for years. Amy had lots of friends, but Charlie was her oldest friend and the two of them had grown up together. Amy made friends easily, and recently she had met Crystal, who she thought was great fun and always up for a laugh. One day Crystal suggested that a group of them should meet up to go ice skating. Amy knew that Charlie would never want to go out with a group of people she didn't know, but she was dying to go. Charlie was shy with big groups and had invited Amy to her place to watch a movie together. Amy understood that Charlie was super sensitive about being left out and would react badly if she found out about the ice-skating invitation. It was pretty hard to get it right. The only advice her mum would give was, 'You've got to solve this problem for yourself.'

51. Ice skating

NB: all adults and young people to take turns asking and answering questions as part of a conversation

A	B	C	D
Who is in the story?	Amy feels Charlie is 'needy', what do you think that might mean?	Why is Amy taking time to make this decision?	← What is your evidence for your view?
Where had Crystal invited Amy to go?	What is Amy's problem?	What solutions are there to Amy's problem?	← What is the best solution for all? Why?
Who did Amy go to for advice?	Why did Amy ask her mum for advice?	Why did Amy's mum not just tell Amy what to do?	← If she did, what do you suspect Amy's mum would advise? Why?
Talk about a time when a friend or someone in your family has been 'needy'.	Talk about this story using the word 'needy'.	Retell this story with your own ending.	Suppose Amy went ice skating without telling Charlie. What might be her motive?
Have you ever found it really hard to decide what to do? (Adults should also talk about their experiences.)			← ask the question to the left first

Use these resources to help think through these specific questions or as needed:

pages 264–308   pages 309–355   pages 356–360   pages 363–378   pages 379–391

52. The sleepover

The whole group were really looking forward to Saturday night, and Hattie had promised it would be the party of the year. Kacy and Karly were so excited they could barely talk about anything else. None of them had been to a sleepover for ages, not since the trouble at Becky's. Karly, who had never been to any of their parties before, was particularly excited. Finally, Saturday came and Kacy and Karly met up and went to Hattie's house. The others had already gathered in Hattie's bedroom. Hattie's mum came up and told them she'd be back at 11:00 p.m. and said 'Don't do anything I wouldn't do.' They all went downstairs and put on some music. Everyone was laughing, dancing and having a great time. Hattie kept turning up the music. Although she was having fun, Karly tentatively said, 'Do you think we should turn it down a bit?' Everyone laughed. Hattie said, 'Don't be so boring.'

52. The sleepover

NB: all adults and young people to take turns asking and answering questions as part of a conversation

A	B	C	D
When was the sleepover?	'Kacy and Karly could barely talk about anything else.' What do you think they might have said?	Hattie's mum said 'Don't do anything I wouldn't do.' What does she mean by this?	Mum didn't tell the girls what they could and could not do. What might be the consequences of this?
Whose house was the party at?	What was the problem?	Why shouldn't the girls make as much noise as they like?	What were Karly's motivations for suggesting the music should be turned down?
Where did they go to listen to music?	How might the neighbours have felt about the party?	The neighbours don't like the noise, but they don't say anything. Why not?	Karly tentatively asked to turn the music down. What are the pros and cons of asking 'tentatively'?
What's happening in this story?	Talk about this story using the word 'uptight'.	If you were feeling 'uptight' and wanted to feel more relaxed, what could you say or do?	The girls think that different things are OK. How could they resolve their differences? What is the best solution here for everyone?

Have you ever been worried about what might happen if things got out of control? (Adults should also talk about their experiences.)

← ask the question to the left first

Use these resources to help think through these specific questions or as needed:

pages 264–308   pages 309–355   pages 356–360   pages 363–378   pages 379–391

53. Stolen scarf

Sue and Yuni went shopping at the new mall together. It was Yuni's introduction to the outrageously expensive shops, and it was fun being out together even if she knew they couldn't afford anything. She was particularly attracted to a very soft scarf but didn't think about buying it because it cost the earth! She went back and stroked it several times before they left the shop. A little later, outside the mall, Yuni was horrified when Sue pulled the scarf out of her rucksack and gave it to her. Her stomach turned. Was she caught on CCTV touching the scarf? Would security think she had stolen it? What was her mum going to say when she saw it? As her heart raced, she desperately tried to think what she could do. Meanwhile Sue skipped along, presuming that Yuni was pleased to have such a gift.

53. Stolen scarf

NB: all adults and young people to take turns asking and answering questions as part of a conversation

A	B	C	D
Who was involved in this story?	When Sue gave her the scarf, what did Yuni's body tell her?	What could Yuni have done to calm down?	Do you think Yuni knows why Sue did it? Why do you think that?
What did Sue give Yuni?	How did Yuni feel when Sue gave her the scarf?	Why does Sue giving her the scarf bother Yuni?	← What evidence supports your view?
What were Sue and Yuni doing at the beginning of the story?	What could Yuni have said to Sue once she had been given the scarf?	Do you agree with what Sue did? Why/why not?	Why might Sue's feelings matter to Yuni? How will that affect what Yuni does next?
Where are Yuni and Sue?	What's going to happen next?	Retell this story with your own ending.	What could Sue do now to sort the problem out? What is the best solution here for both Sue and Yuni?
Have you ever been freaked out when someone did something you thought was wrong? (Adults should also talk about their experiences.)			

← ask the question to the left first

Use these resources to help think through these specific questions or as needed:

pages 264–308   pages 309–355   pages 356–360   pages 363–378   pages 379–391

54. Not again!

Much to his irritation, Travis didn't understand what the teacher was saying, yet again. He hardly ever understood what was going on in this class, because the teacher rabbited on and on. He looked over at the posters on the wall, wondering if they could help him work out what the teacher was saying. He was tired after a day of concentrating hard on things that really didn't make much sense. The teacher, noticing he wasn't looking, asked him a question. He thought he knew the answer, but his mind was racing, as was his heart, and it came out all muddled. He realised it might have sounded rude. Some of the other kids looked at him and sniggered. Travis pushed his desk over and ran out of the classroom. Reflecting afterwards, he wished he hadn't behaved the way he had, because usually he coped better.

54. Not again!

NB: all adults and young people to take turns asking and answering questions as part of a conversation

A	B	C	D
Who did not understand what the teacher was saying?	What was Travis's problem?	Why did Travis not just stay in the room?	What conclusions can you draw about Travis and learning?
Where did this happen?	How did Travis feel when he couldn't answer a question? And afterwards?	In class, what could Travis have done to make himself feel better?	Did the other students understand what being in this class was like for Travis? Justify your view.
Who tried to answer a question?	How did Travis feel about the other students?	Retell this story with your own ending.	Imagine you are the teacher. Tell the story as they would see it.
Who pushed his desk over?	Who could help next time?	Did the teacher know that Travis didn't understand? Why do you think that?	What could Travis and his teacher do differently next time? What is the best solution here?

Have you ever felt too stressed to think? (Adults should also talk about their experiences.)

← ask the question to the left first

Use these resources to help think through these specific questions or as needed:

pages 264–308   pages 309–355   pages 356–360   pages 363–378   pages 379–391

55. Little brother

Yasmin found it hard to believe, but her little brother Tai was now in secondary school. Although he was almost as tall as her and thought he could look after himself, she still liked to keep an eye on him. When he first went to secondary school, Mum told her they had to go together. Tai didn't like it much, but Yasmin made sure he got there safely. A little while ago, Tai had got into trouble with a group of lads because he was shooting his mouth off. Tai had said that the boys had been teasing him about his jacket, and so he was just defending himself. Luckily Yasmin had heard the commotion in the street and frightened them off. She told him to watch his tongue, because if Mum heard him swearing like that there would be serious consequences for him.

55. Little brother

NB: all adults and young people to take turns asking and answering questions as part of a conversation

A	B	C	D
Who is Yasmin's brother?	How does Yasmin feel towards Tai?	↩ Why does Yasmin feel that way?	↩ What evidence do you have to support your view?
Who did Tai get into trouble with?	How did Tai's trouble start?	Tai got angry in the street. What could he have done to make himself feel better?	Are there times when swearing and shouting is justified?
Who does Yasmin tell to 'watch his tongue'?	What 'serious consequences' might there be for Tai if Mum hears him swearing?	Why might Yasmin not tell Mum about Tai's swearing?	At some point in the future, why might Yasmin change her mind and tell her mum about Tai's swearing?
In this story, Yasmin feels 'protective' towards Tai. Tell me about a time when you felt 'protective'.	What is the main issue here?	Retell this story with your own ending.	Talk through the options and decide the best way to prevent any further issues.
Have you ever wished you could protect someone better? Have you ever had someone close to you that kept getting into trouble? (Adults should also talk about their experiences.)			↩ ask the question to the left first

Use these resources to help think through these specific questions or as needed:

pages 264–308   pages 309–355   pages 356–360   pages 363–378   pages 379–391

56. A canoe adventure

It was a perfect day. The sun was shining, the sky was blue and there was a gentle breeze. Sanjiv was with his favourite people: Issy, Natalie and Adam. They had been canoeing along at a bracing speed, but now they were resting, listening to the silence. As they paused, getting their breath back, there was a harsh whistling sound. Natalie laughed because she thought it was Adam mucking about, but then they realised a seal had surfaced beside them and it was also taking a breath before disappearing again. Sanjiv thought, 'This is it; this day couldn't get any better.' They drifted over to the bank where they were going to have a barbecue and Sanjiv hopped out, missed his footing and landed flat on his face in the mud. Issy screamed, Adam laughed, and Natalie looked on in horror. Sanjiv slowly got up, scanning his body for signs of injury. Then he observed his friends carefully and he was struck by their different reactions. And so a plan formed in his mind.

56. A canoe adventure

NB: all adults and young people to take turns asking and answering questions as part of a conversation

A	B	C	D
Who went on this canoe adventure?	How did Sanjiv feel about the day when they saw the seal?	What could he do to make sure he remembers this day and this feeling?	Do you think this group often does this sort of activity? What's your evidence for thinking that?
Where were they?	Why did Natalie laugh at the strange whistling sound?	What do you think is Sanjiv's plan?	Do you think Sanjiv's plan will be the same for all of his friends? Why do you think that?
Finish this sentence: 'Sanjiv thought . . .'	Why was the day so great?	Retell this story, but add in your own ending.	Do you think Sanjiv's earlier mood will affect what he does? How?
What happened to Sanjiv towards the end of this story?	What does 'scanning his body for signs of injury' mean?	Why did the friends all have different reactions to Sanjiv's accident?	From their reactions what could you surmise about each of his friends?
What's your idea of a perfect day, who would be there and what would you be doing? (Adults should also talk about their experiences.)			

← ask the question to the left first

Use these resources to help think through these specific questions or as needed:

pages 264–308   pages 309–355   pages 356–360   pages 363–378   pages 379–391

57. Sunglasses squabble

Jen really wanted to be Matthew's friend because he always seemed to be having fun. But Matthew didn't like her that much, because she was taller than him and she got in the way when he was trying to talk to Priya, who he was particularly interested in. One weekend Matthew and Jen, together with Priya and Nairo, were in the park. Matthew was already trying to distance himself from Jen, because he thought she looked ridiculous in trousers which were too short and too much make-up. She said to him, 'You can take your sunglasses off now, the sun's gone in.' He snapped back at her, 'I'm not wearing them because of the sun you ****!' Matthew and Nairo laughed together but stopped when Jen yelled back at Matthew, 'You are as shallow as a puddle and not as interesting!' Priya looked daggers at Matthew and his heart sank as he noticed Nairo turn his back. He swore at Jen and then at Priya too. Nairo watched as the argument escalated.

57. Sunglasses squabble

NB: all adults and young people to take turns asking and answering questions as part of a conversation

A	B	C	D
Who wanted to be Matthew's friend?	Who started the argument?	Do you think Matthew expected Jen to yell back at him? Why/why not?	← What led you to your conclusion?
Who 'looked daggers' at Matthew?	How did Matthew feel about Priya?	What does 'looked daggers' mean?	Do you suspect that Priya's reaction affected what Matthew did next? (yes/no) Explain why/why not.
Finish this sentence: 'Matthew was already trying to distance himself from Jen because . . .'	How would you describe Matthew and Jen's relationship?	Retell this story and add your own ending.	Whose side will Nairo take in the end do you think? Why do you think that?
What did Jen compare Matthew to?	Matthew's 'heart sank'. Did his heart really move? What happened?	What could Matthew do to calm down?	What is the best solution here for all four involved?
Has anyone ever made a wrong assumption about you because of how you look? (Adults should also talk about their experiences.)			

← ask the question to the left first

Use these resources to help think through these specific questions or as needed:

pages 264–308   pages 309–355   pages 356–360   pages 363–378   pages 379–391

58. How to lose your friends

One evening recently some of Regan's friends were going to a party, but she was too nervous to join them. She didn't say that, but instead pretended to be ill. Her friends called for her anyway and so at the door it was a bit awkward. Tarik tried to persuade her to go, but she persisted in refusing. The next week her friends were planning a trip to the cinema, and Regan expected them to invite her. However, she was thrown off balance when they didn't. From then on, she was consistently excluded, and so she started to bear a grudge. If she heard them talking about an event, she would say things like, 'Oh, I guess I'm not invited to that either?' Her oldest friend, Callum, was very loyal and sometimes he would try to explain things to her, but she thought this was patronising and so she rebuffed him. Another friend, Bobbi, just ignored Regan because it was all getting too embarrassing. Subsequently, when Regan heard she wasn't invited to Tarik's birthday party, she started telling everyone how nasty he was. Tarik was devastated when he overheard her talking about him.

58. How to lose your friends

NB: all adults and young people to take turns asking and answering questions as part of a conversation

A	B	C	D
At the start of the story who was going to a party?	What could Regan have said to her friends about feeling nervous?	Why wasn't Regan honest about feeling nervous?	What might be the consequences of Regan being honest?
Finish this sentence: 'She expected them to invite her, however. . .'	What does 'persisted' mean?	What does 'bear a grudge' mean?	What conclusions can you draw about Regan's friends? What's your evidence for that?
What did Regan do when she heard about Tarik's party?	How did Regan feel after she kept being excluded?	Retell this story with your own ending.	Do you think it's possible for Regan to make up with her friends or is it too late? Why/why not?
What did Tarik do at the beginning of the story?	What's the main issue here?	At the end of the story, what could Tarik do to make himself feel better?	What is the best solution here, particularly for Tarik and Regan?
Have you ever wished you were braver? (Adults should also talk about their experiences.)			

← ask the question to the left first

Use these resources to help think through these specific questions or as needed:

pages 264–308   pages 309–355   pages 356–360   pages 363–378   pages 379–391

59. The fateful lie

Shirin secretly spied on Ashton from a distance, and when she caught sight of the sun glinting on his hair, her heart leapt. Now she had a problem and didn't know what to do. She had only spoken to him once, and unfortunately, she had been so absorbed in keeping him talking that she couldn't remember what he had said. Her friend Omar found it easy to chat to anyone, and so he couldn't understand how ridiculously awkward she felt talking to Ashton. Another friend, Vic, was talking about Ashton describing his good looks, and in a moment of madness Shirin said, 'Oh yeah, we're really close.' Omar's eyes were like saucers when he heard that!

Later, when Omar started teasing Ashton about 'the lovely Shirin,' Ashton had no idea what was going on and got irritated. After Omar spilled the beans, Ashton sent Shirin an abrupt message saying, 'Don't tell lies about me. I barely know who you are!'

59. The fateful lie

NB: all adults and young people to take turns asking and answering questions as part of a conversation

A	B	C	D
Who is in this story?	How did Shirin feel at the beginning of the story?	Why do you think Shirin lied to Vic?	What was Omar's motive for telling Ashton what Shirin had said about him?
What was Shirin doing at the beginning of the story?	← How did she feel about the way she was behaving?	Retell this story with your own ending.	What do you suspect about Ashton from his reaction?
Finish this sentence: 'Omar found it easy to chat to anyone and . . .'	What tells you that Omar was surprised when Shirin said she was close to Ashton?	Did Omar know Shirin was lying to Vic? How do you know?	Do you think Shirin will retaliate against Omar? How do you know?
What did Shirin say to Vic?	Who might Shirin be cross with at the end? Why?	What could Shirin have done to make herself feel better at the end?	What could Shirin do to sort this problem out? What is the best solution here for everyone involved?
Have you ever liked someone so much you did or said something you later regretted? (Adults should also talk about their experiences.)			

→ ask the question to the left first

Use these resources to help think through these specific questions or as needed:

pages 264–308   pages 309–355   pages 356–360   pages 363–378   pages 379–391

60. Some boys are strange creatures

Elsie, Chip and Eric had all been friends since they started school. Although they hadn't always been in the same class or seen each other very much. Elsie thought Chip was the funniest person she knew. Her admiration for his sense of humour alongside his kindness made him a valued friend. When he arrived one day, Chip was his usual smiley self with Eric, but he didn't smile at Elsie. Elsie went over to say hello to them, but only Eric replied. She began to feel uneasy and went cold when Chip said, 'I know you think I'm an awful human, so why are you bothering?' Eric looked shocked and said, 'What's up mate?' 'She knows,' Chip replied. Eric joined Chip in looking at the ground. Elsie had no idea what they were talking about and looked at both of them waiting for an explanation. When none came, Elsie said casually, 'I guess it's a boy thing,' and strode away.

60. Some boys are strange creatures

NB: all adults and young people to take turns asking and answering questions as part of a conversation

A	B	C	D
Finish this sentence: 'Elsie, Chip and Eric have all been friends since. . .'	How did Elsie feel when Chip wouldn't talk to her?	← At this point what could Elsie do to make herself feel better?	How might Chip feel when he looks back on this?
Who was involved?	What does 'admiration' mean?	Why didn't Elsie get angry with Chip?	What can you infer about Elsie from the way she reacted?
Who was Elsie's valued friend?	Summarise what happened in this story.	Tell this story with your own ending.	What might the consequences of this incident be?
Who looked shocked?	Who might know why Chip is behaving like this?	Why do you think Chip might be behaving like this?	Nobody seems OK at this moment. How can they sort it out so that everyone will be satisfied?
Has anyone ever turned on you and you didn't know why? (Adults should also talk about their experiences.)			

← ask the question to the left first

Use these resources to help think through these specific questions or as needed:

pages 264–308   pages 309–355   pages 356–360   pages 363–378   pages 379–391

Attendance sheet

Language for Behaviour and Emotions group

Adult:		Session 1: day and time				Session 2: day and time
Young person	Start Language Level B/C/D	Key skill to focus on *				Dates of group and attendance

* There are three parts to understanding language. Which is your focus?

☐ Saying when you don't understand (comprehension monitoring).

☐ Understanding words (vocabulary).

☐ When people don't say what they mean (figurative language).

Use resources from the toolkit:

pages 264–308   pages 309–355   pages 356–360   pages 363–378   pages 379–391

Attendance sheet

Language for Behaviour and Emotions group

| Adult: Sarah Jones | | Session 1: day and time
Monday 9:00–9:30 | | Session 2: day and time
Thursday 12:00–12:30 | | | | | | | | |

Young people	Start Language Level B/C/D	Key strategy for young person	Dates of group and attendance									
			6/5/19	9.5.19	13.5.19	16.5.19	21.5.19	23.5.19	3.6.19	6.6.19	10.6.19	13.6.19
Grant	B		✓	✓	✓	✓	✓	✓	✓	✗	✓	✓
Dwane	D		✓	✓	✓	✓	✓	✗	✓	✓	✓	✓
Charlotte	C	✓	✓	✓	✓	✓	✗	✓	✓	✓	✓	✓
Olly	C		✓	✗	✓	✗	✓	✗	✓	✓	✓	✗

Key strategy symbols:

* There are three parts to understanding language. Which is your focus?

☑ Saying when you don't understand (comprehension monitoring).
☐ Understanding words (vocabulary).
☐ When people don't say what they mean (figurative language).

Note: If you choose 'understanding language' you also need to tick which section you are focusing on.

Use resources from the toolkit:

pages 264–308   pages 309–355   pages 356–360   pages 363–378   pages 379–391

Toolkit

Saying when you don't understand (comprehension monitoring)

Introduction to comprehension monitoring

Comprehension monitoring is the term used for our continual checking that what we are listening to and reading is making sense. Many young people with SLCN do not do this reliably. Nonetheless, it is an essential skill, because if a listener does not say when they do not understand, speakers usually assume that they do understand. This in turn may lead to misunderstandings which may then be labelled as a lack of cooperation.

Key components of comprehension monitoring skills are:

- checking that the incoming information (heard or read) makes sense,

- recognising gaps in understanding,

- asking for clarification, either spontaneously or when the speaker asks if help is needed, and

- having a range of ways to ask for clarification.

Comprehension monitoring strategies that are beneficial for all young people

Comprehension monitoring is needed throughout life and spans conversation, verbal instructions and reading, it is important in education, work and social interactions. It is important for all young people, so start by developing a culture which supports comprehension monitoring in every type of language task, from chatting with friends to reading Shakespeare.

Model these points and give specific praise such as 'good question!', when young people use them.

- No one understands everything all of the time.

- There is no shame in saying 'I don't know.'

- Comprehension monitoring is a skill, and like all skills, it needs practise.

- We all need a range of ways of saying what we don't understand, and the more information that the listener can provide to the speaker, the better. So saying, 'What?' is not as helpful as 'I don't know what 'compliance' means.'

How to spot if a young person needs support with comprehension monitoring

It is likely that most of the young people you are working with using *LFBE* will need some support with comprehension monitoring. However, using the LFBE profile on page 126, and in particular the 'Saying when you don't understand' section, will help to more specifically tailor the intervention plan. The profile will have highlighted areas that are 'really tricky' or 'tricky sometimes'.

Comprehension monitoring resources provided in this toolkit

Resource	Page
'Why it's important to say when things don't make sense'	267
'Self-awareness rating'	270
'How to check it makes sense'	271
'What to say when you don't understand'	273
'How to let someone know when you don't understand'	274

Teaching comprehension within an LFBE scenario session

The comprehension monitoring tools may be used flexibly to suit the young people's needs and situations, and they are designed to be guides that start discussion but also as reminders to be revisited many times.

In one of the very early *LFBE* sessions, and potentially the very first session, introduce the idea that conversation is a two-way process with three components:

1 Speaker

2 Listener

3 Message

The aim of a conversation is for the message to get from the speaker to the listener. Sometimes the message does not get to the listener because of too much noise in the environment, distractions, mumbling, saying too much, using complicated words or crazy phrases or when the listener is not paying attention. You can have great fun role playing these and even making short videos.

Then introduce 'Why it's important to say when things don't make sense' (page 267). This has been divided into two parts so it can be used flexibly to suit the young people's needs.

The remaining resources are for you to choose from as necessary to meet young people's needs. Select the tools which are most useful and present them one at a time over a number of sessions. Practise in real situations so that the young people understand how to use them e.g. checking understanding of the *LFBE* story, or a passage from a book. Have them to hand in subsequent sessions and remind the group of them at the start of each session.

Carry over to other settings

Comprehension monitoring is a particularly challenging skill to master, so it needs a strong focus not only in the group but also in the classroom or other settings. Let other adults who work with the young people know about the work that is happening in the group and plan for how the work will transfer beyond the group.

The self-awareness rating 'How much do you understand' (page 270) is designed to be used in the classroom and can be used on a whole class level. 'How to check it makes sense' (page 271) and 'What to say when you don't understand' (page 273) can both be printed off and used as displays or during whole class discussions. 'How to let someone know when you don't understand' (page 274) is a useful starting point for a whole class discussion.

Practise comprehension monitoring in class using regular two-minute activities in which the speaker intentionally makes it impossible for the listener to understand, and therefore young people need to use the clarification strategies. This can be extended by making short videos of these activities.

Independence

As with any skill, the aim is for young people to be able to independently apply their skills. From time to time discuss progress with each young person and reflect upon situations where they are now using the skill and where they still need support. Be aware that new or formal settings will make this task much more challenging. Very formal settings such as hearings or court make it extremely challenging to speak up, and so care needs to be taken to ensure that young people can understand to enable fair justice.

Why it's important to say when things don't make sense

To be shared with the young person

Part 1: using general strategies

Sometimes it can be hard to understand or remember everything that a speaker has said.

Sometimes it is hard to listen to what other people say.
Sometimes we get distracted and think about something else.
Sometimes speakers use posh or unusual words or talk for way too long.
Sometimes speakers say things that just don't make sense.
This happens to everyone some of the time.
When people talk, they usually want the other person to understand what they are saying.

If we miss some of the information that we have been told, we might do or say something they didn't expect. Or we might do or say nothing when they wanted us to react. People might think we are stupid, being silly or behaving badly. Sometimes people might think we don't care about them. They might even get very cross with us. Being labelled 'stupid, silly, awkward or uncaring' might seem unfair, especially when we've been trying to make sense of what they said.

That is why it is so important to say something when speakers say things that don't make sense.

Here are some of the things that you can say when things don't make sense. You can say:

- 'I don't understand.'

- 'I don't get it.'

- 'I'm confused.'

- 'Tell me that again.'

Why it's important to say when things don't make sense

To be shared with the young person

Part 2: using specific strategies

To be good at sports you need to practise. To be good at saying when you don't understand also takes practise. Sometimes it will be easy, and you'll think, 'I've got this,' and then other times it will be very hard.

Most people find it hard sometimes to say when they don't understand. Sometimes it is easy to say when you don't understand, and other times it might be embarrassing. Keep practising and it will get easier and you'll get better at it.

When you are listening to somebody talk, constantly think about what they are saying. Does it make sense?

If it doesn't make sense, think of what you can say and when you can say it. Be aware that if you interrupt, some speakers may not be very happy. In a large group you should put up your hand.

Here are some of the things that you can say when things don't make sense. You can say:

- 'I don't understand.'
- 'I don't get it.'
- 'I'm confused.'
- 'Tell me that again.'

Telling the speaker a bit more detail about what you need to know really helps them. Try saying:

- 'I don't get the bit about. . .'
- 'I understand the bit about . . . but not the rest.'
- 'What do you mean by. . .?'
- 'What does . . . word mean?'
- 'You said too much. Please say it one bit at a time.'

Sometimes you might say to someone 'Sorry, I don't understand' and they respond with 'You should have been listening.' If they say this, then you could try saying, 'I was listening but sometimes it is hard for me to understand.'

Sometimes it is hard to say you don't understand, especially in classes or large groups. At these times it is good to speak to the teacher or group leader one to one and agree on some way that you can show when you don't understand.

It takes guts to say when you don't understand, so be brave.

Self-awareness rating

How much do you understand?

I don't understand	Not sure	I understand

- ✂ -

How do you find it?

Really tricky I can't do it Really hard	OK sometimes	No problem I can do it Easy

- ✂ -

How well does the adult help me?

Not great	Ok sometimes	They are great at this

- ✂ -

Understanding of words or phrases

Never heard of it	Heard of it but not sure what it means	Know what it means

😮 How to check it makes sense

Listen and look or concentrate on what you are reading

Check understanding; does it make sense?

- Do you understand all the words?
- Do you understand everything they said?
- Can you work out what the crazy phrases mean (if there are any)?
- Can you work out what they mean to say, even if they are being sarcastic?

Yes

No

If you understand, keep listening or keep reading.

If you don't understand, you need to let someone know.

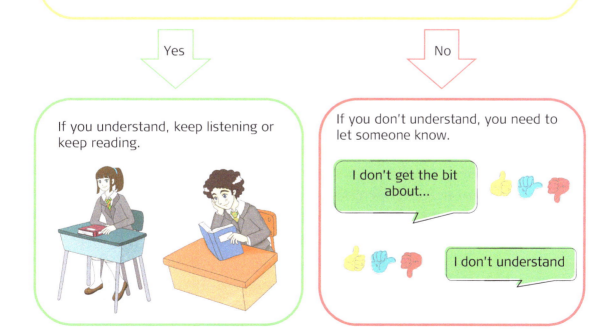

I don't get the bit about...

I don't understand

Does it all make sense?

> ### • Do you understand all the words?
>
> Is the adult using words you don't understand? Sometimes this is OK because you get the general idea of what they are saying. When you start to get confused, you need to do something.
>
> If you are looking at a worksheet, start by underlining all the words you don't know.
>
> ### • Do you miss bits of what people say?
>
> Sometimes people say too much, which can be overwhelming. Other times we can switch off and stop listening. Asking adults to repeat information can help. Sometimes you might need them to say a bit at a time.
>
> ### • Are there any crazy phrases you don't understand?
>
> Adults often use odd phrases that can be hard to understand. Phrases like 'my brain's like a sieve today'. Often people don't even realise they use them. If someone uses a phrase you don't know, tell them.
>
> Writing can be even worse. The author can use all sorts of phrases that can be hard to understand. If you are using a worksheet, underline any odd phrases you don't get.
>
> ### • Do they mean what they say?
>
> People don't always say what they mean. They expect you to work it out. Sometimes they are sarcastic, so they say the exact opposite of what they mean. They might say 'Don't move too fast, will you' when they are actually asking you to move faster. Sometimes they expect you to fill in the gaps. They don't say the opposite thing, but they do expect you to work out the missing bit. They might say 'There's a bin over there.' They expect you to work out that they want you to put your rubbish in the bin. You just need to look out for these situations. Sometimes you will need to check that you have understood.

What to say when you don't understand

When it does not make sense, you can say:

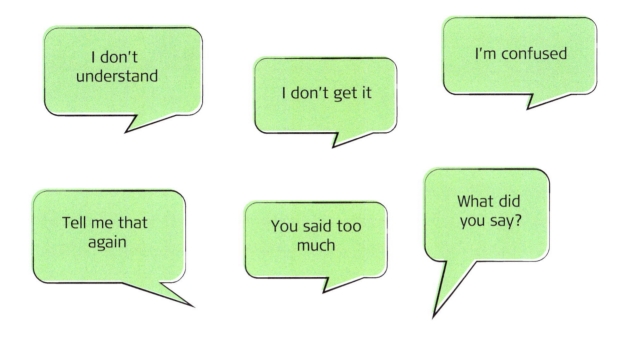

I don't understand

I don't get it

I'm confused

Tell me that again

You said too much

What did you say?

Try and let the person know which bit you don't understand:

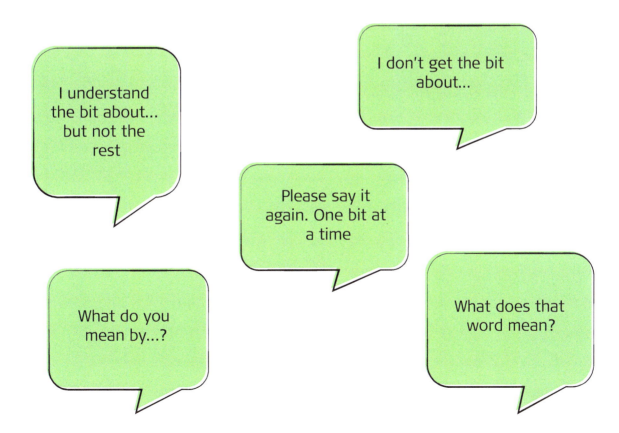

I understand the bit about... but not the rest

I don't get the bit about...

Please say it again. One bit at a time

What do you mean by...?

What does that word mean?

How to let someone know when you don't understand

	Pros What's good about it	Cons What's bad about it.	When is this useful?
Look confused.	It's quiet.	The speaker has to notice you.	OK if waiting to say that you do not understand.
Go and do something else.	No need to listen any more.	The speaker might get angry with you.	Not a good choice unless you want to make the speaker angry.
Put your hand up.	The teacher or group leader knows you need help.	You still need to think of something to say. You need to be brave in front of a group.	Good for big groups.
Signal such as thumbs or coloured card.	The teacher or group leader knows you need help.	Needs to be agreed beforehand. Adult needs to remind young people to use it.	In big groups can be more discrete. You don't have to be brave.

	Pros What's good about it	Cons What's bad about it.	When is this useful?
Say something general like: **I don't understand** • 'I don't understand.' • 'I don't get it.' • 'I'm confused.' • 'Tell me that again.' • 'Help.' • 'You said too much.'	Gets the message across.	The speaker may not understand what you don't understand.	Good, but you may need to say a bit more.
Say something more specific such as: **I don't get the bit about...** • 'I don't get the bit about . . .' • 'I understand the bit about . . . but not the rest.' • 'What do you mean by . . .?' • 'What does . . . word mean?' • 'Can you say a bit at a time?'	Lets the speaker know exactly what you do and don't understand.	Hard to do quickly. You need to keep concentrating and you need to practise doing it.	The best way to show what you do and don't understand.

Understanding words (vocabulary)

😮 Introduction to developing vocabulary

It is estimated that a typically developing student knows approximately 30,000 to 50,000 words by the time they complete their secondary (high) school education (Clark, 1993). For many young people with SLCN, this presents as an enormous challenge but also one for which there is no quick fix. In-depth vocabulary teaching is beyond the scope of this book, and two of the authors have written extensively about this elsewhere (Parsons & Branagan, 2021). If a young person has significant word learning needs then this needs specific and ongoing attention.

Vocabulary learning strategies that are beneficial for all young people

1   Expose young people to a rich language environment that has words at the right level. The words should challenge but not overwhelm.

2   Directly teach important words: choose words carefully and teach methodically within context. Use visual supports and simple definitions as part of this process.

3   Engage young people in word learning by playing word games and showing your own enjoyment of words.

4   Teach word learning strategies, so the young people can take ownership of their word learning. Looking words up in dictionaries is only the start.

All of the above are derived from 'Word Aware' (Parsons & Branagan, 2021).

How to spot if a young person needs support with vocabulary

Analyse the 'Understanding words' section of the *LFBE* profile on page 126, in particular the sections which have been identified as either 'really tricky' or 'tricky sometimes'. This will help in the development of the intervention plan, but it is advised that you continue to monitor understanding of key vocabulary as you progress with the *LFBE* scenarios. It is hard to predict which words young people will and will not know, so be observant.

Vocabulary learning resources provided in this toolkit

Resource	Page
'Why it's important to learn new words'	282
'Tricky words: definitions and symbols'	282
'Word Wizard'	295
'10 steps to learning words independently'	296
'Definitions of words connected with behaviour'	297
'What's that feeling called?'*	314
'Grouping feelings'*	315

*Found in the 'What's that feeling called?' section of the toolkit.

Teaching vocabulary within an LFBE scenario session

The basic process is:

1   Identify words to teach

2   Make a word book of the Word Wizard sheets

3   Introduce one word per group using the Word Wizard

4   Apply this learning to other contexts

5   Build independent word learning skills

1 Identify words to teach

Choose the most useful words to teach. To start with, think about which ones are easier to learn or are most important.

Words can be chosen from:

• 'Tricky words: definitions and symbols' (see page 282).

• Definitions of words connected with behaviour (see page 297) or other unknown words connected with behaviour that are commonly used in your school.

- Unknown words from the scenario.

- 'What's that feeling called?' (see page 314).

- 'Grouping feelings' (see page 315).

2 Make a word book of the Word Wizard sheets

Make each group participant a 'book' of blank Word Wizards (see page 295). Make a front cover and a contents page, so they can be used as a regular word learning tool.

3 Introduce one word per group using the Word Wizard

Introduce the Word Wizard as a tool that helps us all learn and remember new words. Go through the Word Wizard and discuss each component and write down details. Direct young people to write down the same details in their word books. You will need to draw or print off pictures/symbols for each word, but symbols are also provided in 'Tricky words: definitions and symbols' (page 282), 'Definitions of words connected to behaviour' (page 297), 'What's that feeling called?'(page 314) and 'Grouping feelings' (page 315).

There is also additional guidance for adults around teaching emotion words in 'Introduction to talking about feelings' (page 309)

4 Apply this learning to other contexts

Words that are only used in a group setting are less likely to be learnt fully, so plans should be made about how the word can be encountered in other settings. Include other adults and family in this also, but whichever process you decide upon discuss this with the young people regularly.

- Group participants take the Word Wizard from the group and discuss it with another adult. This may be a teacher, support worker or family member.

- Working word walls: display the words (and symbols) on a wall. If this is not possible, make a temporary 'wall' by writing half a dozen or so of the words on a board/piece of paper or emailing the words to relevant teachers or the family. Adults should occasionally use the words and encourage the young people to do so also. The activities listed next can then be applied to words on the wall or paper.

- Talk about the words:

  - Without saying the word directly, one person defines a word and the others guess what the word is. Expand on this by bringing in an adult who is not familiar with the words. This adult stands with their back to the word wall, and so the young people's definitions need to be highly accurate if the adult is to guess correctly.

- Talk about how words might go together. There is no right or wrong answer.

- Individuals indicate which words they like or dislike and say why.

- Choose a synonym of a word on the word wall and discuss how they are similar and different. When is it better to use one rather than the other?

- Match the symbol to the definition. Why this symbol, and could the young people draw an even better one? How is their symbol better?

- Match the words to their definitions, either as a group or individually.

- Notice when the words are used and tally when they are heard or read.

5 Build independent word-learning skills

The aim when teaching any skill is for the young people to apply it independently. After the young people are using the Word Wizard easily, you can then introduce '10 steps to learning words independently'. Many of the skills overlap with the Word Wizard, but it also adds others and can be used less formally. Check through that the participants understand and discuss how well they think they can do each one of the steps. In subsequent sessions:

- Place '10 steps to learning words independently' on the table at the start of the session.

- Remind the young people to look at the tool in the session.

- Model the strategies.

- Encourage use of the strategies.

- Praise spontaneous use of the strategies.

- Support students to use the strategies in the classroom and at home. This can be done through displaying the poster in class and reminding the students of the strategies as well as adding them to word books.

Applying this approach flexibly

- Plan ahead: look at the stories and select words that you anticipate will be challenging for the young people you are working with.

- Spontaneous/responsive teaching: have the tools to hand and when young people identify words that they do not know then go through the teaching process. This works well if comprehension monitoring strategies are also a focus.

- Emotions: the vocabulary teaching process can also be applied to emotions, but extra time needs to be spent on the context and how the word is different from other similar words. See pages 309–355 for further details on teaching emotions.

Further vocabulary guidance

Dictionaries

Dictionaries are an obvious tool for learning vocabulary but should be used with caution as many students will find the language and multiple options confusing. The *Collins COBUILD Primary Learners English Dictionary* (2018) provides straightforward definitions in simple language. This is useful for young people under 11 years of age. The free online version www.collinsdictionary. com has similar definitions under the first tab and has a wider vocabulary. Using dictionaries and applying the definitions meaningfully is a skill which needs specific teaching.

Support for more severe vocabulary needs

If young people have more severe vocabulary needs then they require more specialist support and a referral to Speech and Language Therapy/Speech-Language Pathology is recommended. Some general activities which can be built into the existing support include:

- Pre-teaching the words that are to be taught to the whole group: this will give the young person a head start and increases the likelihood of them being able to access the whole group teaching. It also boosts self-esteem as they can see that they can access learning that was previously impossible.

- Repeat the Word Wizard individually: on a one to one basis go through the Word Wizard with simpler words until the young person has a thorough understanding of all of the steps.

- Play more words games: ensure the young person has more encounters with the new words by playing extra word games. Aim to find games they enjoy, as this will increase motivation.

- Highlight the young person's vocabulary needs to all who work with them. Adults need to remember: when instructions and discussions are important, keep their vocabulary simple.

- Enrich the vocabulary the young person is exposed to by reading aloud to them and/or getting them to listen to audiobooks. Keep the passages short, but do it every day.

References

Clark, E. (1993). *The lexicon in acquisition.* Cambridge: Cambridge University Press.

Collins COBUILD Primary Learners English Dictionary. (2018). Glasgow: Harper Collins.

Parsons, S., & Branagan, A. (2nd edition, 2021). *Word aware 1: Teaching vocabulary, across the day, across the curriculum.* Abingdon, Oxon: Routledge.

See also

Joffe, V. L. (2011). *Vocabulary enrichment programme.* Milton Keynes: Speechmark.

Online resources to accompany Alex Quigley's 'closing the vocabulary gap' www.theconfidentteacher.com/resources/

Sarah Spencer blog about teaching vocabulary to adolescents https://adolescentvocabulary.wordpress.com/top-tips-for-new-word-learning-2/

🫢 Why it's important to learn new words

To be shared with the young person

The average English speaker knows lots of words. Some people say it's 30,000 and others say it's 50,000. That's a lot of words.

Think about an activity that interests you. It can be anything from gaming to sailing to orienteering. Anything. Now think of the special words that you use when talking about that activity. Think about whether your friends or family would know these words. When you first started that activity, you had to learn those new words and without the words you would have soon got stuck. The same is true of any new activity or topic. You need to know the words.

If you don't know the right words then it can make getting your point across extra hard. People might not understand what you are talking about. And if someone is using words you don't understand then that causes problems too.

You can learn words in lots of different ways, but the most important way is just to listen out for them. Try and spot new words when someone is talking or look out for them when you are reading. Ask someone what they mean or look them up in a dictionary. Get interested in words and you will learn more and more.

Because there are so many words to learn it takes a big effort, but keep on going as learning new words will make lots of things easier.

🫢 Tricky words: definitions and symbols

Young people need to understand these words for:

- talking about feelings,

- understanding Level C and D questions in the scenarios which support 'Finding clues and explaining your thinking (inference and verbal reasoning)', and

- solving people problems.

The 'Adult's experience of the word' are examples of things that might happen in an adult's life. If you have a similar real story that shows the meaning of the word, then do use a real example or use both the real example and the example given here. If you want to use these stories as if they are your own, then please do adapt and change as needed (e.g. change husband to wife). Adapt the 'Young person's experience of the word' to suit the young people you are working with.

TRICKY WORDS: DEFINITIONS AND SYMBOLS

Word	Definition (in simple terms)	Words that mean nearly the same thing	Adults' experience of the word	Young person's experience of the word.
Conclusion	What you think is true after you have thought carefully about all the important facts. (Note: Conclusion also means endpoint, but that will need to be taught separately. Focus on one definition at a time.)	Decision	I once had a BBQ and nobody had said they were coming. My first thought was that nobody liked me and so didn't want to come. Then I thought about it carefully and checked my emails and I found out I forgot to send the invites! When I thought about all the facts, I **concluded** that I hadn't invited anybody. I needed to find out all the facts and think carefully to work out what was true.	Have you ever had two friends fall out with each other? How did you come to a **conclusion** about what you could do to make it better? What are all the things you needed to think about to reach a **conclusion**?

Word	Definition (in simple terms)	Words that mean nearly the same thing	Adults' experience of the word	Young person's experience of the word.
Consequences	Something that happened after, as a result of something else.	Result, effect, upshot, outcome, repercussion	It was very cold and my car window was frosted up. I scraped it off, but it was still a bit unclear. I was in a rush so I started to drive. Then I had the sun in my eyes. I couldn't see the bollard in the road so I knocked it over. The **consequence** of not clearing my window properly was knocking over a bollard.	Have you ever had an argument with a teacher? what was the **consequence**? What happened because you had an argument? Have you ever broken something? What was the **consequence**? What happened because you broke it?
Convince	Making someone agree with you. Get them to believe the same thing as you.	Persuade	My family doesn't like going for walks. They think it is boring. I really want to go walking so I try and **convince** them that it will be fun. I tell them about the beautiful place that we are going to see and that we won't walk for long. I tell them that we will go to a cafe and have cake. The cake tends to **convince** them. It makes them think that the walk might be OK.	Have you ever tried to **convince** someone of something? Have you tried to **convince** someone to try a new food? Do you ever try and **convince** your mum/dad/carer that your music is the best? Have you tried to **convince** someone to watch a film or a TV programme?

Word	Definition (in simple terms)	Words that mean nearly the same thing	Adults' experience of the word	Young person's experience of the word.
Evidence	What you see or read that tells you something is true.	Proof	I came downstairs and I thought someone had eaten some more of my leftover birthday cake. I asked all my family. They all said no. Then I found a plate in the living room. There were chocolate cake crumbs on the plate. Now I had **evidence** that someone had eaten some more cake. The cake crumbs on the plate told me.	Have you ever walked in the snow or the sand? What **evidence** would you see that tells you someone has been there before you? If your friend/brother/ sister had sweet wrappers next to them what is that **evidence** of?
Incident	Something significant (usually bad) that happened.	Event	The other day there had been an **incident** on our high street. A man didn't look properly when he was trying to reverse out of a car parking space. An old couple were trying to cross the road.	Has there ever been a serious **incident** at your school? Did something bad happen?

Word	Definition (in simple terms)	Words that mean nearly the same thing	Adults' experience of the word	Young person's experience of the word.
			The car only reversed a little but it bumped into the old lady. There was lots of shouting from the woman's husband and also other people. It was quite an **incident**.	
Infer	Bringing together everything you know to work out what is happening.	Work out	My friend was coming to visit me. I hadn't been outside. When I opened the door, she was all wet. I could easily **infer** that it was raining. As she was wet, the only good reason that explained it is that it was raining.	If you saw a picture of someone's living room and there is a tree in the corner with presents underneath, what could you **infer**? What can you work out about the time of year? Has any of your family ever come downstairs all dressed up? If you didn't know what was happening, what could you **infer**? Why do people normally dress up?

Word	Definition (in simple terms)	Words that mean nearly the same thing	Adults' experience of the word	Young person's experience of the word.
Intention	An idea about what you are going to do.	Aim, purpose	I was staying with my mum and I wanted to help. My **intention** was good. I started to clean the sitting room, but the vacuum cleaner got caught in the fairy lights that were trailing on the floor. The lights were hooked around a beautiful picture on the wall and this pulled the picture from the wall. The picture was so badly damaged it had to be thrown away. My **intention** was to be helpful, but I ended up damaging my mum's picture.	Have you ever **intended** to do something but then forgot about it?

COMPANION @ WEBSITE

Word	Definition (in simple terms)	Words that mean nearly the same thing	Adults' experience of the word	Young person's experience of the word.
Issue	The main problem.	Problem	On my street there is a littering **issue**. People drop litter everywhere, and there are no bins. How can we resolve this **issue**?	What do you have an **issue** with? Are there any **issues** at school?
Justification	A good reason or explanation for something somebody else thinks is wrong.	Good reason	I told my son that I needed some cake. I went shopping and I came back with three cakes. He started to laugh. I said that I thought our neighbours might like one and I got his favourite. I was justified in buying three cakes, as there was a good reason for it.	Have you ever **not** done a task that someone asked you to do? Could you come up with a good **justification** for not doing it? Was there a good reason why you didn't do it?
Motive	The reason for doing something. What made someone want to do something.	Reason	My son was really nice to Granny when she came to visit. He went and got special things for her to eat. He is usually nice to her but this time he was being	When you do work (at school) what is your **motive**? What makes you want to do it? A. I will be told off if I don't do it. B. I do it because I have to. C. I want to learn.

Word	Definition (in simple terms)	Words that mean nearly the same thing	Adults' experience of the word	Young person's experience of the word.
			extra thoughtful. I wondered what his **motive** was. Why was he being extra kind? What did he want? Then I found out. Granny had said that she might give him a bit of money. His **motive** for being nice was wanting the money. That was what made him be extra nice.	Sometimes we have several different motives at the same time.
Observe	What you see happening. Watch carefully. Notice what's important.	Notice, detect	On my balcony we have a bird feeder. I really like to stay indoors and **observe** the birds that come to eat the seeds. At first glance they look alike, but if I **observe** them closely, I can tell which is which.	What do you **observe** about your friends? What do you **observe** when someone has had a haircut?

Word	Definition (in simple terms)	Words that mean nearly the same thing	Adults' experience of the word	Young person's experience of the word.
Opinion	Someone's view about something.	Idea, impression	I really don't like the taste of chicken. In my **opinion,** it's horrible. In my friend's **opinion,** chicken is the tastiest meat.	What's your **opinion** of eating meat?
Perspective	How you or someone else sees things.	View, point of view	Sometimes it is hard to see things from someone else's **perspective.** I was really cross with my husband for not feeding the cat. His **perspective** was that the cat is too fat.	What's your **perspective** on overweight pets? From your **perspective,** which is the best football team?
Pros and cons	Pros are the good things. Cons are the bad things.	Good and bad	I was thinking of moving to a new house but I wasn't sure. The **pros** of moving (what would be good about moving) are: • I would be closer to work. • I would have a bigger house.	What are the **pros and cons** of going on holiday in this country? What are the good things (pros) and what are the bad things (cons)?

Word	Definition (in simple terms)	Words that mean nearly the same thing	Adults' experience of the word	Young person's experience of the word.
			The **cons** (the bad things about moving) • Packing up and moving is really hard work. • I won't know as many people nearby.	
Realise	To become aware of something or understand it.	Understand	I was going to buy a cake, but then I **realised** I didn't have my purse. I suddenly remembered.	Have you ever thought you knew what you were doing but then **realised** you weren't sure?
Regret	Sad about what happened. Wished it hadn't happened.	Sorry	I **regret** being rude to Sarah, as she never forgave me and I lost a friend. I wish I hadn't been rude.	What do you **regret** about arguments you've had? Do you **regret** things you have done? Do you wish you hadn't said or done something?

Word	Definition (in simple terms)	Words that mean nearly the same thing	Adults' experience of the word	Young person's experience of the word.
Resolve	To find a solution, especially when there has been a problem or argument.	Sort it out	We both wanted to do different things on our holidays. The **resolution** was that we had days together and days where we did our own thing. That's how we sorted it out.	How have you **resolved** a difference of opinion? How did you sort it out?
Significant	Really important	Important	The most **significant** thing about the way I look is _____. That is the thing that you would notice first. It is the really important thing.	What is the most **significant** thing that happened in your day? What is the most important/most interesting thing that happened?
Solve	To work it out. Find the answer.	Work it out	My daughter wanted some new jeans. I said they were too expensive. We managed to **solve** the problem because I found the same jeans in a sale.	What's the best way that you've **solved** something?

Word	Definition (in simple terms)	Words that mean nearly the same thing	Adults' experience of the word	Young person's experience of the word.
Surmise	You think something is true, but are not totally sure as you do not have all of the information. A best guess.	Guesswork, deduce, suspect	I **surmised** that he didn't like the food because he didn't eat very much even though he said it was OK. That was what I worked out.	What do you **surmise** when someone doesn't say much about a present you give them? What do you think they are thinking?
Suspect	Something you think is probably true. You don't know but you are making a good guess. Have an idea about something without proof.	Think, believe, hunch	I had been away for the weekend and my husband said that the house had been tidy all weekend. I didn't know if he was telling the truth or not, but I **suspected** he was lying. I **suspected** the house had been really messy but he tidied it up just before I came home.	Are there times that you **suspect** other family members have used your things? Times when you think they did but you weren't sure?

Word	Definition (in simple terms)	Words that mean nearly the same thing	Adults' experience of the word	Young person's experience of the word.
Tactful	Being tactful is when you avoid upsetting or offending people even when you have to tell them something quite bad.	Thoughtful, considerate	My best friend had bought a new dress. She was so pleased with it. When we were at her house she went and tried it on, so she could show me. She came out with a big smile on her face. I looked at her. She looked awful in it. It made her bottom look really big. How could I tell her? I wanted to be **tactful** but I had to tell her. I didn't want her to be upset. 'I am not sure it is my favourite of your dresses' I said **tactfully**. She looked a bit disappointed but I think she got the hint. I never saw her in the dress again.	Has anyone ever given you something that you didn't like? What do you say to be **tactful**, so that you don't hurt their feelings? What would **not** be **tactful**?

Word wizard

Symbol/ picture:

Word

Meaning

Context you could use the word in

Action

What can you think of that will help you remember this word?

Record word in workbook

- Have you heard the word before?
- Where did you read it/ hear it?
- What was it used to talk about?

- Students say the word to the person next to them
- Write the word on a scrap of paper

To help you remember the word:
- Think of the first sound
- Think up a nonsense word that rhymes with it
- Think about how many syllables the word has

Other meanings

Use the word in a sentence

10 steps to learning words independently

1 Be alert.	Listen out for new words when people are talking. Look out for new words when you are reading.
2 Say it.	Say the new word out loud. Think about its sounds, rhyme and syllables.
3 Write it.	Write it down. Think about its letters and parts (prefix and suffix).
4 Find out about its meaning.	Ask someone. Look it up in a dictionary.
5 Expand the meaning.	Think and talk about how the new word is different from other similar words you know. Talk about when you might use the word again.
6 Put it into a sentence.	Write or say it in a sentence.
7 Remember it.	Write it so you can look back at it later: a word book, a word map or the Word Wizard.
8 Don't forget it.	Come back to it from time to time. Give yourself and others quizzes.
9 Use it.	Use the new word when you can and when it's right to.
10 You've got it.	Give yourself a mental tick and notice your achievement.

Definitions of words connected with behaviour

All of the words listed here are included in the 'Behaviour vocabulary assessment' on page 91

Words	Simple, everyday definition	Words that mean nearly the same thing
1 Time out	Take a break. Especially when you need to calm down. Or a place where you go to calm down.	Break, calm down, quiet time
2 Calm down	Relax, especially when you are over excited or angry.	Relax, chill, quiet time
3 Choice	You can have one or pick one. The one you like the best, or the thing you want to do.	Choosing, pick one
4 Disagree	Don't agree. Don't think the same. See things differently.	Argue, clash, fight
5 Positive	A good thing. When people say or do something nice.	Good, right, perfect
6 Point of view	How one person sees things. Different people can have different points of view.	View, each side, both sides
7 Reward	Getting something nice when you do something good.	Sticker, award, well done
8 Cooperate	Go along with what you are asked to do. Work together.	Teamwork, sharing, together
9 Unacceptable	Something is bad or wrong, and so you don't want it.	Bad, wrong, not wanted
10 Respond	Say or do something after something else has happened.	React, answer back, answer, reply

Words	Simple, everyday definition	Words that mean nearly the same thing
11 Inappropriate	Wrong or bad thing to do at this time.	Wrong, bad, mistake unexpected
12 Responsibility	What you have to do. Important things.	Important, serious matter, duty
13 Consequence*	Something that happened after, as a result of something else.	Effect, reaction, follow-up, chain reaction
14 Expectations	What you or someone else wants to happen or think will happen.	Hopes
15 Negotiate	Talking about a problem and trying to sort it out.	Talk, agree, sort it out
16 Compromise	Two people make a deal, but both have had to give in a bit.	Deal, agreement, trade-off
17 Resolve*	To find a solution, especially when there has been a problem or argument.	Iron out, work out, agree, settle
18 Empathy	When you understand how someone else feels. You imagine what it would be like if it was you.	Understand, appreciate, insight
19 Perspective*	How you or someone else sees things	View, viewpoint, understanding, angle
20 Excluded	Not allowed to go somewhere, especially when not allowed to come to school because the rules have been broken. Can also be when groups don't want someone to join in.	Expelled, suspended, banned, ignored, left out

Items marked * are also included in 'Tricky words: definitions and symbols' on page 282.

When people don't say what they mean

Introduction to 'When people don't say what they mean'

The words people use don't always seem to match what the people are trying to say. Routinely both adults and young people use:

- Crazy phrases (idioms/figures of speech).

- Sarcasm.

- Implied meaning.

How to spot if a young person needs support with 'When people don't say what they mean'

Analyse the 'When people don't say what they mean' section of the *LFBE* profile on page 126, in particular the sections which have been identified as either 'really tricky' or 'tricky sometimes'. This will help you in the development of the intervention plan, but it is advised that you continue to monitor understanding of crazy phrases as you progress with the *LFBE* scenarios. It is hard to predict which phrases young people will and will not know, so be observant.

Teaching crazy phrases using LFBE

As you get into scenarios 21–40, a few crazy phrases are used. In scenarios 41–60, crazy phrases are used much more frequently. When working through any of the scenarios, make sure that you are asking the young people if there is anything that they do not understand. If none of the young people identify the crazy phrases, check understanding by getting the young people to explain the meaning of the crazy phrase. If there are any difficulties understanding then follow the teaching sequence on the next page.

It is also useful to think about why people do not always seem to say what they mean. Sometimes it is a kind of 'short cut', and there's an assumption that other people will understand. Sometimes it is to avoid being rude or hurting people's feelings or to express feelings. It can also be a way of being more tactful.

Developing understanding of crazy phrases, sarcasm and implied meaning in day-to-day conversations

Develop adults' awareness.	We all use crazy phrases, sarcasm and implied meaning without really noticing. Start to notice when you use them. Listen to the adults and young people around you. You will be amazed by how much they are used.
Talk about crazy phrases, sarcasm and implied meaning as it is used.	As you naturally use crazy phrases, sarcasm or implied meaning, start to talk about what it means. Check understanding by getting the young person to explain the meaning of what has been said. Talk about misunderstandings.
When you need to get your message across: say exactly what you mean.	When a young person needs to understand and there is no time for discussion, avoid using any crazy phrases, sarcasm or implied meaning. Say exactly what you want in the most straightforward way possible. Make sure all adults are aware that this is necessary.

Resources

Collins Easy Learning English. (2010). *Easy learning English idioms: First edition*. Glasgow: Harper Collins.

Joffe, V. (2013). *Favourite idioms*. Milton Keynes: Speechmark.

Why it's important to know when people don't say what they mean

To be shared with the young person

Sometimes the words people say are different from what they mean. This can be very confusing. To avoid confusion, you need to listen out for when people do this.

There are many ways that people's words are different from what they mean, but the two most challenging are **crazy phrases** (sometimes called idioms or figures of speech) and **sarcasm**.

Crazy phrases

Crazy phrases make what you say more interesting. If you look at the words one by one, they have a very different meaning to the phrase altogether. Here's some examples:

'You hit the nail on the head' means you are exactly right. It does not involve a nail or a hammer or anyone being hit, so it can be a bit confusing. However, imagine you are hammering in a nail. You need to hit the nail <u>exactly</u> on the head to hammer it in. So, when people say 'you hit the nail on the head' they are emphasising that something is exactly right.

'Can't get over it' means surprised or shocked. There's no climbing involved, but you might be so shocked by something that you keep thinking about it and so can't move on or 'get over it.'

Some crazy phrases make no sense at all. 'The bees knees' means something or someone is wonderful. There is no obvious connection at all, and the meaning of many crazy phrases has been lost many years ago.

Listen out for crazy phrases. Ask what they mean. Remember them, so you can use them too.

Sarcasm

Sarcasm is when people say something, but they mean the exact opposite. The speaker might use sarcasm to be funny, sometimes to be mean and sometimes to make a point. To work out if a person is being sarcastic, you need to look at their face and body language but also think about what they might be thinking. Here's a few examples.

Making a point

If you walked into the house with very muddy shoes your mum might say 'Good job you remembered to take your dirty shoes off when you came inside.' She is saying 'you have forgotten to take off your shoes' and is cross or irritated.

Being funny

If your dad dropped a plate and it broke, he might try and make a joke of it and say 'I thought plates usually bounce.' Of course, plates do not bounce, they break.

Being mean

If a girl came to school with some very ugly shoes someone, who is being mean, might say 'Nice shoes.' Of course, the shoes are not nice. Other students might laugh at the girl. But this is not being funny. This is being mean.

It is often very hard to work out when someone is using sarcasm to be funny or to be mean. If you are unsure, ask someone who you can trust.

Definitions of crazy phrases used in the assessment

Many crazy phrases (idioms) are used to manage or talk about behaviour. Below are definitions of the idioms from the crazy phrases assessment on page 95. There will be many more that young people are exposed to.

Crazy phrase	Definition
Button it	Be quiet.
Call it quits	End it now and let's say it is equal no one owes anyone anything.
Clean up your act	Start doing things right, even if you've done wrong things in the past.
Create a scene	Make a fuss or have an argument so that everyone looks at you.
Don't lose your cool	Don't get angry.
Get a grip	Try and stop yourself from being angry, rude or anxious.
Get a move on!	Work or move more quickly.
Get it in the neck	Being told off.
Get on my nerves	It is annoying.
Get cracking	Get started.
Going through a sticky patch	Things aren't going so well at the moment.
Have a go at someone	To criticise or attack someone.
In the dog house	Someone is cross with you and is going to be for quite a long time
It will all end in tears	If this keeps going as it is, someone will end up upset or hurt.

Crazy phrase	Definition
Let's start with a clean sheet	Let's forget anything that has happened before.
Let the side down	Someone has done something disappointing
Not a clue	Confused.
Out of order	Totally wrong and shouldn't have happened.
Pack it in	Stop it.
Shooting your mouth off	Talking loudly and in a way that is likely to make other people feel upset.
Turn over a new leaf	Things have been going wrong. Start again, trying to do the right thing.
Up to your neck	You are in a lot of trouble.
Watch your mouth	Stop saying swear words or rude things.
Get to the bottom of this	Find out what has happened.
Winding someone up	Annoying someone.

Definitions of crazy phrases used in the scenarios

Scenario	Crazy phrase	Definition
19	Could not believe her eyes	Amazed.
20	Dropping hints	Give clues.
22	Down in the dumps	Feeling gloomy.
23	Could not believe her eyes	Amazed.
27	Perpetual fog	Couldn't understand at all.
29	Lump in her throat	Anxious and might cry.
31	Burst out laughing	To laugh suddenly.
34	Erupt like a volcano	To get really cross, really quickly.
36	His brain was on fire	He could think really well.
38	Seed of an idea	Very beginning of an idea.
40	Didn't think twice	Without stopping to think about it.
41	Hive of activity	Lots going on.
42	Blood beginning to boil	Starting to get very angry
43	Got out of bed on the wrong side	Started the day feeling grumpy.
44	Watch like a hawk	Watch very carefully.
45	Your face is such a picture	Your face shows very clearly what you are thinking.
46	Not before time	You have been waiting for this to happen and it has happened at last.

Scenario	Crazy phrase	Definition
47	His head might explode	Someone is feeling so stressed, worried or emotional that it makes it hard to think.
47	You are a real ray of sunshine	Someone who is really happy and positive. Sometimes used sarcastically meaning: You are being grumpy.
48	Nosy parker	Someone who is interested in things which are nothing to do with them.
49	Knock 'em dead	Do something impressive.
49	His/her face fell	His/her face changed to looking disappointed, unhappy or shocked. Stopped smiling.
50	Would not let it lie	Keep talking about something, although others have heard enough
52	Don't do anything I wouldn't do	Behave yourself. (Sometimes it is used in a jokey way, then it means 'have fun and be a bit bad'.).
53	Costs the earth	Really expensive.
53	Stomach turned	Strong reaction, anxious or disgust.
54	Mind raced	Thinking quickly.
54	Rabbited on	Talked too much.
55	Shooting his mouth off	Talking loudly and in a way that is likely to make other people feel upset.

Scenario	Crazy phrase	Definition
55	Watch your tongue	Stop swearing or saying things that might upset others.
57	Looked daggers	To stare angrily at someone because you don't like what they are doing or saying.
57	heart sank	You realise something bad is happening or is going to happen.
58	Bear a grudge	Not forgive someone and continue to treat them badly because of what they did.
58	Thrown off balance	To be confused or upset by something.
59	Eyes were like saucers	Eyes wide with surprise.
59	Spill the beans	To tell things that were meant to be a secret. Gossip.
60	I guess it's a boy thing	This is said by a girl. It means that because she is a girl, she can't understand what a boy is thinking.

Learning new crazy phrases

Have you heard it before?	Have you ever heard this phrase before? Has anyone in the group heard it before?
Predict	Have you any idea what you think it might be? Remember it is a crazy phrase so it can be hard to work out.
	What else was happening when the crazy phrase was used? Are there clues that help you work it out?
Ask or look it up	If you can't work it out, look it up or ask the adult or someone else in the group. Try and use simple words to talk about what the phrase means. Tools that might help: • 'Definitions of crazy phrases used in the assessment' (page 303). • 'Definition of crazy phrases used in the scenarios' (page 305). • www.phrases.org.uk • idioms.thefreedictionary.com • www.idiomconnection.com • www.idiomsite.com
When would the adult use it?	Ask the adult to think of another time they might use this phrase.
When would you use it?	Try and think of another time **you** could use this phrase.
Record the phrase	Record the phrase so that the phrase can be talked about at home and in other group sessions.

Talking about feelings

  Introduction to talking about feelings

Emotional literacy skills involve the ability to monitor one's own and others' emotions, to discriminate between them and to use this information to guide one's thinking and actions. They are key to positive interactions and include:

- Self-perceptions, self-awareness and self-direction.

- Motivation.

- Self-control/self-regulation.

- Relationship skills.

In *LFBE* we focus on:

- What's that feeling called? (naming emotions).

- Dealing with feelings (emotional regulation).

However, the scenarios and resources provided also offer opportunities to discuss a wide range of emotional literacy skills

How to spot if a young person needs support with emotional literacy

Analyse the *LFBE* profile on page 126. Consider the 'Talking about feelings' (emotional literacy) section. This will have highlighted areas that are 'really tricky' or 'tricky sometimes'. This will help you in the development of the intervention plan. Be alert for problems with naming or managing emotions as you work through the scenarios, and if they occur, refer to the resources in this section.

Developing the ability to talk about feelings within an LFBE session

It is very important that adults build a positive relationship with the young person and that they are responsive to them, how they feel and what they want to talk about. It is helpful to have opportunities to talk about feelings but not helpful to be pressured into it. Similarly, we need to suggest a variety of healthy ways to deal with or manage feelings and young people will then find ones that work for them (see page 27 of the guide for more information about building a positive relationship).

Non-judgmental discussions will work best. The basis for this work is discussed in detail in 'The Guide', specifically:

- Communication strategies (page 28).
- Emotional coaching strategies (page 30).
- Using talk to extend young people's thinking (page 32).

Talking about feelings resources provided in this toolkit

Resource to support 'What is this feeling called?'	How it can help	Page
'Where do I feel that emotion?'	It can be difficult to work out what a feeling is, so it might be useful to work out where you feel an emotion in your body.	314
'Grouping feelings'	You might have a rough idea about what sort of feeling it is, and this might help narrow it down. It can also help to link to new, more specific vocabulary.	315
'What's that feeling called?'	A list of words and definitions and contexts where the emotions might happen.	328
'How strong is that emotion?'	Tools for discussion about the intensity of an emotion.	348
'What is the main feeling in the story?'	A list of emotions related to each story.	350

Resource to support 'Dealing with feelings'	How it can help	Page
'Accepting feelings'	Feelings are there for many reasons, and we need to listen to them. There are no 'good' or 'bad' feelings, but the way we react when we feel them can be helpful to us and other people (or not). This tool explains where to start with dealing with feelings; accepting them as useful.	356
'If you **LIKE** a feeling you can. . .'	Sometimes we like a feeling and so it's useful to think about how we can remember it. This tool has ideas about how to do this.	357
'If you **DON'T LIKE** a feeling you can. . .'	Ideas about what you can do with feelings which feel difficult or uncomfortable.	358

Ways you can use these

- Use the tools to start a discussion about when they might be helpful.

- Try them in the *LFBE* sessions when you see these symbols.

- It can be helpful to talk about the main feeling in the story before you read it together, to cue the young person and to start a conversation about real situations where this feeling has or might occur. Remember, the suggested feelings aren't necessarily the 'right' one. Other suggestions might be just as good.

- Remember to have 50:50 conversations, everyone's perspective is important.

- You can use the resources to discuss real events or fictional ones.

- There are lots of pictures and definitions that can be cut out and used in games or artistic activities.

- You can use these tools in drama and creative storytelling and writing activities.

- Play around with the emotion slopes to think about how strong feelings are, either yours or fictional characters.

- Add a number rating to any emotion. 5 is the strongest, 1 is the weakest.

- Group work can be useful to share ideas, especially ways to remember and celebrate positive times and emotions. You can also think about how to create more of these times.

- Over time, the aim is to fade the supports whilst maintaining high levels of student success.

- Praise spontaneous use of these strategies.

- Support young people to use the strategies in the classroom and at home. Siegel and Bryson (2011) say 'name it to tame it'; in other words, if we can label our feelings that helps us to manage them and calm down if necessary. It's worth thinking about strong emotions and learning to label them but **note** this can only happen **after** the event when everyone is feeling calm.

References and additional resources

- www.drdansiegel.com/resources/

- Siegel, D. J., & Payne Bryson, T. (2011). *The whole-brain child: 12 revolutionary strategies to nurture your child's developing mind, survive everyday parenting struggles, and help your family thrive.* Delacorte Press, New York.

- 'Mind Reading' is a unique reference work covering the entire spectrum of human emotions. Using the software, you can explore over 400 emotions, seeing and hearing each one performed by six different people. www.jkp.com/uk/mindreading

- www.actionforhappiness.org/

Why it's important to talk about feelings

To be shared with the young person

Feelings really are very important. Feelings are with us all day, every day. Even when we don't notice feelings, they are there. Sometimes we might feel OK. Sometimes we might feel fantastic. Sometimes we might feel sad. And other times we might feel angry. We all feel these things sometimes. That's OK.

Sometimes we're not sure how we feel until we do or say something that causes problems. The first thing to do is just to notice feelings. Sometimes people feel feelings in different parts of their body. Notice where you feel different feelings. It sometimes takes practice to spot feelings. Some can be very hard to notice, so keep practicing. Even adults, who've had lots of practice, sometimes take a long time to spot some feelings.

Once we notice feelings, we can give them a label. There are many different feelings and so there are many different labels. Knowing these labels helps us to think about them more, and it also helps to tell others about them more. If you tell someone that you were 'surprised' by a big dog they might react very differently from how they would if you said you were 'frightened' by the big dog. Saying the right label is important.

Talking about feelings is very important because it helps us take more control of them. Find people you can talk to about your feelings. You can start by saying 'I need to talk about how I am feeling.' Once you know how you are feeling and can talk about it, then you can get better at accepting your feelings, remembering them if they feel good and changing them if they feel uncomfortable.

What's that feeling called? (naming emotions)

 Where do I feel that emotion?

Pick a range of emotions and talk about where you might feel these emotions in your body. This helps us recognise those emotions as they happen. You could use the 'Grouping feelings short version' as a place to start (page 325).

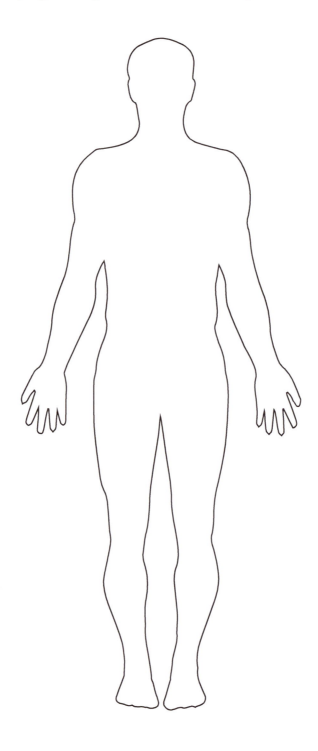

Grouping feelings

There are many different ways of grouping emotions together. Use this list as a starting point to:

- Introduce new emotion words that are related to ones the young person knows.

- Discuss how words are similar and different.

- Discuss the intensity of emotion words. Use the 'How strong is that emotion' chart on page 348 to help.

- Talk about where you feel emotions in your body. Use the body chart on page 314.

- Talk about words that might fit into other groups.

Emotion categories

There are many different ways to categorise words. Use this as a discussion point. There are no good or bad, right or wrong emotions but some of them feel good (positive) and some are less comfortable (negative).

THESE ARE THE CATEGORIES WE'VE USED TO GROUP THE EMOTION WORDS:

Negative emotions	Positive emotions	Other
Afraid	Happy	Interested
Embarrassed	Caring	Surprised
Sad	Admiration	Self-aware
Left out	Positive relationship-related	
Anger	Confident	
Resistant	Content	
Meaning to be bad	Looking forward	
Stressed	Excited	
Anxious	Other positive	
Uneasy		
Confused		
Uncertain		
Loss of focus		
Negative relationship-related		
Other negative		

Alphabetical list of emotions with page numbers (list runs across two pages)

	P		P		P		P		P		P
Absorbed	324	Cheerful	322	Dread	320	Hopeful	323	Nosy	324	Silly	321
Admiration	322	Comfortable	323	Eager	323	Hopeless	318	Outraged	319	Soothed	323
Affectionate	322	Confident	323	Embarrassed	318	Horrified	318	Oversensitive	321	Stern	321
Afraid	318	Confused	320	Enjoy	322	Hurt	321	Overwhelmed	319	Stressed	319
Alert	324	Content	323	Entertained	322	Impatient	319	Panic	319	Stubborn	319
						Impulsive	320				
Amazed	324	Controlled	321	Envy	321	Inspired	323	Patronised	321	Surprised	324
Amused	322	Cooperative	322	Excited	322	Interested	324	Peaceful	323	Tender	322
Angry	319	Cross	319	Excluded	319	Intrigued	318	Playful	324	Tense	323
Annoyed	319	Cruel	319	Expectant	319	Irritated	323	Pleased	319	Terrified	322
Anticipation	323	Curious	324	Forgetful	324	Jealous	320	Protective	321	Thoughtful	322
Anxious	320	Daring	323	Forgiving	323	Joy	322	Proud	322	Thoughtless	323
Argumentative	319	Deceitful	319	Frantic	319	Judging	319	Regret	321	Threatened	321
Ashamed	318	Defensive	319	Frenzied	319	Kind	319	Rejected	322	Tired	318
Astonished	324	Dejected	318	Friendly	318	Left out	322	Relieved	318	Uneasy	323
Attracted	322	Desperate	322	Frightened	319	Livid	318	Resentful	319	Uncertain	320

	P		P		P		P		P		P
Awkward	320	**Despondent**	318	**Frustrated**	319	**Lonely**	318	Resigned	320	**Uncomfortable**	320
Bewildered	320	Devastated	318	**Generous**	322	Longing	321	**Sad**	320	Unsure	320
Bitter	319	**Disappointed**	318	Gentle	322	**Lovesick**	321	**Safe**	323	**Upset**	318
Bored	320	**Disgusted**	321	Glad	322	**Loving**	322	**Satisfied**	323	**Uptight**	320
Brave	323	Dislike	321	**Glum**	318	**Loyal**	322	**Scared**	318	Venomous	319
Calm	323	**Discouraged**	318	**Grief**	318	Motivated	324	Scheming	319	Wary	320
Carefree	323	Displeased	318	**Grumpy**	318	**Mystified**	320	Self-aware	324	**Worried**	320
Caring	322	Distracted	320	**Guilty**	321	**Nasty**	319	Self-conscious	318		
Cautious	318	**Distressed**	320	Happy	322	**Needy**	321	Shocked	324		
Cheated	319	**Down**	318	**Hate**	319	**Nervous**	320	Shy	318		

Words that are in **bold** have more in-depth information in 'What's that feeling called?' (page 328). This includes definitions, related words and prompts to get adults to talk about their experience of the words and to get young people to talk about their experience of the word.

Negative emotions					
Afraid	**Afraid**	**Cautious**	**Frightened**	Horrified
	Scared	Terrified	Threatened	
Embarrassed	**Ashamed**	**Embarrassed**	Self-conscious	**Shy**
Sad	**Despondent**	Dejected	Devastated	**Disappointed**
	Discouraged	Displeased	**Down**	**Glum**
	Grief	**Grumpy**	Hopeless	**Sad**
	Upset			
Left out	Excluded	**Left out**	**Lonely**	Rejected

Anger	Angry	Annoyed	Bitter	Cheated
	Cross	Frustrated	Hate	Irritated
	Livid	Outraged	Venomous	
Resistant	Argumentative	Defensive	Resentful	Stubborn
Meaning to be bad to others	Cruel	Deceitful	Nasty	Scheming
Stressed	Desperate	Frantic	Frenzied	Impatient
	Overwhelmed	Panic	Stressed	Tense

Negative emotions

Anxious	Anxious	Distressed	Dread	Nervous
	Uptight	Worried		
Uneasy	Awkward	Uncomfortable	Uneasy	Wary
Confused	Bewildered	Confused	Mystified	
Uncertain	Uncertain	Unsure		
Loss of focus	Bored	Distracted	Forgetful	Impulsive
	Thoughtless			

Negative relationship-related feelings		Controlled	Envy	**Hurt**	**Jealous**
		Judging	**Lovesick**	**Needy**	**Oversensitive**
		Patronised			
Other negative feelings		**Disgusted**	Dislike	**Guilty**	Longing
		Regret	Resigned	Stern	Silly
		Tired			

Positive emotions

Happy	Amused	Cheerful	Enjoy	Entertained
	Glad	Happy	Joy	Pleased
Caring	Affectionate	Caring	Loving	Gentle
	Kind	Protective	Tender	
Admiration	Admiration	Attracted		
Positive relationship-related feelings	Cooperative	Forgiving	Friendly	Generous
	Loyal	Thoughtful		

Positive emotions	Confident	Brave	Confident	Daring	
	Content	Calm	Carefree	Comfortable	Content
		Peaceful	Relieved	Safe	Satisfied
		Soothed			
	Looking forward	Anticipation	Expectant	Hopeful	Inspired
	Excited	Eager	Excited		
	Other positive feelings	Playful	Proud		

Other					
	Interested	Absorbed	Alert	**Curious**	**Interested**
		Intrigued	Motivated	**Nosy**	
	Surprise	Amazed	Astonished	**Shocked**	Surprised
	Self-aware	Self-aware			

11 Grouping feelings short version

Negative emotions					
Afraid		**Afraid**	**Cautious**	Terrified	Threatened
Embarrassed		**Ashamed**	**Embarrassed**	Self-conscious	**Shy**
Sad		**Upset**	**Disappointed**	**Sad**	**Grumpy**
Left out		Excluded	**Left out**	**Lonely**	Rejected
Anger		**Angry**	**Annoyed**	**Irritated**	**Frustrated**
Resistant		**Argumentative**	Defensive	Resentful	**Stubborn**
Stressed		**Overwhelmed**	**Panic**	**Stressed**	**Tense**
Anxious		**Anxious**	**Dread**	**Nervous**	**Worried**

Positive emotions	Uneasy/unsure/confused	Awkward	Confused	Uncomfortable	Unsure
	Negative relationship-related feelings	Controlled	Hurt	Jealous	Needy
	Other negative feelings	Bored	Disgusted	Guilty	Tired
	Happy	Cheerful	Enjoy	Happy	Pleased
	Caring	Kind	Caring	Protective	Gentle
	Positive relationship-related feelings	Cooperative	Forgiving	Loyal	Generous
	Confident	Brave	Confident	Daring	

Positive emotions	Content				
		Calm	Comfortable	Relieved	Safe
	Looking forward				
		Anticipation	Expectant	Hopeful	Inspired
	Excited				
		Eager	**Excited**		
	Other				
		Proud			
Other	Interested				
		Curious	**Interested**	**Nosy**	
	Surprise				
		Amazed	Astonished	**Shocked**	**Surprised**

Words that are in **bold** have more in-depth information in 'What's that feeling called?' (page 328). This includes definitions, related words and prompts to get adults to talk about their experience of the words and to get young people to talk about their experience of the word.

11 What's that feeling called? (emotional literacy)

The 'Adult's experience of the word' gives examples of things that might happen in an adult's life. If you have a similar real story that shows the meaning of the word then do use a real example or use both the real example and the example given here. If you want to use these stories as if they are your own, then please do adapt and change as needed (e.g. change husband to wife). Adapt the 'Young person's experience of the word' to suit the young people you are working with.

Word	Definition	Words that mean nearly the same thing	Adult's experience of the word	Young person's experience of the word.
Admiration	To think something or someone is beautiful, clever or skilful.	Easier word: respect.	I really **admire** gymnasts. I don't know how they manage to move their bodies in that way.	What sort of people do you **admire**? Singers? Politicians? Actors? Vloggers? Sportsmen/ women? Friends? Why do you **admire** them? What makes them special?
Affectionate	Showing how much you like someone.	Easier words: friendly, warm.	I have a friend who is very **affectionate**, always hugging everyone when she meets them.	Do you have any pets? Or does someone you know have a pet? Do you stroke them in an **affectionate** way? In a way that shows how much you like them?
Afraid	When you don't want to go near something, it makes your heart go faster.	Easier words: frightened, nervous, scared.	I really don't like other people's barking dogs. It makes me **afraid** of the fierce barking dog.	What would you rather not do or go near because you are **afraid**? What might a small child be **afraid** of?

Word	Definition	Words that mean nearly the same thing	Adult's experience of the word	Young person's experience of the word.
Amused	Finding something funny or entertaining.	Easier words: laughing, pleased.	My children are always **amused** when Gran tells a joke. They never find it funny when I tell one.	What makes you laugh? Are you **amused** by clips of animals doing stupid things?
Angry	Really upset about something that someone has said or done	Easier words: annoyed, cross.	I was **angry** when I thought someone was trying to hurt me on purpose.	When did you last shout at someone because you were angry? What makes you **angry**?
Annoyed	A bit angry.	Other word: irritated	I was **annoyed** when someone used my cup at work and left it dirty by the sink.	What **annoys** you? What might make you a bit upset or irritated?
Anticipation	Feeling excited that something nice is about to happen.	Easier words: excited, looking forward to.	I got tickets to see my favourite musical. I had to wait for ages. I kept thinking about how brilliant it was going to be. There was so much **anticipation**.	What things do you look forward to? What things do you **anticipate**?
Anxious	Thinking something bad might happen or has already happened.	Easier words: nervous, worried.	I get really **anxious** when I have to stand up and speak in front of people. I am worried that I won't know what to say.	Do you get **anxious**? What do you worry about?

Word	Definition	Words that mean nearly the same thing	Adult's experience of the word	Young person's experience of the word.
Argumentative	Often disagrees, likes to argue.	Harder words: confrontational, contrary.	Sometimes I just disagree for the fun of it. I like being **argumentative**.	Do you ever feel like arguing? Do you know someone who just wants to say the opposite of whatever you think? Has anyone ever said you were **argumentative**?
Ashamed	Feeling bad because you or someone else did something wrong or looked silly. You don't want other people to know.	Easier words: embarrassed, guilty.	When I was a teenager, there was one boy who always got left out. I never really spoke to him. I wish I had. I feel **ashamed** that I never tried to be friendly.	Have you ever had a spot on your face that you were **ashamed** of? Was it so big that you didn't want anyone to see? Have you ever had clothes that are so ugly that you wouldn't want anyone to know you had them? Are you **ashamed** of them?
Awkward	When you seem embarrassed or don't know what to do in a situation.	Easier word: embarrassed.	It was my best friend's birthday and I forgot. I didn't give her a card or ring her. I felt really **awkward**. I didn't know what to do to make it any better.	Do you ever feel **awkward** when you meet new people? Do you know what to do or say? Have you ever told someone something, then realised you weren't supposed to tell? Was that **awkward**?

Word	Definition	Words that mean nearly the same thing	Adult's experience of the word	Young person's experience of the word.
Bewildered	Really don't understand.	Easier word: confused.	Sometimes when I'm driving using the satnav, I can't take in what it's telling me as well as drive the car. The road and the display don't always look the same and I get **bewildered**.	Do you ever feel people are saying too much or giving you too much information? Does that make you feel confused and **bewildered**? Do you get **bewildered** when you are trying to learn something new?
Bitter	Can't forgive something. You keep feeling angry about it.	Harder word: hostile.	I try not to be **bitter** about upsetting things that happened a long time ago. I try not to be angry anymore.	Is there anything you find it hard to stop thinking about? Something you still feel cross about? Do you know anyone who 'bears a grudge'? Are they **bitter** about something?
Bored	Tired of something that is not interesting.	Harder word: uninterested.	I get **bored** with watching the TV when I can tell what's going to happen next.	Do you have any lessons that make you want to go to sleep? When were you last **bored**?
Brave	Doing something even though it might be difficult or scary.	Harder words: daring, fearless.	I know it will hurt a bit but I'm **brave** about giving blood because it might save someone's life.	What do you do, even though you know it might be tricky or scary? Do you need to be **brave** to talk to new people? Do you get scared of heights or spiders? Are you **brave** or do you run away?

Word	Definition	Words that mean nearly the same thing	Adult's experience of the word	Young person's experience of the word.
Calm	No strong feelings, not anxious or worried.	Easier words: cool, quiet, still.	I find sitting and looking at my fish tank makes me feel **calm**. I feel relaxed and happy.	What do you do to relax or **calm** down? Have you ever been anywhere that felt very peaceful? Does being by yourself make you feel **calm**?
Caring	Being kind, looking after someone.	Easier word: kind.	The **caring** professions included jobs like being a nurse, or people who look after children or old people.	Do you know someone who would help you if you needed them to? How have they been **caring**? Who is the most **caring** person you know?
Cautious	Being careful so nothing bad happens.	Easier words: careful, thoughtful.	I am **cautious** about driving in the fog. You really can't see very far and I am worried I might have an accident so I drive very slowly and carefully.	Have you ever got hurt doing something? Will you be **cautious** about it another time? Will you be more careful next time?
Cheated	Someone was not honest or fair and they got what they wanted, you missed out.	Easier word: tricked. Harder words: resentful, ripped off.	We were just playing a game but my son said he'd help me. Then he used the information I gave him to win. I felt **cheated**, he said it was all part of the game!	Have you ever played with anyone who didn't follow the rules? Have you ever **cheated**?

Word	Definition	Words that mean nearly the same thing	Adult's experience of the word	Young person's experience of the word.
Cheerful	Happy and expecting things to go well.	Easier word: happy. Harder words: jolly, joyful.	I am **cheerful** when I leave work and I have nothing else to do in the evening. It puts me in a good mood.	What makes you smile? What do you look forward to? Are you **cheerful** when these things happen?
Comfortable	Feeling at ease and relaxed.	Easier word: relaxed.	I am **comfortable** with my friends; I don't have anything to worry about.	Who do you find easy to talk to? Are you **comfortable** being with anyone in your class?
Confused	Don't know what to think or do.	Easier word: muddled.	Sometimes I am **confused** about what people want; they say they want one thing then they change their mind. What do they really want?	Have you ever **confused** someone by saying too much or getting muddled about what you want to say?
Content	Peacefully happy.	Easier word: pleased. Harder word: satisfied.	When I'm sitting reading a brilliant book with the cat on my lap, I am **contented.** I am happy. I don't want to do anything else.	Have you ever felt that you have everything you need? Do you have a hobby that makes you **content**?
Cooperative	Able to work with others to achieve something together.	Easier words: helpful, team player.	Successful teams are very **cooperative**; they work together.	Who would you choose to work with on a project? Who is the most **cooperative** person you know?
Cross	See angry			

Word	Definition	Words that mean nearly the same thing	Adult's experience of the word	Young person's experience of the word.
Cruel	Doing something on purpose to make someone upset or hurt.	Easier words: hurtful, nasty.	I hate it when people are **cruel** to animals. They keep them in small places and don't look after them properly.	Are there any characters on TV that are **cruel**? They try to be mean on purpose?
Curious	Keen to find out about something.	Easier words: interested, nosy.	I am **curious** about people I meet. I want to know what sorts of things they are interested in.	Do you want to find out 'whodunnit' when you watch a police drama? Are you **curious** about why they might have committed a crime?
Daring	Very brave.	Harder words: bold, courageous.	Sometimes I feel I am being **daring** when I disagree with someone very powerful. It is quite scary, but I do it anyway.	Do you know anyone who has climbed a high mountain or gone on a dangerous trip? Can you think of any famous people who are **daring**?
Desperate	No hope. Don't know what to do to sort something out. Things are so bad that you will try and do anything to sort it out.	Easier words: anxious, frantic, worried.	I felt **desperate** when I was late for work and I could not find my car keys. I ran about looking for them, getting very stressed.	Can you think of a character in a film or book who is **desperate**? Someone who had no hope or didn't know what to do to sort a problem out?

Word	Definition	Words that mean nearly the same thing	Adult's experience of the word	Young person's experience of the word.
Despondent	You feel unhappy because you don't think you can sort something out.	Easier words: depressed, down, hopeless, sad. Harder words: downhearted, dejected, glum, miserable.	When I was learning French, I used to get really **despondent**. However hard I tried, I still did really badly. I felt down that I couldn't get better at speaking French.	Do your parents/carers ever get **despondent** about anything? Do they ever get **despondent** about the cooking, cleaning or general mess? Do they feel that it will never get sorted?
Disappointed	Unhappy because something was not as good as you wanted it to be.	Easier words: frustrated, upset.	I was **disappointed** when I got a dress. It looked great online, but when I got it, it looked horrible.	Have you ever been given a present you really didn't like? Were you **disappointed** that you didn't get what you wanted?
Disgusted	Something you really don't like.	Harder word: revolting	I was **disgusted** when I put something in the bin and saw there were maggots in it. I was **disgusted** when I saw all the rubbish on the beach.	What makes you feel sick? Are you **disgusted** by any kind of food? Do people do anything that makes you **disgusted**?
Distressed	Very upset or very worried.	Harder words: misery, suffering.	I was **distressed** when my cat got run over, he was crying so loudly. It upset me to see him hurt.	Have you ever been **distressed** by something you saw on TV? What might **distress** a small child? What might make them very upset or worried?

Word	Definition	Words that mean nearly the same thing	Adult's experience of the word	Young person's experience of the word.
Down	Feeling unhappy or depressed.	Easier word: unhappy. Harder word: depressed.	I had a bad day last week. Everything seemed to go wrong. I was late for work, I tripped over, I spilt my coffee. I just felt **down** and wanted the day to be over.	What might make you feel **down**? How do you stop feeling **down**?
Dread	You know something is going to happen and you keep thinking that it will be bad.	Easier words: fear, worry.	I **dread** going to the dentist. I get really worried that they will want to give me a filling. I always worry about it for ages before I go.	What film character would you **dread** coming to your house? What would you be worried that they would do? Are there any lessons that you **dread**? What are you worried will happen in the lesson?
Embarrassed	Very uncomfortable, aware of yourself or someone else close to you. You think you or someone else stands out or looks silly.	Harder words: ashamed, self-conscious.	I was **embarrassed** when I walked into the wrong lecture room and everyone turned to look at me.	Have you ever seen someone who's **embarrassed** going red in the face? Has your mum/dad/carer ever done something that was **embarrassing**?
Excited	Looking forward to something.	Harder words: eager, enthusiastic.	I am very **excited** about going on holiday because I'll see all my family.	Do you remember being very **excited** about anything when you were younger?

Word	Definition	Words that mean nearly the same thing	Adult's experience of the word	Young person's experience of the word.
Forgiving	Stop feeling angry at someone for what they did.	Easier word: understanding. Harder word: excuse.	My cat is very **forgiving**, soon after I stepped on him accidentally, he came and sat on my lap.	Have you ever **forgiven** a friend for upsetting you, because they didn't mean to?
Friendly	Helpful and kind. Being nice. Someone who is happy to talk to other people.	Harder words: pleasant, welcoming.	I know someone who is very **friendly.** He always says hello to people and is always happy to see them.	Do you know anyone (maybe from a film) who is very **friendly**?
Frightened	See afraid			
Frustrated	Something didn't go as well as you'd hoped, you can't do something you want to.	Easier words: angry, upset.	I got very **frustrated** when trying to use a new computer programme; it took me ages to work it out and I kept making mistakes.	Has anyone ever got **frustrated** with you when you wouldn't do what they wanted? What makes you feel **frustrated**?
Generous	Keen to give time, money or help.	Harder word: big-hearted.	I have a friend who is always **generous**, she has something good to say about everyone and is always willing to help.	Is anyone **generous** to you? Was there a time when you were willing to share and be **generous**?
Glum	Quiet and very sad.	Easier words: downhearted, gloomy.	Sometimes I feel **glum** after visiting a relative who was very ill. I can't stop being sad.	Do you ever get **glum** in the middle of winter? How do you stop yourself being **glum**?

Word	Definition	Words that mean nearly the same thing	Adult's experience of the word	Young person's experience of the word.
Grief	Great sadness when someone dies.	Easier word: heartache. Harder word: sorrow.	I felt **grief** when my Nana died, I kept feeling sad all the time.	Have you ever lost a person or pet you loved? Did you feel **grief**?
Grumpy	In a bad mood.	Harder words: grouchy, irritable.	I get **grumpy** when I haven't slept very well. I can end up being cross with my children for no good reason.	What makes you **grumpy**?
Guilty	When you feel bad because you have done something wrong.	Harder word: shame	There were two pieces of chocolate cake left from the party. I ate them both. I felt really **guilty** when my husband wanted a slice.	Have you ever eaten something then felt **guilty** about it? You wished you hadn't eaten it? Have you ever done something to your brother/sister/friend and then felt **guilty** about it? You felt bad afterwards.
Hate	You **really** don't like something.	Harder word: loathe.	I **hate** Brussels sprouts. They make me feel sick just looking at them.	Which film characters **hate** each other?
Hurt	Emotional or physical pain.	Harder words: miffed, offended, harmed.	I was **hurt** when I wasn't invited out with a group of friends. I was really sad that I couldn't go.	Have you ever been **hurt** when someone said something thoughtless or nasty?

Word	Definition	Words that mean nearly the same thing	Adult's experience of the word	Young person's experience of the word.
Impatient	Annoyed by having to wait.	Harder word: exasperated.	Sometimes I get **impatient** when I'm driving, when people are going slowly and I want to get home quickly.	What makes you **impatient**? Why is it so hard to wait or get it right?
Interested	Wanting to spend time on something and find out about it.	Easier word: curious. Harder words: attentive, fascinated.	I'm **interested** in all sorts of things and I'm always reading and listening to podcasts.	Is there anything at school that you're **interested** in? What social media **interests** you?
Irritated	See annoyed.			
Jealous	Unhappy because someone else has things you want, or is good at things you can't do.	Harder words: bitter, envious.	Sometimes I'm **jealous** of my son who has travelled all around the world. I wish I could do that.	Do you think anyone gets treated better than you? Are you **jealous** about that?
Joy	Very happy.	Easier word: delight.	Seeing my family when I haven't seen them for a while gives me great **joy**.	What do you look forward to? Do you have any hobbies that give you **joy**?
Judging	Having and expressing a negative opinion about something.	Easier word: deciding.	I try not to be **judging** but it's hard when people are aggressive or unkind. I end up thinking badly of them.	Do you sometimes feel that people are **judging** you? Do you think they think bad things about you without really knowing you?

Word	Definition	Words that mean nearly the same thing	Adult's experience of the word	Young person's experience of the word.
Kind	Wanting to help, especially if someone is hurt or upset.	Easier words: caring, gentle.	I try to be **kind** when people are behaving badly and listen to them.	Who is **kind** to you? Who do you try to be **kind** to?
Left out	Sad because other people are together and you aren't part of the group.	Easier words: alone, lonely.	I hate it when I hear that two of my friends have done something nice with each other. I end up feeling **left out**. I wish I had been invited.	Have you ever had friends that go and do things together and you aren't invited? Do you feel **left out**?
Lonely	Sad because of being alone or without friends.	Easier word: alone.	Sometimes it's **lonely** when I'm working and I know other people are having fun.	Have you ever felt **lonely** when you went somewhere new or started a new school? Have you ever wished you had a friend with you?
Lovesick	Missing someone that you love so much that you find you can't do everyday things.	Easier word: obsessed. Harder words: infatuated, pining.	I remember being so **lovesick** over someone that I daydreamed about him all day.	Have you seen any films/TV where a character is so **lovesick** that they do silly things? All they can think about is that one person.
Loving	Being very kind, showing care for someone. Showing someone a lot of love.	Easier words: caring, warm.	My Nana was very **loving,** she gave us great big hugs and spent ages playing with us. She always made me feel special.	If someone was **loving** what things might they do?

Word	Definition	Words that mean nearly the same thing	Adult's experience of the word	Young person's experience of the word.
Loyal	Being supportive of someone no matter what happens.	Easier words: faithful, reliable, trustworthy.	I am **loyal** to my friends even when they are ill and grumpy. I am still nice to them.	People say dogs are very **loyal**, do you agree? They always like their owner best.
Mystified	Really not understanding something.	Easier words: confused, puzzled.	I am **mystified** about why people like watching violence in films. I cannot understand it.	Do people sometimes do things that make no sense? Are you **mystified** by that?
Nasty	Wanting to hurt or upset.	Easier word: horrible.	In stories and films, there are often characters, the baddies, who are **nasty** and who just want to kill or hurt others.	Who is the **nastiest** film/book character you know? Who really likes hurting or upsetting people?
Needy	Not having food, housing, affection or love. Someone who wants your attention all the time.	Harder word: deprived.	My friend's dog is very **needy**, he always wants to be stroked, played with or fed.	Do you know anyone who is **needy**? Do they always need something from you? Are there groups of people who are **needy**?
Nervous	Feeling frightened or worried about something that is happening or might happen.	Easier words: anxious, frightened, worried.	I like to ride but I get really **nervous** on a horse. I like to be on really old, gentle horses because it makes me less **nervous**: I don't worry as much.	Some people can make us **nervous**. We keep thinking they are going to tell us off. Is there anyone you know that makes you **nervous**?

Word	Definition	Words that mean nearly the same thing	Adult's experience of the word	Young person's experience of the word.
Nosy	You are interested in things that you shouldn't be.	Harder words: curious, snooping.	When I travel on the train, I am really **nosy** about what people are doing. I like to know what they are doing. I know it is nothing to do with me, but I am really interested.	Have you ever read someone's texts when you knew it was nothing to do with you? Were you just a bit **nosy**, wanting to know what they said?
Outraged	Very angry.	Harder words: enraged, infuriated, livid.	I am **outraged** when I hear about people being cruel to children or animals. It makes me so angry.	Is there anything that makes you so angry you can't think straight? Are you **outraged** by something that someone does?
Oversensitive	If you are over sensitive about something, you are easily upset about it.	Harder word: vulnerable.	When I was a teenager, I used to be **oversensitive** about my hair. I hated anyone looking at it.	Do you know anyone who is **oversensitive**? They get upset really easily? What else do you notice about them?
Overwhelmed	Feelings that are too big to deal with.	Easier words: dazed, stunned.	Sometimes when lots of people are talking to me at once and asking me to do things, I get **overwhelmed**. I don't know what to do.	Have you ever just wanted to run and hide because you felt **overwhelmed** with what was going on? There was just too much going on. Have you ever **overwhelmed** someone else by being over excited about something? Did they find it hard to cope with you being so excited?

Word	Definition	Words that mean nearly the same thing	Adult's experience of the word	Young person's experience of the word.
Panic	A sudden fear that might seem too big to deal with.	Harder words: alarm, dread, horror, terror.	When I realised I was driving down a bus lane and didn't know how to get out, I felt **panic**. I didn't know what to do.	Have you ever seen anyone **panic** and not know what to do? Has it ever happened to you?
Peaceful	Quiet and calm.	Easier word: restful. Harder word: non-violent.	I think being in nature, by the sea or a forest is **peaceful.** It is really relaxing there.	What makes you feel **peaceful**? Any particular music or places?
Playful	Likes having fun and having a laugh.	Easier words: full of fun, lively. Harder word: jolly	Someone I work with is very **playful,** he is always joking and teasing people	Are you someone who likes being silly and **playful**?
Protective	To look after someone. To make sure they don't get hurt.	Easier word: caring	When children are very little, you need to be very **protective**. You spend all your time trying to make sure they are safe.	Do you ever feel **protective** towards anyone? Do you try and make sure they are OK?
Proud	Pleased about something you have done.	Easier words: delighted, satisfied.	I was **proud** that my friend has become a stand-up comic. It is amazing that she is able to talk in front of all those people.	What have you done well at? Is there anything that you've put a lot of effort in? Are you **proud** of it?

Word	Definition	Words that mean nearly the same thing	Adult's experience of the word	Young person's experience of the word.
Relieved	Something bad didn't happen.	Easier words: pleased, thankful.	I was **relieved** when I didn't get a parking ticket! I thought I was going to get one because I was late back to the car.	Did you feel something bad might happen, then **relieved** when it didn't?
Sad	Unhappy.	Harder words: miserable, sorrowful.	I was **sad** when my cat died.	Have you ever seen anything **sad** on the news that made you want to cry?
Safe	You won't get hurt.	Harder words: harmless, protected.	Children are kept **safe** by seatbelts in a car.	Where do you feel **safe**? Somewhere you feel happy and relaxed, where nothing bad is going to happen.
Satisfied	Having enough to make you happy. You got what you wanted or needed.	Easier words: contented, pleased.	I was **satisfied** with the work that I did last week. It was good enough.	Were you **satisfied** by your last meal? Was it what you wanted or needed?
Scared	See afraid			
Shame	See guilty or ashamed			
Shock	Something suddenly happens. Usually it isn't nice.	Easier words: amazed, surprise.	I was looking after a friend's dog and he slept on the kitchen floor. I was **shocked** when I came down and found poo and wee all over the kitchen floor. I didn't expect to find that.	What could I do that would **shock** you? What could I do that that would really surprise you?

Word	Definition	Words that mean nearly the same thing	Adult's experience of the word	Young person's experience of the word.
Shy	Not happy with people they don't know.	Harder words: cautious, nervous.	I am **shy** when I have to go into a room full of people I don't know. I never know what to say to them.	Do you know anyone who is **shy?** Would you be **shy** about standing on stage and talking to lots of people?
Stressed	Finding something too hard makes you feel uncomfortable.	Easier words: anxious, tense, worried.	I get **stressed** if I don't have enough time to do things properly. It really upsets me.	Do you know anyone who is **stressed** about having too much to do? What are they like?
Stubborn	Won't change their mind or do things differently.	Easier word: determined. Harder word: Strong-willed.	I find it difficult when people are too **stubborn** to try another way of doing things. They just don't want to listen to anything new.	Do you know anyone who is so **stubborn** that they never change their mind?
Surprised	Something you didn't expect.	Easier words: amazed, shocked.	I was **surprised** when the head teacher started dancing in assembly.	Have you ever been **surprised** by something unusual someone did?
Tender	Showing gentleness and sympathy.	Easier words: caring, kind.	The nurse was kind and **tender** when he took my bandage off. He really took his time and tried to do it really gently.	Have you had a **tender** feeling towards a child or small animal? What did you want to do?

Word	Definition	Words that mean nearly the same thing	Adult's experience of the word	Young person's experience of the word.
Tense	Feeling nervous or worried so it's hard to think or be relaxed, muscles get tight.	Easier word: jumpy. Harder word: edgy.	I get **tense** when I sit at my computer working at something difficult. My shoulders get all tight.	What or who makes you **tense**? Just thinking about something/someone can make you feel a bit nervous or worried.
Uncertain	Not sure.	Easier words: unknown, unsettled.	I'm **uncertain** about what car I'm going to get next. I really don't know yet.	Are you **uncertain** about what you'll be doing in a years' time? Do you know yet?
Uncomfortable	Slightly worried or embarrassed and not relaxed and confident.	Other words: edgy, tense, uneasy.	I'm **uncomfortable** when I know I'm going to be late. I am a bit worried about it. When I was a child, I used to feel **uncomfortable** when my granny gave me a kiss. She had hairs on her chin. I didn't like the feeling of it.	Do you feel **uncomfortable** when you meet new people? Is it hard to relax and be yourself?
Upset	To make someone unhappy, disappointed or worried.	harder word: distressed.	I was **upset** when I found out my children had eaten all the cake. The cat was **upset** when I took him to the vets. He was not at all happy to be there.	Do you get **upset** if someone tells you what is going to happen when you watch a film? Do you get **upset** when you see people suffering on the news?

Word	Definition	Words that mean nearly the same thing	Adult's experience of the word	Young person's experience of the word.
Uptight	Anxious, angry and tense.	Easier words: anxious, bothered, troubled.	I get **uptight** when the house is in a mess. I know it doesn't really matter, but I just can't relax.	Is there anyone who make you feel **uptight**?
Worried	Troubled about a problem. Keep thinking about something bad that might or did happen.	Easier words: bothered, uneasy.	I **worry** about how well I'll be able to work when I haven't slept well. I think about how hard work will be.	Do you know anyone who **worries** a lot? They keep thinking about bad things that might happen.

▐▌ How strong is that emotion? (Emotion slopes)

You can use the emotion slopes or numbers to think about the intensity of an emotion. If a person is **angry**, how **angry** are they? Are they really **angry**? If so, they might rate the **anger** at 4 or even a 5.

Angry

1 Weak	2	3	4	5 Strong

▐▌ How strong is that emotion? (Example)

This might also mean that there might be a better word for really **angry**. Have a look on page 318 at the grouping of emotions. Related words are given together. So, in the **anger** line there is:

Angry	Annoyed	Bitter	Cheated
Cross	Frustrated	Irritated	Livid
Outraged	Venomous		

Are there any words that might really get across how **angry** the person could be? Is the person **livid**? Or **outraged**? Remember these words don't mean exactly the same thing. You may need the emotion words definitions (What's that feeling called?) on pages 329–347 to help.

How strong is that emotion? (Completed emotion slope)

You can try and put the words in order of how strong the feelings are. You can't be exact, as the words mean slightly different things. Also, people have different views. It is all a basis for discussion. Angry might look a bit like this:

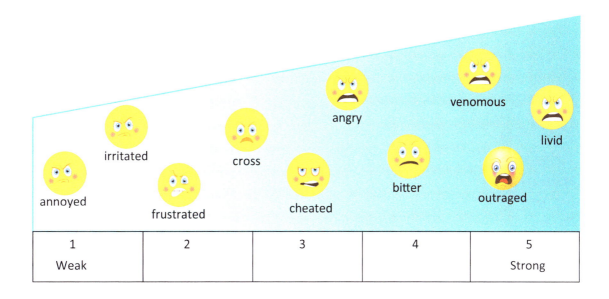

1	2	3	4	5
Weak				Strong

⏸ How strong is that emotion?

1	2	3	4	5
Weak				Strong

(11) What is the main feeling in the story

This is a list of the emotions that are associated with each scenario. Young people may come up with other words. Sometimes they need some support to expand their vocabulary of emotions or look at the story with more depth. The aim isn't that the young people have to use these exact words. Use the scenarios and toolkit as a springboard for discussion.

Tools available

- All these words are grouped with symbols in 'Grouping feelings' (page 315).

- All the words in **bold** have more in-depth information in 'What's that feeling called?' (page 328). This includes definitions, related words and prompts to get adults to talk about their experience of the words and to get young people to talk about their experience of the word.

	Main feeling	other feelings
Assessment scenario 1	Shy	Excited, nervous, proud
Assessment scenario 2	Jealous	Confident, **upset**
Assessment scenario 3	Nosy	Confused, proud, surprised
Assessment scenario 4	Guilty	Deceitful, devastated, **proud**, **satisfied**, threatened, unsure

	Story title	Main feeling	Other feelings
1	**Granny's house**	**Comfortable**	**Annoyed, cautious**
2	**New home**	**Safe**	Pleased
3	**Cute new puppy**	**Joy**	**Impatience**, tired

	Story title	Main feeling	Other feelings
4	**Runny nose**	**Disgusted**	**Excited**
5	**Long holiday**	**Lonely**	Longing
6	**Boring game**	**Cheerful**	**Bored,** relieved
7	**Picnic**	**Forgiving**	**Cross**
8	**The storm**	**Frightened**	**Calm,** tired
9	**Motocross**	**Interested**	**Curious**
10	**Mrs Mad Head**	**Upset**	**Playful,** self-conscious
11	**Late home**	**Angry**	**Awkward, embarrassed**
12	**Fishing**	**Calm**	Enjoy
13	**A sudden soaking**	**Surprised**	**Annoyed, excited,** thirsty
14	**New school**	**Friendly**	**Relieved, scared**
15	**After the match**	**Grumpy**	**Annoyed,** enjoy, irritated, tired
16	**The party**	**Excited**	**Angry, disappointed**
17	**Holiday birthday**	**Cheated**	**Disappointed, worried**
18	**Peppermint thief**	**Brave**	**Exciting,** loyal, **upset,** wary
19	**Street tree**	**Caring**	Astonished, **interested, surprise**
20	**Present from dad**	**Disappointed**	**Excited,** expectant, **upset**
21	**End of year**	**Generous**	**Excited, sad**

	Story title	Main feeling	Other feelings
22	Artwork	Satisfied	**Disappointed**, discouraged, frustrated, **worried**
23	Favourite band	Desperate	Amazed, **excited**, **worried**
24	Fetch!	Cruel	**Amused**, **bored**, frenzied
25	New trainers	Embarrassed	Envious, **excited**, **judging**, **proud**
26	Bus ride betrayal	Worried	Cruel, thoughtless
27	Frustrating French	Confused	**Ashamed**, **dread**, hopeless
28	The forgotten washing up	Frustrated	Absorbed, **angry**, forgetful, **left out**
29	One step at a time	Cautious	Anxious, eager, **excited**, dejected, focussed
30	Broken bike	Cooperative	**Annoyed**, **frustrated**, pleased, unsure
31	Class entertainment	Daring	**Amused**, displeased, silly, stressed
32	Lift home	Uncertain	**Anxious**, confident, tired, unsure
33	The prom	Uncomfortable	**Amused**, anxious, **dread**, happy, silly
34	Volcanic tea	Outraged	Enjoyment, controlled, glad, livid

	Story title	Main feeling	Other feelings
35	**Basketball game**	**Loyal**	Cruel, **proud**, unsure
36	**Maths breakthrough**	**Proud**	Eager, focussed, glad
37	**Who cares about football?**	**Impatient**	**Excited**, eager, **disappointed**, glad, **frustrated**
38	**A big fat ginger cat**	**Tender**	Enjoyment, inspired, **interested**, love, pleasure, **worry**
39	**Bus trip**	**Relieved**	**Angry**, **annoyed**, fun, hopeful, pleased
40	**Lost and found**	**Curious**	Eager, **relieved**, unsure
41	**Poor Ralf**	**Grief**	Intrigued, unsure
42	**Exam results**	**Jealous**	**Annoyed**, happy, **proud**
43	**Bad day**	**Glum**	**Caring,** despondent, **kind**, self-aware, thoughtful
44	**Little cousins**	**Affectionate**	Alert, **anticipating**, happy, soothing
45	**Quidditch**	**Bewildered**	Confident, **confused**, entertained
46	**Finally!**	**Peaceful**	Amusing, frantic, **overwhelmed**, **relieved**
47	**Noisy breakfast**	**Overwhelmed**	Anxious, cheerful, eager, happy, **sad**, thoughtful
48	**Phone call**	**Tense**	**Afraid**, distracted, gentle, **sad**

	Story title	Main feeling	Other feelings
49	**Bike chain sculpture**	**Amused**	Alert, intrigued, horrified, motivated, pleased, **relieved**
50	**Answering back**	**Argumentative**	**Angry, annoyed, irritated, playful,** stern, **stubborn**
51	**Ice skating**	**Needy**	Eager, fun, **oversensitive, shy, worried**
52	**The sleepover**	**Uptight**	Carefree, enjoyment, **excited, worried**
53	**Stolen scarf**	**Panic**	Attracted, carefree, fun, horrified, resigned, terror
54	**Not again!**	**Distress**	**Confused,** cruel, **irritated,** regret, **stressed,** tired
55	**Little brother**	**Protective**	Amazed, defensive, dislike
56	**A canoe adventure**	**Content**	**Amused,** horrified, **peaceful,** scheming, **shocked,** wary
57	**Sunglasses squabble**	**Judging**	**Angry, amused,** discouraged, eager, **interested,** rejected venomous
58	**How to lose all your friends**	**Bitter**	**Embarrassed,** excluded, devastated, **disappointment,** hurt, **loyal, nervous,** patronised, resentful, **uncomfortable**

	Story title	Main feeling	Other feelings
59	**The fateful lie**	**Lovesick**	Amazed, **awkward**, **confused**, **excited**, impulsive, **irritated**
60	**Some boys are strange creatures**	**Mystified**	**Admiration**, horrified, resigned, **uncomfortable**, uneasy

Dealing with feelings

Accepting feelings

All feelings are important and there for a reason.

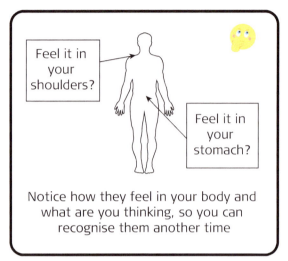

Feel it in your shoulders?

Feel it in your stomach?

Notice how they feel in your body and what are you thinking, so you can recognise them another time

I feel angry but I don't have to hit someone

Remember that your feelings are **not** you, they come and go. You have a choice about what to do about them and how to react.

I am feeling embarrassed

I am feeling excited

I am feeling irritated

Give the feelings a name

Sometimes we are too stressed to think and we need to calm down first. Pause.

If you LIKE a feeling you can. . .

Draw or write something to help you remember it and what made it happen

Make a collection of things that will remind you of it

We just talked for ages. We didn't talk about anything special ...

Talk about it, tell the story

That was just like the other time ...

Think back to other times like that

If you DON'T LIKE a feeling you can. . .

Name it then it won't seem so bad

Tell someone you trust about it, say how you feel

Try to come up with a solution to the problem that caused it. You could use problem solving frames (page 382-387)

Ask for help

Distract yourself; do something interesting, take a deep breath, count to ten, listen to music

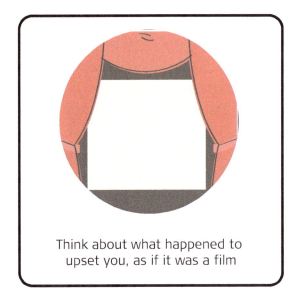

Think about what happened to upset you, as if it was a film

If you DON'T LIKE a feeling you can. . .

Tell yourself; 'it's OK I can get through it', 'this is a problem I can solve', 'I can try again', or 'it doesn't really matter'

Move; run, jump, walk, dance

Go somewhere calm and quiet

You might also want to be grateful for worrying thoughts which are trying to keep you safe, so you can say to yourself 'thanks, but I'm OK'

If you have negative thoughts, remember they are just thoughts, you don't have to believe everything you think!

Do something kind for someone else

If you DON'T LIKE a feeling you can...

Remember good things, or things you're grateful for, or a time when you were relaxed and happy

Wait, if you don't keep thinking about it, the feeling will go in a few seconds.

Keep away from the people or situation that upsets you

Calm down by putting a hand on your chest (and maybe one on your belly) and take some slow deep breaths

Try to see it from another point of view, perhaps how another person might see the situation

Finding clues and explaining your thinking (inference and verbal reasoning)

 ## Why it's important to find clues and explain thinking

To be shared with the young person

When someone is talking, the listener's job is to try and work out what the speaker means. Quite often when people talk, they don't always say exactly what they mean.

Listeners can work out what speakers mean by listening to the words, but also by thinking about the situation, looking at the speaker's face and their body and adding it to what they already know.

It can be a challenging task, but the stories in this book will help you practise these skills. You will listen to the words, think about the situation and look at the faces and bodies in the pictures. Then you can practise working out what the story means and answering some questions. Some of the questions will be easy and some will really make you think.

Things that will generally help you:

- What do I know about this situation already? What might you think or do in this situation?

- Does the story make sense? If not, ask what it means.

- If you can't remember some of the story ask for it to be read again.

- Put yourself in the character's shoes. What would you do? How would you feel?

- Think about why things have happened.

- Think about what might happen next.

For most of the questions, there are no right or wrong answers. It is about trying to work it out and then choosing the answer you think is best. It is OK if other people have different answers.

A selection of Language for Behaviour and Emotions questions

Level A	Level B	Level C	Level D
Tell me what happened.	Who has been affected?	What's important?	What's your evidence for thinking that?
Who was involved?	How have you been affected?	How have others been affected?	How sure can you be of your opinion? (What supports your view?)
What is X doing?	What do you think about it now?	What's needed to make things right?	What is X's motive?
Where are they?	What could they say or do?	What could X do next time, so this does not happen?	What can you infer from what you saw/heard/read?
Has it happened to you?	What's going to happen next?	What might happen if. . .?	What led you to your conclusion?
• How did you feel? (Simple, single emotion)	What does X mean?	Why? / Why not?	How can you be sure?
• What did you say?	Why? (obvious)	How do you know?	What made you realise?
• What did you do?	When?	Why wouldn't / shouldn't. . .?	What are the consequences of that?
Sentence completion.	How did they feel?	What might have caused this to happen?	What do you suspect?
What did they do?	Tell me how you. . .	How could you solve the problem?	What did you observe that made you think that?
What did they say?	If (obvious)	What is the best thing to do? Why?	How might x feel when they look back on this?
What did you notice happening?	What is the problem/ main issue here?	How could it be done differently?	What might have made X behave in this way?
Make a face like X (person in story).	Tell me three things you know about.	Why might X see the issue differently?	Tell me how they would resolve their differences/ come to an agreement. Talk through the steps.
	Who could help?	Why does it bother them?	What is the best solution? Why?
	What were they thinking?	What would they say happened?	If you consider it from X's view, does that change our opinion? How?
		What were they trying to do?	If someone else disagreed with your point of view, how would you defend it?
		Do you agree with what X did? Why /why not?	
		Did he/she believe what the other person was saying?	
		What does that crazy phrase (idiom) mean?	

References

Blank, M., Rose, S. A., & Berlin, L.J. (1978). *The language of learning: The preschool years*. New York: Grune & Stratton.

https://www.iirp.edu/news-from-iirp/time-to-think-using-restorative-questions

The story (narrative)

 ## Introduction to narrative

Being able to tell a story clearly, in the right order without missing out any key points is very important, as almost every conversation includes telling stories to each other. Narrative skills are also key to reading, comprehension and writing. Having a clear narrative of events of one's own history is also crucial for mental health.

To tell a good story we need to be able to:

- Remember the events.

- Recognise the key points.

- Put the information in the right order.

- Recognise what the problem is/problems are.

- Talk about how people solve the problem(s).

- Identify the consequences of actions.

- Understand the characters' (or people's) motivations, perspectives and emotions.

- Have the words to describe what happened.

- Have the grammar to form the sentences.

- Tell the story in an interesting and engaging way, including non-verbal skills.

How to spot if a young person needs support with telling stories

- Analyse the 'The story (narrative)' section of the profile on page 126, in particular the sections which have been identified as either 'really tricky' or 'tricky sometimes'. This will help you in the development of the intervention plan.

- You may have undertaken formal narrative assessments which have shown areas of need.

Although it is important to identify specific needs, all young people will benefit from some support with telling stories.

Narrative resources provided in this toolkit

Resource	Page
'Why it's important to be able to tell stories'	367
Three 'Story frames' *LFBE* levels **A**, **B**, **C/D**	368
Worked examples of all the Story frames	373

Developing narrative skills within an LFBE scenario session

- In one of the early *LFBE* sessions, use the tools to start a discussion about when they might be helpful. Pick which frame is going to be most useful. The frames relate to the young person's language level (either **A***, **B** or **C/D**).

- * If a young person is at Language Level **A,** they will find it hard to access the *LFBE* programme but they may well need to explain what has happened. This frame is intended to support day-to-day narrative.

- You could start a session by reading the intended scenario and use this story as the starting point. As a group, develop the story so that it includes all of the narrative components (as outlined on the story frames). Repeat the story and complete the chosen story frame as a group. Students can then retell the story including all the components.

- Most of the scenarios contain a narrative-related question. These are marked by a 📖 symbol. When you get to this question, use the appropriate story frame as a guide.

It is important to work together to fill in the story frames and have a 50:50 conversation about the story.

Use the frames as a basis for talking about what has happened or to make up stories.

- Talk about a recent real event from your own life. It works best if something went wrong or was different from your expectations. Refer to a story frame as you tell your story. With the individual/small group, go back over your story and ask the young people to identify each component of the story. Instruct the young people to draw a stick figure for each element of the story structure. Using the story frame as support, the young people then retell the story. Once completed, highlight each story structure component used or missing.

- One person can start a story and another can think of what happens next, using a story frame as a prompt.

- Use the frames to analyse known stories or ones they are learning about.

- Make up your own frames that help with particular story tasks, like explaining how to do a task, or as the basis for drama, or to think about things that might happen.

In general

- When telling a story, a young person may make errors in vocabulary or grammar. Try not to worry about this too much, as the focus is on the 'key points' in a narrative and getting them in the right order. However, you may wish to repeat the story using the appropriate language which gives them an accurate model.

- Over time, the aim is to fade the supports whilst maintaining high levels of student success.

- Praise spontaneous use of strategies.

- Support students to use the strategies in the classroom and at home.

There are also other commercial resources that can be used to develop narrative skills.

Aimed at 7–11 year olds	From Oral to Written Narrative, Black Sheep Press	A programme to develop stories beyond the basic 'who', 'where', 'when', 'what happened' and 'in the end'. Can be used with whole classes.

Aimed at young people 11+	Narrative intervention Programme (V. Joffe, 2011)	In-depth intervention programme to develop narrative skills
	Secondary Talk Narrative, KS3-4 Black Sheep Press	A range of story frames to support a variety of narrative tasks

References

Apparicio, V., & Shanks, B. (2015). *Oral to written narrative.* Keighley, West Yorkshire: Black Sheep Press.

Joffe, V. L. (2011). *Narrative intervention programme.* Milton Keynes: Speechmark.

Shanks, B. (2010). *Secondary talk narrative.* Keighley, West Yorkshire: Black Sheep Press.

Why it's important to be able to tell stories

To be shared with the young person

When you first hear the word 'stories' you might think of the kind of stories that are in books, in films or ones you write. Stories are more than this as they can be about real events or be made up.

Many of our conversations are in the form of stories. We tell stories to explain or describe real or imaginary events. They might be about what happened in the war or what happened in our favourite show on TV. These stories can become important when we have been involved in or seen something happening and others want to know more.

Learning to tell stories is sometimes complicated and hard. You need to think about what you want to say, and then you need to put it into words. It takes skill and practise to get good at telling stories. Learning to tell stories is a good thing to do, because when you tell a good story to people you can really get your point across.

Story frame *LFBE* Language Level A

Who was there?	
Where were they?	
What happened?	
So then what happened?	
How did it end?	

Story frame *LFBE* Language Level B

When did it happen?	
Who was there?	
Where were they?	
What happened?	
What's the problem?	

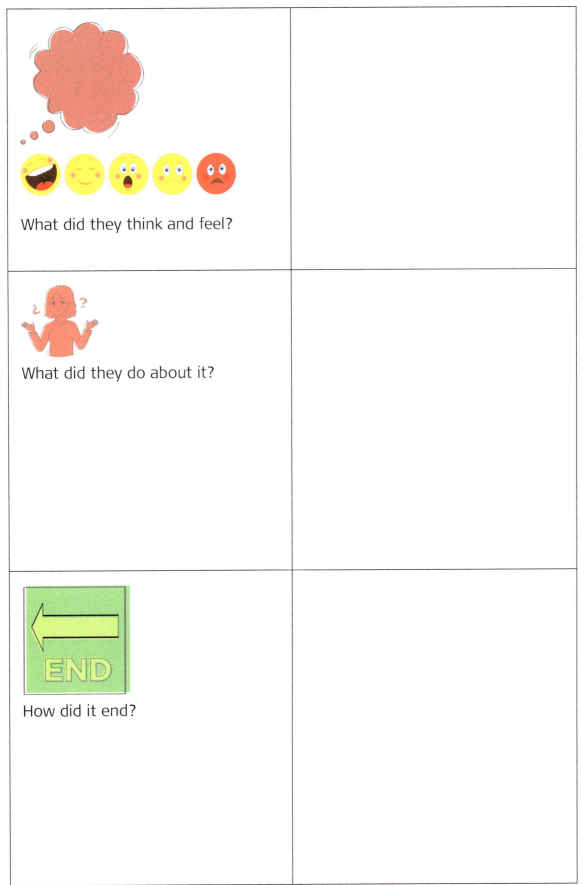

What did they think and feel?

What did they do about it?

How did it end?

Story frame *LFBE* Language Level C/D

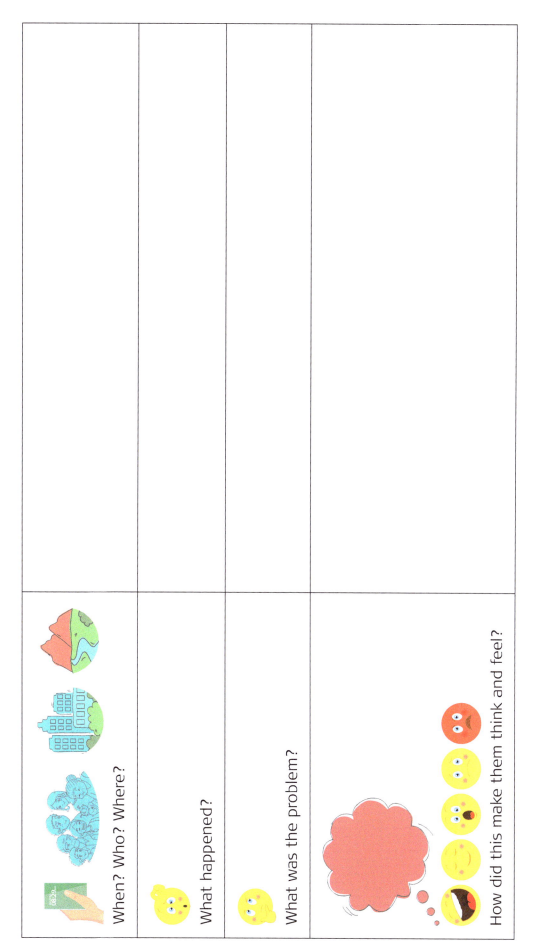

When? Who? Where?

What happened?

What was the problem?

How did this make them think and feel?

What was their plan to sort it out?	What did they do to sort the problem out?	How did it end? How was it sorted out? What effect did that have? What were the consequences?	How did they think and feel at the end?

Story frames worked examples

There are three worked examples for the same story. This allows young people to use the right level of questions to think about the story. The story used is Scenario 30: Broken bike on page 198.

30 Broken bike

Sofia was riding her bike home from school one day when part way home her chain came off. Sofia tried several times to put it back on, but it just would not go. She was just about to start pushing her bike home when Reza, a boy from her class, came along and offered to help. Sofia wasn't convinced that he'd be able to fix it. Reza tried several times to get the chain back on but without any luck. 'I think we can do it if we do it together,' suggested Sofia. And within a moment it worked! The chain slotted into place, and Sofia's bike was fixed again. They high-fived and Sofia rode off home.

Story frame *LFBE* Language Level A

Who was there?	Where were they?	What happened?	So then what happened?	How did it end?
Sofia and Reza	On the way home from school	She was riding home and her bike chain came off.	Sofia tried to fix the bike. Then Reza tried to fix it. Then they tried to fix it together.	The chain was fixed. Sofia could go home on her bike.

Story frame *LFBE* Language Level B

When did it happen?	After school
Who was there?	Sofia and Reza
Where were they?	On the way home
What happened?	Sofia was riding home.

What's the problem?	Her chain came off
What did they think and feel?	She was worried that she would have to walk home. She didn't know if she could fix it.
What did they do about it?	Sofia tried to fix it. Reza tried to fix it. They tried to fix it together.
How did it end?	It worked when they did it together. She got to cycle home.

Story frame *LFBE* Language Level C/D

When? Who? Where?	Sofia & Reza were on the way home from school.
What happened?	Sofia was riding home.
What was the problem?	Sofia's bike chain came off. Sofia wasn't convinced Reza could fix it. Reza thought he could get the chain back on by himself.
How did this make them think and feel?	Sofia was worried that she would have to walk home. She didn't know if she could fix it.

		3. Reza offered to help	5. Sofia thought they could do it together
	1. Sofia thought she would try to fix it herself	4. He tried and failed	6. They worked together
	2. She tried and failed		

What was their plan to sort it out?

What did they do to sort the problem out?

They got the chain back on.

END

How did it end? How was it sorted out? What effect did that have? What were the consequences?

They were both pleased. Sofia was relieved she didn't have to walk home.

How did they think and feel at the end?

Solving people problems

 An introduction to solving people problems

All of the skills taught within the *LFBE* approach support verbally solving interpersonal problems, but this final stage brings all of the skills together and applies them more explicitly to problem-solving. During the course of the intervention, and with support, we expect that young people will take the skills they have been learning 'off the page' and apply them to their lives. This can be very difficult, particularly when young people need to apply these still developing skills to situations that are emotionally charged. This section of the toolkit provides a range of tools and guidance to support young people to apply their learnt skills.

How to spot if a young person needs support with solving people problems

Analyse the 'Solving people problems' section of the profile on page 126, in particular the sections which have been identified as either 'really tricky' or 'tricky sometimes'. This will help you in the development of the intervention plan. Although it is important to identify specific needs, all young people will benefit from some support with solving people problems.

Resources to support solving people problems provided in this toolkit

Resource	Page
'Why it's important to learn how to solve people problems'	381
Three problem-solving frames *LFBE* Language Levels **A***, **B** and **C/D** for problem-solving about the **scenarios**	382, 384, 386
Worked examples of all the previous problem-solving frames	388–391
Three problem-solving frames *LFBE* Language Levels **A***, **B** and **C/D** for solving people problems that the young person encounters in **everyday life**	383, 385, 387

* If a young person is at Language Level A, they will find it hard to access the *LFBE* programme but they may well need to solve people problems. An easier frame can also be helpful sometimes.

Developing solving people problems skills within an LFBE *scenario session*

Solving people problems involves all the skills developed in this programme. Therefore, the task of solving the problems is an *LFBE* Language Level D task. In most of the scenarios there is a 'solving people problems' task. These are marked with ✓. If you have young people who are working at *LFBE* Language Level D, then they will naturally come across this task. Introduce the 'Solving people problems frame *LFBE* Language Level C/D' (page 386). As a group, work through all the prompts and talk about different options. Remember it needs to be an equal conversation and adults need to participate as much as the young people. If solving people problems has been identified as a particular focus, ensure you spend time on this task. If the young people are not yet at *LFBE* Language Level D but solving people problems is a priority, then it is possible to still target this skill but at the appropriate level. Just choose the 'Problem-solving frame' at the appropriate language level and adults can support and model.

'Why it's important to learn how to solve people problems' (page 381) is an introductory story which may be used to explain to young people the reason for targeting this skill.

Make sure that the young person has regular practise at solving people problems and using the frames within the structure of the *LFBE* sessions. Once they are confident at using the frames within the *LFBE* sessions, then the equivalent personal (as opposed to scenario) frames can be applied to real-life situations. Remember real life is inevitably harder as there are usually strong emotions involved.

Young people also need to understand the language of problem-solving especially the words 'solution' and 'consequences'. Use definitions on page 283 and 'Introduction to developing vocabulary' on page 276.

Why it's important to learn how to solve people problems

To be shared with the young person

Everyone finds it difficult to get on with other people sometimes. This can happen anywhere: at home, school, college or when you're out together. Sometimes it can be difficult to get on with people you really like as well as those you don't like so much. This can mean we get into arguments, get upset or 'fall out'.

Other people might not understand what we're thinking, feeling or saying. We might not understand what the other person is thinking, feeling or saying. Sometimes the other person might not be trying to upset us, but it might feel like that.

It can be very upsetting if we don't understand someone else. It's sad if someone we like no longer wants to talk to us because we have fallen out.

Even if we don't like a person, we might have to see them or work with them, so it's better to find a way to be together without arguing or fighting. If we have problems with people we like, it's important to think about how to make things better between us. It's good to sort it out and get on with them again.

Problem Solving Frame LFBE Language Level A

For scenarios

Who was there?

Where were they?

What happened? (Use stick men and speech bubbles)

What's the problem? (Talk through what is happening and try and think about what the problem might be)

These are some things they could do to make it better (adults list options):

Which one could they do?

Problem Solving Frame LFBE Language Level A

Personal

Who was there?

Where were they?

What happened? (Use stick men and speech bubbles)

How did you feel?

What did you think?

These are some things you could do to make it better (adults list options):

Which one will you do?

Problem Solving Frame LFBE Language Level B

For scenarios

What happened?

Person 1: _____   Person 2: _____

What is the main problem for person 1?

What is the main problem for person 2?

How did that make them feel?

How did that make them feel?

What were they thinking?

What were they thinking?

How can they make it better?

What could they say?

What could they do?

Who can help?

What might happen next?

What might happen next?

What might happen next?

What's the best thing to do?

✓ Problem Solving Frame LFBE Language Level B

Personal

What happened?

You	The other person
What is the main problem for you?	**What is the main problem for them?**
How did that make you feel?	**How did that make them feel?**
What were you thinking?	**What were they thinking?**

How can you make it better?

What could you say?	What could you do?	Who can help?
↓	↓	↓
What might happen next?	What might happen next?	What might happen next?

What's the best thing to do? ✓

Problem Solving Frame LFBE Language Level C/D

For scenarios

Person 1:_____

Person 2:_____

What would they say happened?	What would they say happened?
How did that make them feel? ⏸	How did that make them feel? ⏸
Why does this bother them?	Why does this bother them?
What were they thinking?	What were they thinking?

How can you solve it? Think of different ways to sort the problem. Listen to thoughts, listen to reasons, listen to feelings.	What might be the consequences of these solutions? What might happen if you did this?

Option 1 ➡

Option 2 ➡

Option 3 ➡

What is the best solution that works for both people, so both people end up feeling ok? ✓

Problem Solving Frame LFBE Language Level C/D

Personal

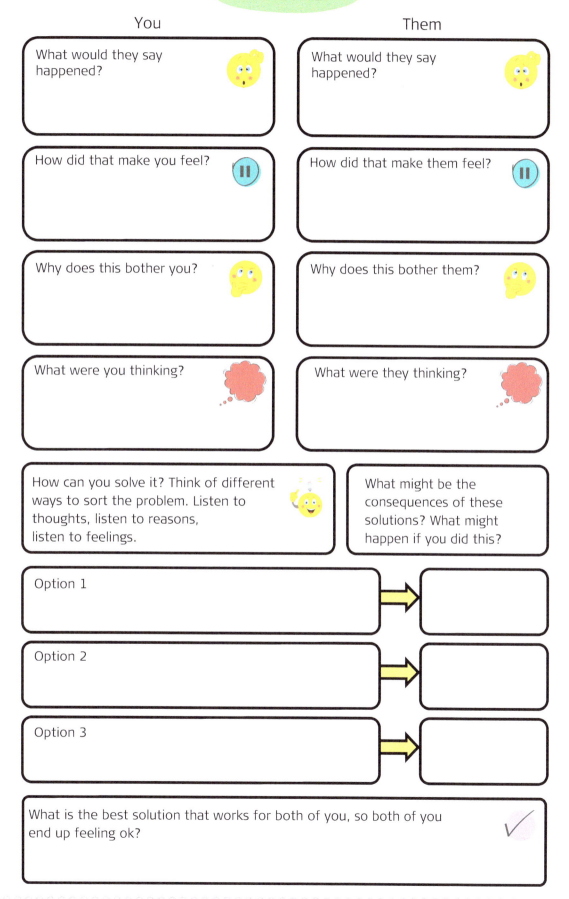

You	Them
What would they say happened?	**What would they say happened?**
How did that make you feel?	**How did that make them feel?**
Why does this bother you?	**Why does this bother them?**
What were you thinking?	**What were they thinking?**
How can you solve it? Think of different ways to sort the problem. Listen to thoughts, listen to reasons, listen to feelings.	**What might be the consequences of these solutions? What might happen if you did this?**

Option 1 →

Option 2 →

Option 3 →

What is the best solution that works for both of you, so both of you end up feeling ok? ✓

✓ Solving people problems worked example

There are three worked examples for the same problem. Each allows young people to use the right level of questions to think about the problem. The story used is 'Fetch!'

24 Fetch!

Rhys and Daniel had been out for most of the day, and they were now bored. They were in the park when they saw a dog, but they couldn't see an owner. The boys found a stick, and they threw it for the dog. The dog chased the stick and brought it back, but the next time Rhys threw it the stick hit the dog on the head. Daniel thought this was funny. The dog didn't seem to mind and still brought the stick back. Daniel threw the stick, and it hit the dog again. This time it nearly hit his eye. Daniel laughed again, this time louder, and picked up the stick again aiming it at the dog.

Problem Solving Frame LFBE Language Level A

Who was there?

Rhys and Daniel

Where were they?

In the park

What happened? (Use stick men and speech bubbles)

They were throwing a stick for the dog. Daniel thought it was funny. He tried to hit the dog with the stick.

What's the problem? (Talk through what is happening and try and think about what the problem might be)

The dog could get hurt.

These are some things you could do to make it better (adults list options):

1. Walk away
2. Tell Daniel to stop
3. Do nothing

Which one could they do?

walk away

Problem Solving Frame LFBE Language Level B

For scenarios

What happened?

Rhys and Daniel were throwing a stick for the dog. The dog got hit by accident, then Daniel though it was funny and tried to hurt the dog.

Person 1: Rhys   **Person 2:** Daniel

What is the main problem for person 1?

His friend is hurting the dog

What is the main problem for person 2?

He doesn't have a problem

How did that make them feel?

He is uncomfortable. Worried about the dog.

How did that make them feel?

Happy. It's making him laugh.

What were they thinking?

He doesn't like the dog getting hurt

What were they thinking?

How funny it is.

How can they make it better?

What could they say?

'Stop, that the dog could get hurt.'

What could they do?

Go somewhere else

Who can help?

He could look for the dog's owner.

What might happen next?

His friend might tell him to stop being stupid. He might stop.

What might happen next?

They would go away from the dog.

What might happen next?

The owner could take the dog away.

What's the best thing to do?

Problem Solving Frame LFBE Language Level C/D

For scenarios

Person 1: Rhys   **Person 2:** Daniel

What would they say happened? Daniel was trying to hurt the dog with the stick.	What would they say happened? He was having a laugh. It was funny when the stick hits the dog.
How did that make them feel? He is uncomfortable. Worried about the dog.	How did that make them feel? Happy. It's making him laugh.
Why does this bother them? His friend is hurting the dog	Why does this bother them? It doesn't.
What were they thinking? I wish he would stop throwing the stick at the dog.	What were they thinking? This is fun.

How can you solve it? Think of different ways to sort the problem. Listen to thoughts, listen to reasons, listen to feelings.	What might be the consequences of these solutions? What might happen if you did this?

Option 1 Do nothing	➡	The dog could get hurt.
Option 2 Tell Daniel to stop.	➡	He might not stop. He might.
Option 3 Say 'this is boring lets go somewhere else'.	➡	He would stop

What is the best solution that works for both people, so both people end up feeling ok?   *Option 3*   ✓